PREVENTING CHILD MALTREATMENT

Preventing Child Maltreatment
Community Approaches

Edited by
KENNETH A. DODGE
DORIANE LAMBELET COLEMAN

Foreword by J. B. Pritzker

THE GUILFORD PRESS
NEW YORK   LONDON

© 2009 The Guilford Press
A Division of Guilford Publications, Inc.
72 Spring Street, New York, NY 10012
www.guilford.com

Printed in the United States of America

This book is printed on acid-free paper.

Last digit is print number: 9   8   7   6   5   4   3   2   1

Library of Congress Cataloging-in-Publication Data

Preventing child maltreatment : community approaches / edited by Kenneth
A. Dodge, Doriane Lambelet Coleman.
    p. cm. — (Duke series in child development and public policy)
  Includes bibliographical references and index.
  ISBN 978-1-59385-973-2 (hardcover)
  1. Child abuse—United States.   2. Abused children—Services for—United States.
3. Social work with children—United States.   I. Dodge, Kenneth A.   II. Coleman,
Doriane Lambelet.
  HV741P727 2009
  362.76′709756—dc22

                                                              2008053346

About the Editors

Kenneth A. Dodge, PhD, is the William McDougall Professor of Public Policy Studies and Professor of Psychology and Neuroscience at Duke University, where he is also Director of the Center for Child and Family Policy. He has been honored with the Distinguished Scientific Contribution Award from the American Psychological Association and the Senior Scientist Award from the National Institutes of Health.

Doriane Lambelet Coleman, JD, is Professor of Law at Duke University, where she teaches courses and seminars on children and the law, among other topics. Her scholarship focuses on the impact of culture on the ways in which women and children are treated in the law. Her most recent work is concerned with child maltreatment in immigrant families and the legal ethics of pediatric research.

Contributors

Robert T. Ammerman, PhD, ABPP, Department of Pediatrics, Cincinnati Children's Hospital Medical Center, University of Cincinnati College of Medicine, Cincinnati, Ohio

Pilar Baca, RN, MSN, Department of Pediatrics, University of Colorado Denver School of Medicine, Denver, Colorado

Christina Christopoulos, PhD, Center for Child and Family Policy, Duke University, Durham, North Carolina

Robert Cole, PhD, School of Nursing, University of Rochester Medical Center, Rochester, New York

Doriane Lambelet Coleman, JD, Duke University Law School, Durham, North Carolina

Deborah Daro, PhD, Chapin Hall at the University of Chicago, Chicago, Illinois

Kenneth A. Dodge, PhD, Center for Child and Family Policy, Duke University, Durham, North Carolina

John Eckenrode, PhD, Family Life Development Center and Department of Human Development, College of Human Ecology, Cornell University, Ithaca, New York

Charles Henderson, MA, Department of Human Development, College of Human Ecology, Cornell University, Ithaca, New York

John Holmberg, PsyD, Department of Pediatrics, University of Colorado Denver School of Medicine, Denver, Colorado

Harriet Kitzman, RN, PhD, School of Nursing, University of Rochester Medical Center, Rochester, New York

Cindy S. Lederman, JD, Juvenile Justice Center, 11th Judicial Circuit, Miami, Florida

Dennis Luckey, PhD, Department of Pediatrics, University of Colorado Denver School of Medicine, Denver, Colorado

Peter A. Margolis, MD, PhD, Department of Pediatrics, Cincinnati Children's Hospital Medical Center, University of Cincinnati College of Medicine, Cincinnati, Ohio

Gary B. Melton, PhD, Institute on Family and Neighborhood Life, Clemson University, Clemson, South Carolina

Robert Murphy, PhD, Center for Child and Family Health, Durham, North Carolina, and Department of Psychiatry and Behavioral Sciences, Duke University, Durham, North Carolina

Karen O'Donnell, PhD, Department of Pediatrics and Department of Psychiatry and Behavioral Sciences, Duke University, Durham, North Carolina, and Center for Child and Family Health, Durham, North Carolina

David L. Olds, PhD, Departments of Pediatrics, Psychiatry, and Preventive Medicine, University of Colorado Denver School of Medicine, Denver, Colorado

Ronald J. Prinz, PhD, Department of Psychology, University of South Carolina, Columbia, South Carolina

Frank W. Putnam, MD, Department of Pediatrics, Cincinnati Children's Hospital Medical Center, University of Cincinnati College of Medicine, Cincinnati, Ohio

Desmond Runyan, MD, DrPH, Departments of Social Medicine and Pediatrics, University of North Carolina School of Medicine, Chapel Hill, North Carolina

Judith B. Van Ginkel, PhD, Department of Pediatrics, Cincinnati Children's Hospital Medical Center, University of Cincinnati College of Medicine, Cincinnati, Ohio

Michael S. Wald, MA, JD, Stanford Law School, Stanford, California

Jane Waldfogel, PhD, Columbia University School of Social Work, New York, New York

Adam Zolotor, MD, MPH, Department of Family Medicine, University of North Carolina School of Medicine, Chapel Hill, North Carolina

Foreword

The physical maltreatment of young children in the United States is a social policy problem that leaves a moral blemish on our society and imposes a barrier to the economic growth of our citizenry. Ever since Dr. Henry Kempe alerted us all to the plight of the "battered syndrome" child over 35 years ago, the official rates of child maltreatment in the United States have been measured at tragically high levels. Every year in the United States, about a million children are officially substantiated as maltreated. Furthermore, every study conducted on the topic concludes that the actual rate of maltreatment is far greater than official statistics tell us.

In spite of governmental and philanthropic spending of millions of dollars and countless professionals trying their best to prevent children from being maltreated, it is not clear that we have yet learned how to keep our children safe from physical abuse and neglect. Heart-warming case stories and promising programs do provide some glimmers of hope, but we have not yet been successful in lowering the measured population rate of maltreatment among our children. Of those programs that exist, few have been evaluated adequately, and those that have demonstrated some positive outcomes have been implemented only in small doses and consequently have not reached all of their targeted families.

Moreover, communitywide efforts have been too sporadic and too poorly funded to yield any truly measurable impact. Nationwide campaigns are welcomed, but their aspirations exceed their realities. New approaches must be developed and evaluated rigorously, approaches that bring together leaders in science and our communities to forge effective strategies for preventing maltreatment of children.

The focus of this volume is to bring together the best in scientific theory and evidence, stimulate thinking about community-based realities of the policy and practice world, determine the best utilization of the philanthropic community, and generate new ideas that could achieve real-world change in child well-being. This is a highly ambitious and morally imperative task, but the authors of these chapters provide us with the directions that we must take.

This volume grew out of a national conference that was held at Duke University in October 2007, and funded through The Children's Initiative: A Project of the J. B. and M. K. Pritzker Family Foundation. About 150 nationally renowned scholars, policymakers, and community leaders assembled for 2 days of thought-provoking discussions regarding the state of knowledge and promising ideas for community approaches to preventing child maltreatment. This book brings together the work of the invited speakers at the conference, who have thoughtfully considered what we know, what we need to know, and how we can make progress in significantly reducing this seemingly intractable problem.

At this time, we confront economic challenges that have not been witnessed in over 75 years. Funding cutbacks often appear inevitable, as difficult choices must be made. It would be easy to conclude that because of the times, the growing demand for resources to support basic human needs might crowd out spending precious dollars on science and rigorous evaluation of our efforts. However, it is precisely in challenging times that we *must* attend to our children's safety and we *must* use science to hold our investments accountable. This volume keeps us on that course.

> J. B. PRITZKER
> *The J. B. and M. K. Pritzker Family Foundation*

Contents

PREVENTING CHILD MALTREATMENT

Introduction

Community-Based Prevention
of Child Maltreatment

Kenneth A. Dodge *and* Doriane Lambelet Coleman

Systematic efforts to prevent child maltreatment within families have grown rapidly over the past several decades, since Dr. Henry Kempe's seminal article describing the horrors of the "battered child syndrome" (Kempe, Silverman, Steele, Droegemueller, & Silver, 1962) and Knitzer's (1982) scathing indictment of how communities have failed to protect their children. Many innovative interventions have been implemented with families across the nation. However, most of these interventions have been directed toward individual families and have received little rigorous empirical scrutiny. Skeptics have doubted the overall effectiveness of this movement in reducing the rate of child abuse, at least in part because the maltreatment phenomenon is often closely linked to deficiencies within the community (Daro & Cohn-Donnelly, 2002). Efforts to fix individual families without also attempting to fix their communities or the community-based structures that lead to maltreatment are unlikely in the long run to result in a reduction of the incidence of child abuse. What has been lacking is thus a community-based approach to population-wide prevention that is implemented systematically and evaluated rigorously. Recently, three developments have conspired to bring new attention to this challenge and to produce this book and the research that is reported here.

First, clinical scientists who have been developing and implementing interventions for individual families have questioned whether their worthy efforts are reaching the large number and diversity of families for which these interventions might be effective. For example, David Olds and colleagues (Chapter 2, this volume) developed a nurse-practitioner home-visiting program that has been deemed effective in preventing child abuse through rigorous randomized trials, but its impact on lowering the child abuse rate for an entire community (let alone a state or a nation) is probably nil if it cannot be disseminated systematically to penetrate that entire community. The need to bring individual interventions "to scale" has been increasingly recognized as a high priority.

Second, social scientists have formulated theories and amassed empirical evidence that the perpetration of child abuse within a family is affected by factors at the community level. Bronfenbrenner and Morris (2006) proposed an ecological theory that within-family behavior is affected by community factors such as norms, support systems, and culture. Empirical findings from the National Survey on Children's Health (Wilkenfield, Lippman, & Moore, 2007) indicate that more than 25% of the nation's children live in neighborhoods that are described as moderately low or very low in family support. Coulton, Korbin, Su, and Chow (1995) found that these factors make a difference in community rates of child maltreatment: Communities in which families feel that they have little efficacy to help each other indeed have higher rates of maltreatment.

Third, policymakers have become increasingly interested in accountability in government. That is, they are interested not only in seeing that prevention programs are provided for families but also in ensuring that these programs are effective, that they have the impact that is intended.

The outcome of these converging forces has been a surge in consideration of community-based approaches to preventing child maltreatment. These approaches vary in their focus on the reform of public social service agencies versus grassroots campaigns to change cultural norms. And they vary in their conceptual basis and the target of their efforts. This book assembles several of the most noteworthy of these approaches, as a "state-of-the-community" overview of this new community movement.

The book is organized in three parts. Part I establishes the scientific basis for community-based efforts to prevent child maltreatment. Specifically, in Chapter 1, Deborah Daro sets out the history of the relationship between science and child abuse prevention, describing both the phases through which prevention efforts have passed and the appropriately significant part that basic and applied research "has played ... in shaping prevention programming and assessing its impacts on children and families." Examining the modern focus on community-based prevention programs, Daro argues that "as the prevention field places increased emphasis on altering context as well as individual behaviors, a ... shift is ... needed in the scientific paradigm" away from the "randomized clinical trials" that sustained earlier efforts, to "a multifaceted research lens" that can "provide policymakers and program planners the array of information necessary to identify and address the conceptual and adaptive challenges" inherent in these modern efforts.

Part II describes several of the most effective community-based child maltreatment prevention programs. Olds and colleagues begin in Chapter 2 with a description of the Nurse–Family Partnership, a home-visiting program that pairs nurses with low-socioeconomic-status women and their families with the goal of "improving the neurodevelopmental, cognitive, and behavioral functioning of the child by improving prenatal health, reducing dysfunctional care of the child early in life ... and enhancing family functioning and economic self-sufficiency." This evidence-based program has been subject to multisite evaluation and successfully replicated in 310 counties across the country. The Nurse–Family Partnership is generally recognized by experts in the field as the gold standard of U.S.-based home-visiting programs (e.g., Runyan & Zolotor, Chapter 6).

In Chapter 3, Prinz describes a "new and emerging paradigm for the prevention of child maltreatment that is based on a public-health-compatible model." This model provides for universally available parenting programs and services designed to enhance the health, welfare, and safety of children. Using the Triple P—Positive Parenting Program as an example of how this paradigm has been operationalized, Prinz explores both its capacity to destigmatize the prevention effort and how it can be made cost-effective using a tiered approach to interventions based on individual families' needs.

In Chapter 4, Dodge, Murphy, O'Donnell, and Christopoulos describe the Durham Family Initiative (DFI), whose objective is to "translate a science-based social-ecological model of how within-home child maltreatment develops, along with knowledge of public policy and practice, into a preventive system of care to reduce the population rate of child maltreatment in Durham County, North Carolina." Program implementation involving a holistic, community-based approach to child maltreatment prevention began in July 2002. Empirical outcomes attributable to the program have been substantial and positive, including a reduction in the official rate of substantiated maltreatment in relation to comparison counties.

In Chapter 5, Melton describes Strong Communities, a South Carolina-based initiative to restore the role communities traditionally played as partners in families' efforts to raise safe and healthy children. In contrast with other models for community-based prevention described in this book, Strong Communities relies on and seeks to promote a culture of volunteers and volunteerism to provide services and support to families in need. Led by outreach workers and premised on the fact that most maltreatment is caused not by evil parents but by parents who simply need help doing right by their children in often difficult circumstances, citizens throughout the target communities engage in a multiplicity of strategies to increase the likelihood that "families will be able to obtain help where they are, when they need it, in a form in which they can use it with ease and without stigma."

Finally, in Chapter 6, Runyan and Zolotor describe the Period of PURPLE Crying, a community-based educational campaign designed to prevent a specific form of child maltreatment, shaken baby syndrome or abusive head trauma. As applied in Keeping Babies Safe in North Carolina, the campaign is a state-wide effort involving the provision of information about shaken baby syndrome to parents and others "(1) in the newborn nursery, (2) in community settings, for example, at either a prenatal visit to a health department or a well-child care visit to a health department or primary care provider within 2 weeks of the child's birth, and (3) through a [paid and earned] media campaign." Ultimately, the goal is to saturate the public with relevant information about the practice so that, as was the case with the integrated campaign against sudden infant death syndrome, a new culture of infant care emerges.

Part III discusses several significant policy and practice issues implicated by community-based efforts to prevent child maltreatment. Ammerman, Putnam, Margolis, and Van Ginkel first focus on methods for quality improvement in child abuse prevention programs in Chapter 7. Their particular aim is to ensure that program quality remains high as successful prevention models are replicated in diverse environments. Thus, they describe the essential features of effective quality improvement approaches and explain how these features were applied to ensure that quality was maintained in the replication of one model program, Every Child Succeeds.

In Chapter 8, Waldfogel describes the dilemma faced by child protective services (CPS) as it seeks simultaneously to remove children from abusive homes and successfully to assist some of the same families to prevent child maltreatment in the future. She makes the case for programs that provide for a "differential response" by child protective services to cases that implicate serious abuse on the one hand and neglect on the other. In jurisdictions adopting differential response, simple neglect cases are treated in a non-adversarial manner, so that families are able to work with social workers as partners rather than opponents in the effort to promote their children's well-being.

Coleman, in Chapter 9, focuses on the privacy implications of community-based efforts to prevent child maltreatment. She describes these implications and discusses aspects of those efforts that are particularly promising in resolving the tension between privacy and effective assistance. She concludes with the outlines of a proposal for reforming the child maltreatment reporting system that addresses a principal concern of those who seek to secure the trust and buy-in of targeted families: the dilemma of the home visitor who is simultaneously a mandated reporter.

In Chapter 10, Judge Lederman explores the structural and policy-based reasons for why courts are largely absent from discussions about community-based child maltreatment prevention efforts; she argues that with appropriate training in child development and knowledge about evidence-based parenting programs, judges could become important partners in these efforts. She concludes with a description of a court-based prevention program that has been successfully implemented in her jurisdiction and that can provide the basis for such collaborations in the future.

Finally, in Chapter 11, Wald examines the merits of community-based efforts to prevent child maltreatment from the perspective of policymakers who seek simultaneously to foster the conditions necessary for children to have good childhoods and good chances of success as adults *and* to invest in competing proposals to achieve these ends. From this perspective, he argues that efforts designed to prevent child maltreatment, including those that are intended to address simple neglect, are less likely to be supported (and thus to be effective) than are investments in education-based initiatives designed to promote positive parenting and child well-being. Concomitantly, he argues that child protective service agencies as currently conceived should be limited to working with families in which children have suffered or are at risk of suffering "significant injuries."

Together, the chapters in this book provide a state-of-the-science-and-practice treatise on the prospects for community approaches to the prevention of child maltreatment.

REFERENCES

Bronfenbrenner, U., & Morris, P. A. (2006). The bioecological model of human development. In R. Lerner (Ed.), *Handbook of child psychology: Vol. 1. Theoretical models of human development* (pp. 793–828). Hoboken, NJ: Wiley.

Coulton, C. J., Korbin, J. E., Su, M., & Chow, J. (1995). Community level factors and child maltreatment rates. *Child Development, 66,* 1262–1276.

Daro, D., & Cohn-Donnelly, A. (2002). Charting the waves of prevention: Two steps forward, one step back. *Child Abuse and Neglect, 26,* 731–742.

Kempe, C. H., Silverman, F. N., Steele, B. F., Droegemuller, W., & Silver, H. K. (1962). The battered-child syndrome. *Journal of the American Medical Association, 181,* 17–24.

Knitzer, J. (1982). *Unclaimed children: The failure of public responsibility to children and adolescents in need of mental health services.* Washington, DC: Children's Defense Fund.

Wilkenfield, B., Lippman, L., & Moore, K. A. (2007, September). Neighborhood support index. *Child Trends Fact Sheet* (Publication # 2007-28). Available at *www.childtrends.org/Files/child_Trends-2007_09_18_FS_NeighborhoodIndex.pdf.*

PART I

THE SCIENTIFIC BASIS FOR THE COMMUNITY PREVENTION OF CHILD MALTREATMENT

CHAPTER I

The History of Science and Child Abuse Prevention

A Reciprocal Relationship

Deborah Daro

Over the past 40 years, efforts to prevent child maltreatment have moved through various stages—public and professional recognition of the problem, experimentation with a wide range of prevention programs addressing one or more factors believed to increase a child's risk for maltreatment, and the development of systemic and contextual reforms to better integrate and sustain these diverse interventions (Daro & Cohn-Donnelly, 2002). Throughout this history, research, both basic and applied, has played a critical role in shaping prevention programming and assessing its impacts on children and families. From Henry Kempe's landmark research in the 1960s through the brain research of the 1990s, those developing, implementing, and funding child abuse prevention efforts have been driven, in part, by what the data have told them.

Community context and neighborhood resources have long been considered key factors in determining a child's relative risk for maltreatment and poor developmental outcomes. Neighborhood conditions can significantly influence child maltreatment rates (Garbarino, Kostelny, & Dubrow, 1991), juvenile delinquency (Brody et al., 2001), early child behavior problems (Linares et al., 2001), and later deviance (Simons et al., 2002). The causal status of neighborhood effects is still unclear, because families are known to self-select neighborhoods. How neighborhoods shape these developmental pathways, furthermore, is even less well developed (Burton & Jarrett, 2000; Leventhal & Brooks-Gunn, 2003). One proposed explanation suggests that neighborhood conditions impact child development by shaping a parent's normative and resource options (Chaskin, 1997). These options, in turn, influence parenting practices, the quality of the home environment (Leventhal & Brooks-Gunn, 2003), and the availability of parenting resources (Jencks & Mayer, 1990)—all of which may produce individual or collective effects on children. It is not surprising, therefore, that efforts to enhance community capacity or "to alter the context in which parents rear their children" have emerged as promising strategies for improving outcomes with respect to child abuse, infant mortality and morbidity, school performance, juvenile crime, and youth violence (Daro, 2000; Gorman-Smith & Tolan, 1998; Shonkoff & Phillips, 2000). These strategies offer hope of preventing child maltreatment and, if implemented with scientifically rigorous evaluation, may provide a strong test of the causal role of the community.

This chapter examines the evidentiary base that has guided the child abuse prevention planning process toward the current focus on community prevention efforts. At each evolutionary stage, the research methods of greatest utility have shifted as public policy concerns have transformed from capturing the extent of the problem, to understanding its underlying causes, to determining how best to treat, and, ultimately, prevent its occurrence. As the prevention field places increased emphasis on altering context as well as individual behaviors, a comparable shift is again needed in the scientific paradigm. Sustaining a meaningful relationship between science and practice will require adjustments not only by those implementing programs but also among those examining program impacts. A knowledge development model that places singular and preeminent emphasis on randomized clinical trials may be less appropriate today than in the past. In response to this challenge, the chapter suggests the development of a rich research toolbox, one that places equal emphasis and value on designs to assess program and policy efficacy, and their effectiveness. The chapter argues that a multifaceted research lens is needed to provide policymakers and program planners the array of information necessary to identify and address the conceptual and adaptive challenges facing efforts to expand and replicate community prevention efforts.

DEFINITION AND AWARENESS

Modern public and political attention to the issue of child maltreatment is often pegged to Henry Kempe's 1962 article in the *Journal of the American Medical Association* on the "battered child syndrome" (Kempe, Silverman, Steele, Droegemueller, & Silver, 1962). Although several medical articles had appeared as early as the 1940s describing subdural hematomas and long bone fractures suggestive of maltreatment (Caffey, 1946; Silverman, 1953), Kempe's work differed from these earlier efforts in two key respects. First, the work established an empirical estimate of the problem broader than single-site clinical studies. Kempe and his colleagues examined hospital emergency room X-rays for 1 year in 70 hospitals around the country and surveyed 77 district attorneys. They documented more than 300 cases of suspected maltreatment in hospital emergency rooms and 447 cases prosecuted by district attorneys. Among the children treated in hospital emergency rooms, 11% had died and more than 28% had suffered permanent brain damage. In addition to providing preliminary estimates of the scope of the problem, this effort and similar surveys (DeFrancis, 1963; Merrill, 1962) offered physicians and other frontline respondents "diagnostic clues" for identifying potential victims as well as those children facing imminent harm. The public, as well as professionals, began developing a picture of the typical abuse case, one that defined the problem as a young child who suffered injury as a result of overburdened parents or caretakers using extreme forms of corporal punishment or depressed single mothers failing to provide for their children's basic emotional and physical needs.

    Second, Kempe explicitly linked his research to a public policy option. He proposed the adoption of a system that would facilitate the ability of professionals and others concerned with a child's well-being to report their concerns officially so that children would be protected and services provided. Such child abuse reporting laws were rapidly adopted across the United States. Between 1963 and 1967, all states and the District of Columbia passed child abuse reporting laws, a trend that one author labeled one of the most rapid diffusions of a legislative innovation to occur in the 20th century (Nelson, 1984). Federal reporting guidelines were established in 1974 with the authorization of the first Federal Child Abuse and Neglect Prevention and Treatment Act. These guidelines encouraged states to establish specific child welfare agencies to accept reports, in part, as a result of survey research. David Gil's 1965 public opinion poll asked respondents under what conditions they would be comfortable reporting families whom they suspected as being involved in maltreatment to local authorities. Only 23% of the respondents indicated they would report to the police, whereas 45% said they would report such cases to social service agencies (Gil, 1970).

    As the research base expanded, it became clear that the child abuse problem was both more common and more nuanced than initially imagined. Disappointment with single-factor theories of abuse or neglect led to the adoption of more complex, ecological frameworks (Belsky, 1980; Bronfenbrenner, 1979; Cicchetti & Rizley, 1981; Garbarino, 1977). These interactive models were reflected in more inclusive definitions of what constituted a reportable act of maltreatment (Newberger, 1983). Although physical abuse was initially the most common form of maltreatment reported to authorities, these early cases rarely reflected the degree of harm and intentionality documented in the clinical cases observed by Kempe and colleagues (1962) or documented in court records and newspaper files. The early pool of reported cases confirmed that abuse resulted from poor adult functioning, but also noted that environmental factors (such as poverty, limited access to healthcare and supportive services) were far more common among known cases than had been suggested by the initial clinical studies (Gil, 1970). Then, as now, poor families and families of color were overrepresented in child welfare caseloads, underscoring the reality that children were often not intended victims of dysfunctional parenting but, rather, of the collateral damage resulting from a chaotic and poorly resourced environment.

In addition to reflecting the problem's complexity, subsequent implementation research on the reporting system and child welfare practice found the initial public policy response inadequate. In a survey of 450 physicians in the late 1960s, for example, many remained uninformed and said they never considered child abuse as a potential problem among their clients ("Child abuse laws—are they enough?", 1967). Reluctance to report at-risk children formally was further complicated by the growing body of research indicating that such reports often failed to result in the provision of therapeutic services to victims or the range of supports families under stress required to avoid repeated maltreatment (Schene, 1998). As foster care caseloads grew and available resources for services diminished, a system that merely identified a child only after he or she had been victimized proved unsatisfactory.

One response to this situation was a call for an increased number of prevention services. If little could be offered a child once abuse patterns were identified, the more promising path appeared to be the development of a continuum of services that address many of the causal factors associated with an increased likelihood for abuse. The primary message drawn from the initial child abuse research and public policy response was that there should be an expansion of interventions and, of course, more research.

BUILDING A SERVICE CONTINUUM

The 1980s was a period of significant expansion in public awareness of child maltreatment, research on its underlying causes and consequences, and the development and dissemination of primary and secondary prevention efforts. During this period two distinct paths in prevention planning emerged—interventions targeting reductions in physical abuse and neglect (including emotional neglect and attachment disorders) and interventions targeting reductions in child sexual abuse (Daro, 1989). Programs in the first group emanated from research that suggested physical abuse and neglect resulted from a parent's lack of knowledge, resources, and emotional capacity. These prevention strategies included, among others, services to new parents, general parenting education classes, parent support groups, family resource centers, and crisis intervention services such as hotlines and crisis nurseries (Cohn, 1987). In contrast, the target population for sexual abuse prevention became potential victims, not potential perpetrators. Three factors contributed to this pattern: the social discomfort surrounding sexuality, the difficulty in developing voluntary treatment options for offenders, and the absence of clear risk factors identifying potential perpetrators or victims (Daro, 1994). Strategies within this framework included a number of education-based efforts, provided on a universal basis, to teach children the distinctions between good, bad, and questionable touching and the concept of body ownership or the rights of children to control who touches their bodies and where they are touched (Wurtele & Miller-Perrin, 1992). These educational programs also encouraged children and youth who had been victimized to report these incidents and seek services.

Few prevention efforts were dismissed during this period on the basis of outcome evaluations. Programs were disseminated on the basis of their theoretical and emotional appeal more than because of any significant evidence of their effectiveness. In part, this rush to develop and disseminate a plethora of prevention efforts reflected the broad range of disciplines focusing on the needs of abused children and their families. The emerging child abuse field benefited from the involvement of a variety of sectors, including traditional health, education, and social service professionals as well as an array of corporations, civic leaders, and community advocates. By the 1980s, combating child abuse had become a central theme among philanthropic and community service efforts being promoted by the National Basketball Association, MasterCard, the Ad Council, corporations such as Freddie Mac and Target, and a number of social fraternities and sororities. At least three national organizations focused exclusively on child abuse, coordinating child abuse intervention and prevention efforts across the country and disseminating promising practices (Cohn, 1987).

Research efforts to understand the prevalence and epidemiology of abuse also became more robust during this period. Expanded, more sophisticated, population-based surveys were conducted, many on a regular basis, providing more reliable estimates of the problem's incidence and prevalence. The federal National Center on Child Abuse and Neglect (NCCAN) commissioned two national incidence studies in the 1980s to establish trend data on the number of possible maltreatment cases observed by a diverse array of professionals and the degree to which these cases were referred for formal interventions (U.S. Department of Health and Human

Services [USDHHS], 1981, 1988). In addition, federal legislation required states in 1988 to begin moving toward a more consistent method for summarizing data on the number, characteristics, and outcomes of reported cases of maltreatment. Although wide variation continued in the definition of abuse, in service availability, and in public policy both within and across states, this period was one in which a more uniform understanding of the problem emerged. Innovations were more rapidly shared across states as a function of federally funded national conferences and emerging professional and institutional networks, such as state-sponsored Children's Trust and Prevention Funds, state chapters of the National Committee to Prevent Child Abuse, and the American Professional Society on the Abuse of Children.

As with the prior evolutionary stage, research efforts underscored both the strengths and limitations of a broadly defined service continuum. Although the new array of interventions most certainly assisted many families and addressed several of the most egregious problems and lack of options identified in early clinical studies, not all families were well served by this system. The existing prevention continuum, although logical, missed an important aspect underlying the ecological theories of maltreatment: the additive and interdependent impacts of multiple factors on a parent's ability to care for his or her child. The prevention continuum had done a good job in creating a market of services that addressed the needs of many parents able to negotiate the diverse set of options. It was far less successful in creating a system that could attract and retain families who did not know they needed assistance or, if they recognized their shortcomings, did not know how to access help (Daro, 1993). Reaching these families would require not just more services, but specific services that were sensitive to how a diverse array of chronic and acute circumstances might influence parents' perceptions of their children, their role as parents, and their willingness to change. A prevention menu that merely suggested a diverse array of service options without also offering explicit strategies for how to integrate these efforts across disciplines and circumstances proved disappointing and, in many instances, ineffective.

In addition, the research underscored the fact that many prevention efforts were not as conceptually clear as first thought. Service dosage and duration were often insufficient to sustain the complex behaviors and attitudes the prevention programs targeted. Furthermore, programs often were not implemented with a keen attention to quality, further reducing their ability to maximize impacts.

Similar difficulties were being noted within the child welfare system. In an attempt to sustain an effective public child welfare response in light of expanded caseloads and competing visions and expectations, a series of federal legislative reforms over the past 20 years have directed states to make "reasonable efforts" to prevent out-of-home placement and to promote family reunification or find permanent homes for children who had to be placed (Myers, 2006). The primary emphasis of these reforms has vacillated among a number of alternatives (e.g., prevention, family preservation, permanency, and adoption). However, federal fiscal incentives have consistently favored alternative placement options (Wulczyn, Barth, Yuan, Harden, & Landsverk, 2005). And, increasingly, the public has viewed the child welfare response system as more punitive than therapeutic and as having a disproportionate impact on the lives of poor families and children of color (Courtney et al., 1996).

Although many models proved insufficient, notable success was reported with new parents, particularly when services were offered at the time a woman became pregnant or at a child's birth (Daro, 1989). Emergent brain research and longitudinal studies on early intervention programs implemented in the 1970s and 1980s underscored what Kempe had suggested years ago—start early if you want to change the trajectory of the parent–child relationship and the development of children.

THE DEVELOPMENTAL PARADIGM

In response to the disappointment with the child abuse service continuum, prevention planners shifted their imagery from the horizontal to the vertical (Daro, 2000). Attention was paid to the temporal life course. No longer were all prevention efforts considered equal in importance or impact. Rather, the goal shifted from offering a range of services to planning and delivering prevention efforts in a more orderly manner, beginning with a strong foundation of support for every parent and child, available when a child is born or a woman becomes pregnant. Subsequent prevention services such as parent support groups, early childhood education programs, parenting education options, or family counseling services could then be added to this universal base in response to the specific emerging needs presented by the growing child or the evolving parent–child relationship.

A central feature of this developmental approach was an increased focus on expanding the availability of home visitation services to newborns and their parents. Drawing on the experiences of Western democracies with a long history of providing universal home visitation systems and emerging evidence of the model's utility in the United States, the U.S. Advisory Board on Child Abuse and Neglect concluded that "no other single intervention has the promise of home visitation" (USDHSS, 1991, p. 145). The seminal work of David Olds and his colleagues, showing initial and long-term benefits from regular nurse visiting during pregnancy and a child's first 2 years of life, provided the most robust evidence for this intervention (Olds, Sadler, & Kitzman, 2007). Equally important, however, were the growing number of home visitation models being developed and successfully implemented within the public and community-based service sectors. Although less rigorous in their evaluation methodologies, these models demonstrated respectable gains in parent–child attachment, access to preventive medical care, parental capacity and functioning, and early identification of developmental delays (Daro, 2000).

During this period, stronger linkages also were established with the child development community to understand better how research in this domain (both basic and applied) might best inform child abuse prevention efforts. In addition, higher priority was given to holding program planners accountable for outcomes—good intentions were no longer sufficient. The importance of evidence-based practice within the field of child abuse prevention was reflected in more rigorous program evaluations, including an increase in the number of randomized controlled trials, more rigorous quasi-experimental designs, and an expanded use of quality assurance systems to track performance (Daro, 2007).

After implementing home visitation programs for more than a decade, the prevention field is again critically examining its progress. Over the past 15 years numerous researchers have examined the effects of home visitation programs on parent–child relationships, maternal functioning, and child development. These evaluations have also addressed such important issues as costs, program intensity, staff requirements, training and supervision, and the variation in design necessary to meet the differential needs of a diverse new-parent population. Attempts to summarize this research have drawn different conclusions. In some cases, the authors conclude that the strategy, when well implemented, does produce significant and meaningful reduction in child-abuse risk and improves child and family functioning (American Academy of Pediatrics, Council on Child and Adolescent Health, 1998; Geeraert, Van den Noorgate, Grietens, & Onghena, 2004; Guterman, 2001; Hahn et al., 2003). Other reviews draw a more sobering conclusion (Chaffin, 2004; Gomby, 2005). In some instances, these disparate conclusions reflect different expectations regarding what constitutes "meaningful" change; in other cases, the difference stems from examining different studies or placing greater emphasis on certain methodological approaches (e.g., randomized controlled studies).

Home visitation, although promising, does not produce consistent impacts. Not all families are equally well served by the model; retention in long-term interventions can be difficult; identifying, training, and retaining competent service providers is challenging, particularly when the strategy is designed to be offered widely and integrated into existing early intervention systems. And although home visitation programs are substantial in both dosage and duration, even intensive interventions cannot fully address the needs of the most challenged populations—those struggling with serious mental illness, domestic violence, and substance abuse, as well as those rearing children in violent and chaotic neighborhoods. Such challenges can stymie and limit the impacts of even a highly skilled home visitor (Boo, 2006).

A recurring theme in many prevention domains, whether the focus is on child abuse prevention, school readiness, or child health and well-being, is the importance of context (Earls, 1998). A community's normative standards influence parenting practices as well as the likelihood that a parent will seek out and use supportive services, request assistance for themselves, or offer help to their neighbor. As the field reflected on the strengths and limitations of home-based early intervention, the conceptual lens expanded to include an explicit consideration of defining the pathways that families might use to draw support from their neighbors and their neighborhoods to create a supportive context for their children when such a context did not exist.

THE COMMUNITY PARADIGM

With these lessons in mind, the field is embracing a programmatic vision that places equal emphasis on altering community context and improving individual parenting. The objective of this paradigm is to create safe and nurturing environments for all children, communities in which parents are supported through both formal services and normative values that foster mutual reciprocity. In building these communities, carefully crafted research efforts will be needed to identify promising strategies and direct the planning process. Strategies for creating safe and nurturing environments within neighborhoods with high concentrations of poverty and disorganization are far from self-evident. Although our knowledge base is not perfect, certain historical lessons suggest that community prevention efforts hold the greatest promise if they are bounded by at least three parameters.

First, it remains important to focus on the first few years of life. Nothing we have seen to date in the research suggests that an emphasis on offering assessment and support at the time a woman become pregnant or gives birth is misplaced. None of the critiques of home visitation have contradicted the simple fact that the first 3 years of a child's life have enormous influence. Thus, if one is seeking to prevent child abuse by strengthening community context, doing so through strengthening and expanding early intervention efforts offers the potential for rich rewards.

Second, community initiatives will need to embrace an array of strategies, including both those that focus on changing individuals and those that seek to change community context. In selecting specific strategies, it will be important for program planners and policymakers to continue to invest in strategies that have been developed and refined through careful research. Although specific program models found to be effective through randomized trials are excellent candidates for community-based initiatives to adopt, the specific utility of any model program needs to be monitored in light of the particular context and culture in which it is being implemented. Integrating an evidence-based perspective into community initiatives will require multiple methodologies, including implementation studies that examine the relative merits of various program inputs (e.g., staff qualifications and training, appropriate target populations, service content and curriculum, program management, and supervisory systems). This knowledge base might be generated by a range of methods that compare performance and sustainability across various institutional settings, outcome domains, and community contexts, using randomization methods or by examining trends within administrative data over time.

Third, it will be important to establish systems at both the state and local levels that encourage a culture of continuous program improvement—one in which there is full transparency in program operations and impacts and a willingness to learn from one's experience and the experiences of others. Such transparency is essential for maximizing the opportunities to recognize those elements of community context and organizational infrastructure that will nurture an environment in which individualized services have a greater opportunity to succeed. Full transparency can also contribute to a clearer understanding of how best to embed targeted interventions within a universal system of support for all new parents. Limiting efforts to only those with "problems" has done little to change normative context in either patterns of service utilization or parental practices. And the process often results in marginalized programs that are the first to be cut in times of budget distress. Not everyone needs intensive services; however, few manage without the help of someone. Communities that offer universal supports to all new parents offer an opportunity to both normalize the process of seeking and receiving help around the time a child is born and engage a higher proportion of those families reluctant to accept targeted interventions for fear of stigmatization.

THE SHIFTING RESEARCH PARADIGM

Evaluation theorist Thomas Cook has proposed that the future of program evaluation rests on a "three-legged stool"—better methods, better theory, and better synthesis (Cook, 1997). Given the range of technical and adaptive challenges the field faces in building a research agenda to advance notions of community prevention, Cook's (1997) advice is particularly noteworthy. Continued advances to prevent social dilemmas deeply embedded in both the individual and the cultural milieu will require keen attention to fostering better programs, better theory, and better synthesis.

An important initial step in creating supportive communities will be to develop and implement high-quality interventions that are the subject of high-quality research. Improving our interventions and knowledge base can most certainly benefit from additional randomized control studies, provided that we can specify the intervention and limit its exposure. Equally important, however, is to enhance our understanding about how services are delivered. Better, more robust implementation studies are needed to document the most efficient ways to replicate programs and take them "to scale." In truth, some issues will surface only after programs have been widely disseminated and moved beyond venues where researchers control all of the critical variables. Program managers and practitioners need to be adaptable problem solvers, and researchers need to engage with them in this learning process. In this respect, evaluation designs need to be developed with an eye toward informing practice as well as science.

In considering intervention strategies, it will become increasingly important to look beyond those efforts that target individual participants and cast a critical eye toward those strategies that weave discrete services into an effective system of care. Focusing on how individualized services are linked together and managed through comprehensive systems of care have long been the subject of innovation and debate in children's mental health (Bickman, 1996; Saxe, 1988) and child welfare (Waldfogel, 1998). More recently, similar discussions have emerged among primary health care, early learning, and child abuse prevention providers as states have expanded efforts to provide more comprehensive assistance to pregnant women and new parents (Daro & McCurdy, 2008). Common strategies emerging from these discussions include common assessment tools to identify a family's critical needs across various interventions, identifying shared outcomes across multiple institutional settings, implementing common staff training and standards for supervision, establishing consistent quality assurance indicators and monitoring compliance with these indicators, and structuring tangible goals for organizational partnerships. These strategies, like individual programs, need to be carefully assessed over time and adjusted to reflect their capacity to achieve stronger system-level performance.

Second, community prevention efforts will require stronger theoretical models that can link the proximate outcomes of service availability and neighbor-to-neighbor interactions to the more distal outcomes that drive public policy. Monitoring the number and characteristics of child abuse reports, in the absence of a more complete understanding of the factors that govern reporting behavior or the use of formal and informal supports, will yield little useful information. Reform initiatives, particularly those that are complex, multifaceted, and intended to test new ideas, need to be structured and implemented in a manner that recognizes the importance of both learning and practice. If the interest is in determining a concept's efficacy, selection bias in communities and individual participants has to be reduced by implementing research designs that allow for some type of randomization to varying conditions. If the interest is in determining a concept's feasibility, it may be best to focus on implementing the idea within a community or institutional context that offers the most favorable environment for its incubation. In either case, a reform initiative needs to be guided by a strong theoretical model that links program strategies to specific outcomes and to be subjected to an evaluation method appropriate for its specific complexity and reach.

Finally, better synthesis will increasingly challenge program planners to "look over the fence" and see how others define their problems and craft their solutions. Child abuse prevention planners often advocate adopting a public health approach to preventing maltreatment but often ignore the underlying message in public health—that is, to heed the importance of context. Wallack and Lawrence (2005) have described community building as embracing a sense of interconnectness in which the ability of individuals to act in ways supportive of their own health and the health of their children is influenced, in part, by the environment and cultural imperatives we collectively set for ourselves. Reductions in the rate of smoking, in the rate of fatalities due to drunk driving, and the increased use of safety devices such as car seats have, at their core, a set of specific behaviors by which individual citizens feel empowered to take personal action to ensure collective outcomes. In addition, structural changes, such as the establishment of no smoking areas, criminal penalties, and financial disincentives, also play a role in creating a context or environment in which it becomes easier (or more likely) to act differently. Community child abuse prevention will become a reality when a comparable set of behaviors are in place that facilitate the ability of parents to provide nurturing and supportive environments for their children and to help others in their community achieve these same outcomes. Such behaviors might include discipline methods that do not rely on corporal punishment, parent–child interactions that facilitate language development and early learning opportunities, and parental involvement in any institution or program in which their child is enrolled.

CONCLUSION

Maximizing the potential of community prevention efforts will require considerable effort from many domains. Just as prevention services have changed over the years to respond to the changing needs of families, researchers need to reconsider the relative value and utility of a diverse array of analytic methods. Enhanced management information systems provide tools that allow us to track program implementation, service utilization, and impacts with improved specificity and accuracy. More sophisticated statistical modeling and analytic methods allow for a more rigorous examination of research questions even in the absence of random assignment.

Community change initiatives have long been a central component of efforts to combat poverty, social isolation, and urban decline. The success of these initiatives has hinged on the ability of program planners to achieve a balance between community development or capacity-building goals and the need to produce tangible "products" or solutions to the core issue at hand (Hannah, 2006). Simply advocating infrastructure development can led to gentrification—producing replacement, not reform; focusing only on empowerment often results in continued disinvestment and further physical deterioration and resident disillusionment.

A similar balanced response faces community-based child abuse prevention initiatives. Although the specific ways in which community influences parenting are not fully specified, many believe these impacts are a combination of parents drawing on the parenting practices and values of their neighbors in determining their normative standards of childrearing, and the physical resources available in the community in terms of services and instrumental supports (Zielinski & Bradshaw, 2006). One strategy for community change efforts seeking to reduce child maltreatment is to emphasize building social capital and creating an environment of mutual reciprocity. A second strategy is to develop, implement, and assess an array of formal services and institutional relationships that will support families when friends and neighbors are unable or unwilling to provide assistance. In the first case, the challenge is to recognize those social dilemmas and environmental challenges that indeed require a social response that is difficult to achieve in the absence of public investment or professional skills. In the second instance, the challenge is to recognize the inherent limitations to public resources and the importance of creating a culture in which seeking and offering assistance to meet one's parenting responsibilities is normative. Both elements—individual motivation and a strong formal service infrastructure—are indeed important. As they have in the past, scientists will need to partner with practitioners and policymakers to determine the appropriate array of options. Maximizing this partnership opportunity will require researchers to craft their own balance, one that draws on a wide array of evaluation methods.

REFERENCES

American Academy of Pediatrics, Council on Child and Adolescent Health. (1998). The role of home-visitation programs in improving health outcomes for children and families. *Pediatrics, 10*(3), 486–489.

Belsky, J. (1980). Child maltreatment: An ecological integration. *American Psychologist, 35*, 320–335.

Boo, K. (2006, February 6). Swamp nurse. *The New Yorker*, pp. 54–65.

Bickman, L. (1996). A continuum of care: More is not always better. *American Psychologist, 51*, 689–701.

Brody, G. H., Conger, R., Gibbons, F. X., Ge, X., Murry, V. M., Gerrard, M., et al. (2001). The influence of neighborhood disadvantage, collective socialization, and parenting on African American children's affiliation with deviant peers. *Child Development, 72*(4), 1231–1246.

Bronfenbrenner, U. (1979). *The ecology of human development: Experiments by nature and design*. Cambridge, MA: Harvard University Press.

Burton, L. M., & Jarrett, R. L. (2000). In the mix, yet on the margins: The place of families in urban neighborhood and child development research. *Journal of Marriage and the Family, 62*, 1114–1135.

Caffey, J. (1946). Multiple fractures in the long bones of infants suffering from chronic subdural hematoma. *American Journal of Roentgenology, 56*, 163–173.

Chaffin, M. (2004). Is it time to rethink Healthy Start/Healthy Families? *Child Abuse and Neglect, 28*, 589–595.

Chaskin, R. (1997). Perspectives on neighborhood and community: A review of the literature. *Social Service Review, 71*, 521–547.

Child abuse laws—are they enough? (1967). *Journal of the American Medical Association, 199*, 101–104.

Cicchetti, D., & Rizley, R. (1981). Developmental perspectives on the etiology, intergenerational transmission, and sequelae of child maltreatment. In R. Rizley & D. Cicchetti (Eds.), *New directions for child development: Developmental perspectives in child maltreatment* (pp. 32–59). San Francisco: Jossey-Bass.

Cohn, A. (1987). Our national priorities for prevention. In R. Helfer & C. H. Kempe (Eds.), *The battered child* (4th ed., pp. 444–445). Chicago: University of Chicago Press.

Cook, T. (1997). Lessons learned in evaluation over the past 25 years. In E. Chelimsky & W. Shadish (Eds.), *Evaluation for the 21st century* (pp. 30–52). Thousand Oaks, CA: Sage.

Courtney, M., Barth, R., Duerr Berrick, J., Brooks, D., Needell, B., & Park, L. (1996). Race and child welfare services: Past research and future directions. *Child Welfare, 75*(2), 99–137.

Daro, D. (1989). *Confronting child abuse: Research for effective program design*. New York: Free Press.

Daro, D. (1993). Child maltreatment research: Implications for program design. In D. Cicchetti & S. Toth (Eds.), *Child abuse, child development, and social policy* (pp. 331–367). Norwood, NJ: Ablex.

Daro, D. (1994). Prevention of childhood sexual abuse. *The Future of Children, 4*(2), 198–223.

Daro, D. (2000). Child abuse prevention: New directions and challenges. In D. Hansen (Ed.), *Motivation and child maltreatment of the Nebraska Symposium on Motivation* (Vol. 46, pp. 161–220). Lincoln: University of Nebraska.

Daro, D. (2007). *Home visitation: Assessing progress, managing expectations.* Chicago: Chapin Hall Center for Children and the Ounce of Prevention Fund.

Daro, D. A., & McCurdy, K. P. (2008). Interventions to prevent child maltreatment. In L. S. Doll, S. E. Bonzo, J. A. Mercy, & D. A. Slett (Eds.), *Handbook of injury and violence prevention* (pp. 137–156). New York: Springer.

Daro, D., & Cohn-Donnelly, A. (2002). Charting the waves of prevention: Two steps forward, one step back. *Child Abuse and Neglect, 26,* 731–742.

DeFrancis, V. (1963). *Child abuse—preview of a nationwide survey.* Denver: American Humane Association.

Earls, F. (1998). Positive effects of prenatal and early childhood interventions. *Journal of the American Medical Association, 280*(14), 1271–1273.

Garbarino, J. (1977). The human ecology of child maltreatment: A conceptual model for research. *Journal of Marriage and the Family, 39,* 721–735.

Garbarino, J., Kostelny, K., & Dubrow, N. (1991). What children can tell us about living in danger. *American Psychologist, 46,* 376–383.

Geeraert, L., Van den Noorgate, W., Grietens, H., & Onghena, P. (2004). The effects of early prevention programs for families with young children at risk for physical child abuse and neglect: A meta-analysis. *Child Maltreatment, 9*(3), 277–291.

Gil, D. (1970). *Violence against children: Physical child abuse in the United States.* Cambridge, MA: Harvard University Press.

Gomby, D. (2005, July). *Home visitation in 2005: Outcomes for children and parents* (Invest in Kids Working Paper No. 7). Washington, DC: Committee for Economic Development, Invest in Kids Working Group. Available at *www.ced. org/projects/kids.shtml.*

Gorman-Smith, D., & Tolan, P. (1998). The role of exposure to community violence and developmental problems among inner-city youth. *Development and Psychopathology, 10,* 101–116.

Guterman, N. (2001). *Stopping child maltreatment before it starts: Emerging horizons in early home visitation services.* Thousand Oaks, CA: Sage.

Hahn, R., Bilukha, O., Crosby, A., Fullilove, M., Liberman, A., Moscicki, E., et al. (2003). First reports evaluating the effectiveness of strategies for preventing violence: Early childhood home visitation. *Morbidity and Mortality Weekly Report: Recommendations and Reports, 52,* 1–9.

Hannah, G. (2006). Maintaining product–process balance in community antipoverty initiatives. *Social Work, 51*(1), 9–19.

Jencks, C., & Mayer, S. (1990). The social consequences of growing up in a poor neighborhood. In L. Lynn Jr. & M. McGeary (Eds.), *Inner-city poverty in America* (pp. 111–186). Washington, DC: National Academy Press.

Kempe, C. H., Silverman, F., Steele, B., Droegemueller, W., & Silver, H. (1962). The battered child syndrome. *Journal of the American Medical Association, 181*, 17–24.

Leventhal, T., & Brooks-Gunn, J. (2003). Children and youth in neighborhood contexts. *Current Directions in Psychological Science, 12*, 27–31.

Linares, L. O., Heeren, R., Bronfman, E., Zuckerman, B., Augustyn, M., & Tronick, E. (2001). A mediational model for the impact of exposure to community violence on early child behavior problems. *Child Development, 72*, 639–652.

Merrill, E. (1962). Physical abuse of children: An agency study. In V. DeFrancis (Ed.), *Protecting the battered child*. Denver: American Humane Association.

Myers, J. (2006). *Child protection in America: Past, present and future*. New York: Oxford University Press.

Nelson, B. (1984). *Making an issue of child abuse*. Chicago: University of Chicago Press.

Newberger, E. (1983, April 11). *The helping hand strikes again*. Testimony given before the Subcommittee on Family and Human Services, Committee on Labor and Human Resources, U.S. Senate.

Olds, D., Sadler, L., & Kitzman, H. (2007). Programs for parents of infants and toddlers: Recent evidence from randomized trials. *Journal of Child Psychology and Psychiatry, 48*(3, 4), 355–391.

Saxe, L. (Ed.). (1988). *Children's mental health: Problems and services*. Durham, NC: Duke University Press.

Schene, P. (1998). Past, present and future roles of child protective services. *The Future of Children, 8*(1), 23–38.

Shonkoff, J., & Phillips, D. (2000). *From neurons to neighborhoods: The science of early childhood development*. Washington, DC: National Academy Press.

Silverman, F. N. (1953). The roentgen manifestations of unrecognized skeletal trauma in infants. *American Journal of Roentgenology, 69*, 413–426.

Simons, R. L., Lin, K. H., Gordon, L. C., Brody, G. H., Murry, V., & Conger, R. D. (2002). Community differences in the association between parenting practice and child conduct problems. *Journal of Marriage and Family, 64*, 331–345.

U.S. Department of Health and Human Services, National Center on Child Abuse and Neglect. (1981). *First national study of the incidence and severity of child abuse and neglect*. Washington, DC: U.S. Government Printing Office.

U.S. Department of Health and Human Services, National Center on Child Abuse and Neglect. (1988). *Second national study of the incidence and severity of child abuse and neglect*. Washington, DC: U.S. Government Printing Office.

U.S. Department of Health and Human Services, U.S. Advisory Board on Child Abuse and Neglect. (1991). *Creating caring communities: Blueprint for an effective federal policy for child abuse and neglect*. Washington, DC: U.S. Government Printing Office.

Waldfogel, J. (1988). *The future of child protection: How to break the cycle of abuse and neglect*. Cambridge, MA: Harvard University Press.

Wallack, L., & Lawrence, R. (2005, April). Talking about public health: Developing America's "second language." *American Journal of Public Health, 95*(4), 567–570.

Wulczyn, F., Barth, R. P., Yuan, Y.-Y. T., Jones Harden, B. J., & Landsverk, J. (2005). *Beyond common sense: Child welfare, child well-being, and the evidence for policy reform.* New York: Aldine-Transaction.

Wurtele, S., & Miller-Perrin, C. (1992). *Preventing child sexual abuse: Sharing the responsibility.* Lincoln: University of Nebraska Press.

Zielinski, D., & Bradshaw, C. (2006). Ecological influences on the sequelae of child maltreatment: A review of the literature. *Child Maltreatment, 11*(1), 49–62.

PART II

COMMUNITY EFFORTS TO PREVENT CHILD MALTREATMENT

Preventing Child Abuse and Neglect with Home Visiting by Nurses

David L. Olds, John Eckenrode, Charles Henderson,
Harriet Kitzman, Robert Cole, Dennis Luckey,
John Holmberg, *and* Pilar Baca

THE HISTORY OF HOME VISITING
TO PREVENT CHILD MALTREATMENT

In 1977 our team began conducting a series of randomized controlled trials of a program of prenatal and infancy home visiting by nurses for socially disadvantaged families in which the mother had no previous live births. In the ensuing 30-year period, after finding replicated program effects on a range of maternal and child health outcomes targeted by the program, we gradually began moving this program, now known as the Nurse–Family Partnership (NFP), from the laboratory to national replication, paying careful attention to the faithful replication of its essential elements as it is offered to new communities.

One of the more important findings from our original trial of this program, conducted in Elmira, New York, with a primarily white sample, was that children who were born into the most socially disadvantaged families were less likely to have indicated cases of abuse or neglect in their first 2 years of life than were their counterparts in the control group. Although this effect was only a trend ($p = .07$), it was promising in that it was corroborated by observations of parenting and conditions in the home, as well as reviews of children's emergency department encounters and injuries found in their medical records (D. L. Olds, Henderson, Chamberlin, & Tatelbaum, 1986).

We were encouraged, but believed that until the program effects were replicated with minorities living in urban environments, until the effects were
found to endure, and until we had clear methods of faithfully reproducing
the program itself in new communities, we should hold off on offering it
for public investment (D. L. Olds, Hill, O'Brien, Racine, & Moritz, 2003).
MacMillan and colleagues (2005) have noted that many home visiting
advocates were eager to begin advancing a national child abuse prevention
initiative and relied on the results of the Elmira trial of the NFP to make a
case for public investment in universal home visiting following a variety of
home visiting models delivered by a variety of visitor types.

Healthy Families America

In 1991 the U.S. Advisory Board on Child Abuse and Neglect identified
child maltreatment as a national emergency and recommended that a system of universal home visiting be established to prevent it (U.S. Advisory
Board on Child Abuse and Neglect, 1991). The Advisory Board promoted
national expansion of Hawaii Healthy Start (HHS), a program of paraprofessional home visiting beginning in the newborn period, that appeared to
prevent maltreatment in a nonrandomized study. In response to the Advisory Board's recommendation, the National Committee to Prevent Child
Abuse (known now as Prevent Child Abuse America) created Healthy
Families America (HFA), a national initiative designed to disseminate the
Hawaii model throughout the United States. In 2007, HFA programs were
operating in 430 locations throughout the United States and Canada (*www.
healthyfamiliesamerica.org*). At the time HFA was initially promoted, there
were no randomized controlled trials of this program, but today a series of
randomized controlled trials has been conducted on the HHS program and
its HFA spin-offs in Alaska, New York State, and San Diego. Moreover,
the original Hawaii Healthy Start program has been examined in a well-
conducted randomized controlled trial in Hawaii.

The results of these trials have been disappointing (Chaffin, 2004),
leading the Coalition for Evidence-Based Policy (2008) to conclude that
HHS is a program proven not to work. Although some of the trials (i.e.,
Healthy Families New York State and San Diego) found program effects
on some aspects of self-reported parenting behavior and beliefs (including
reports of abusive behaviors), there were no effects on childhood injuries
or other objectively measured outcomes consistent with the prevention
of maltreatment. A program effect on observed features of the environment, child development, and parent report of child behavior at age 2
was found in the Alaskan trial (Duggan et al., 2005), but a corresponding
effect on child development in San Diego did not endure (Landsverk et
al., 2002).

Duggan and colleagues (2005) concluded that one of the reasons the Hawaiian and Alaskan programs did not work is that they were implemented poorly, but the San Diego program was an augmented version of HFA that was implemented extraordinarily well. These findings suggest that the disappointing results observed for HFA programs are not likely to be explained simply by poor implementation, but are more likely attributable to fundamental challenges with program design. It is important to note, however, that HFA is conducted with substantial variation among its program sites, so it is possible that there are strong HFA programs producing beneficial effects.

Parenting Programs

Several studies have evaluated the impact of parent support programs on child maltreatment. A trial of the Parents as Teachers (PAT) program, using official records, reported that parents in this program had fewer instances of child maltreatment (Wagner & Clayton, 1999). Over a 2-year period covered by the intervention, 2.4% of the control group and 0% of a group that received PAT augmented with case management services had "opened" cases of child abuse and neglect. A group that received PAT alone had 1.3% opened cases, whereas a group that had case management alone had 2.7% opened cases. The low rates of opened cases, low rates of completed follow-up assessments in the trial, and investigators' use of one-tailed tests in this trial raise concerns about the meaning of these findings, especially given that there were no clinically meaningful impacts of PAT shown in tests of child development or observations of the home environment, outcomes that might corroborate the findings based on official records. The combination of PAT and case management was reported to have improved parents' reports of child development and their reported acceptance of their children's behavior, but these findings would be strengthened with corroboration by objective measures and rigorous statistical tests.

Finally, there are parenting interventions, not necessarily conducted in the home, based on teaching parents child behavioral management skills that show substantial promise. In series of randomized controlled trials both Triple P (Sanders, 1999) and Incredible Years (Webster-Stratton, 1994) have been found to improve parents' skills in management and regulation of child behavior. There is reason to expect that improved parenting and regulated child behavior can reduce the prevalence of child abuse and neglect.

Issues in Evaluating Prevention Programs

We wish to emphasize that producing program effects on official records of child maltreatment is an extraordinarily high standard for parenting and home visitor interventions, given that home visitors are mandated reporters likely to promote the detection of maltreatment, through both formal and informal mechanisms, that otherwise would go undetected (D. L. Olds, 1980; D. Olds, Henderson, Kitzman, & Cole, 1995). Moreover, official records pick up only a small portion of the maltreatment that actually occurs. In a study conducted in North and South Carolina, the rate of physically abusive parenting found in a representative sample of parents in those states was 40 times higher than rates of abuse found in child protection service records (Theodore et al., 2005). This finding means that, depending on the thoroughness of community detection systems, home-based interventions may lead to an increase in official records of maltreatment. At the very least, surveillance bias may mask the preventive effect of such programs on the occurrence of actual maltreatment.

To make the assessment of maltreatment even more complicated, parent report by itself does not provide compelling evidence of program impact. If study samples are large enough and the systems of official reports of maltreatment are accurate, then studies should track official records of maltreatment, but such studies also need to include observations of children's homes, qualities of caregiving, and objective measures of child well-being to give a comprehensive picture of whether an intervention has prevented maltreatment (D. L. Olds & Henderson, 1989). The studies reviewed here emphasize just how complicated it can be to obtain an understanding of whether home-based interventions prevent child abuse and neglect (Mac-Millan et al., 2005).

In this chapter we summarize the program of research conducted on the NFP, giving particular attention to its impact on child maltreatment, and we describe our efforts to help new communities develop the program well outside of research contexts.

THE NURSE–FAMILY PARTNERSHIP

The NFP is a program of prenatal and infancy home visiting by nurses for low-income mothers—who have had no previous live births—and their families. Forty percent of all births in the United States are to mothers bearing first children, so the portion of the population that may be served by this program is substantial. The NFP focuses on improving the neurodevelopmental, cognitive, and behavioral functioning of the child by improving prenatal health, reducing dysfunctional care of the child early in life (including child abuse and neglect), and enhancing family functioning and economic self-sufficiency. These early alterations in biology, behavior, and family context are expected to shift the life course trajectories of children living in highly disadvantaged families and neighborhoods away from psychopathology, substance use disorders, and risky sexual behaviors (D. L. Olds, 2007).

Part of the effect of the program is now thought to be accomplished by moderating environmental risks that interact with genetic variations to increase the risk for poor child health and development. In evaluating this program, it is important to understand its theoretical and empirical foundations and the role that dysfunctional caregiving plays in our thinking about the program's long-term impact on adolescent health and development.

Theory-Driven

The NFP is grounded in theories of human ecology (Kitzman, Yoos, Cole, Korfrmacher, & Hanks, 1997; D. L. Olds, Luckey, & Henderson, 2005), self-efficacy (D. Olds et al., 1998), and human attachment (D. L. Olds, 2005). Together, these theories emphasize the importance of families' social contexts and individuals' beliefs, motivations, emotions, and internal representations of their early parenting experiences, in explaining development.

Human ecology theory, for example, emphasizes that children's development is influenced by how their parents care for them, which is, in turn, influenced by characteristics of their families, social networks, neighborhoods, communities, and the interrelations between them (D. L. Olds et al., 2005). Drawing on this theory, nurses attempt to enhance the material and social environment of the family by involving other family members, especially fathers, in the home visits and by linking families with needed health and human services (D. L. Olds, 1980).

Parents help to select and shape the settings in which they find themselves, however (Plomin, 1986). Self-efficacy theory provides a useful framework for understanding how women make decisions about their health-related behaviors during pregnancy, their care of their children, and their own personal development. This theory suggests that individuals choose those behaviors that they believe (1) will lead to a given outcome and (2) they themselves can successfully carry out (Bandura, 1977). Individuals' perceptions of their likely success influence their choices and determine how much effort they put forth to get what they want in the face of obstacles.

The program therefore is designed to help women understand what is known about the influence of their behaviors on their own health and that of their babies. The home visitors help parents establish realistic goals and small achievable objectives that, once accomplished, increase the parents' reservoirs of successful experiences. These successes, in turn, increase the women's confidence in taking on larger challenges.

Finally, the program is based on attachment theory, which posits that infants are biologically predisposed to seek proximity to specific caregivers in times of stress, illness, or fatigue in order to promote survival (Bowlby, 1969). Attachment theory posits that children's trust in the world and their later capacity for empathy and responsiveness to their own children, once they become parents, are influenced by the degree to which they formed an attachment with a caring, responsive, and sensitive adult when they were growing up, which affects their internal representations of themselves and their relationships with others (Main, Kaplan, & Cassidy, 1985).

The program therefore explicitly promotes sensitive, responsive, and engaged caregiving in the early years of the child's life (Dolezol & Butterfield, 1994). To accomplish this, the nurses help mothers and other caregivers review their own childrearing histories and make decisions about how they wish to care for their children in light of the way they were cared for as children. Finally, the visitors seek to develop an empathic and trusting relationship with the mothers and other family members because experience with such a relationship is expected to help women eventually trust others and to promote more sensitive, empathic care of their children.

Epidemiological Foundations

Focus on Low-Income, Unmarried, and Teen Parents

The NFP registers low-income women having first births and thus enrolls large numbers of unmarried and adolescent mothers. These populations have relatively high rates of the problems the program was designed originally to address (e.g., poor birth outcomes, child abuse and neglect, and diminished parental economic self-sufficiency) (Elster & McAnarney, 1980; Overpeck, Brenner, Trumble, Trifiletti, & Berendes, 1998). Women bearing first children are particularly receptive to this service, and to the extent that they improve their prenatal health, care of their firstborns, and life course, they are likely to apply those skills to subsequent pregnancies and births (D. L. Olds, 2002, 2006).

Program Content

The NFP seeks to promote protective factors and reduce specific risks for poor birth outcomes, neurocognitive impairments, child abuse and neglect, injuries, and compromised parental life course (Figure 2.1). The reduced exposure to prenatal toxicants, child abuse and neglect, and untoward family environments is expected to shift the child's health and development toward greater behavioral regulation and interpersonal and cognitive competence, eventually leading to reduced exposure to and engagement with antisocial, deviant peers.

Interrupting Gene × Environment Interactions

Given recent evidence on the interplay between genes and environments (Rutter, Moffitt, & Caspi, 2006), we have broadened our conceptual model of the program to incorporate this emerging evidence. The NFP probably produces part of its effects by interrupting gene × environment interactions that have been found to increase the risk for low birth weight (Wang et al., 2002), impulsive and oppositional behavior (Kahn, Khoury, Nichols, & Lanphear, 2003), violent behavior, depression, and psychosis (Caspi et al., 2002; Rutter et al., 2006). Environmental adversities increase the risk for poor outcomes in the presence of susceptibility variants of functional polymorphisms, termed "genetic vulnerabilities" in Figure 2.1.

Prenatal Health Behaviors

Prenatal tobacco and alcohol exposures increase the risk for fetal growth restriction (Kramer, 1987), preterm birth (Kramer, 1987), and neurodevelopmental impairment (e.g., attention-deficit disorder, cognitive and language delays) (Fried, Watkinson, Dillon, & Dulberg, 1987; Mayes, 1994; Milberger, Biederman, Faraone, Chen, & Jones, 1996; D. L. Olds, 1997; D. L. Olds, Henderson, & Tatelbaum, 1994a, 1994b; Sood et al., 2001; Streissguth, Sampson, Barr, Bookstein, & Olson, 1994). Children born with subtle neurological perturbations resulting from prenatal exposure to stress and substances are more likely to be irritable and inconsolable (Clark, Soto, & Bergholz, 1996; Saxon, 1978; Streissguth et al., 1994), making it more difficult for parents to enjoy their care. Improved prenatal health thus helps parents become competent caregivers.

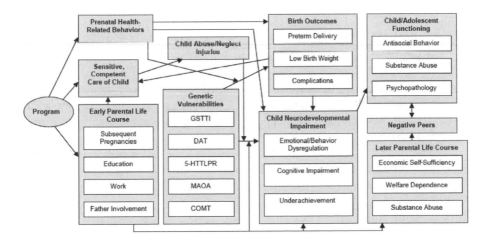

FIGURE 2.1. General conceptual model of program influences on maternal and child health and development.

The impacts of tobacco and alcohol exposure on birthweight and dys-regulated behavior are increased in the presence of susceptibility variants of functional polymorphisms. A polymorphism in the *GSTTI* gene, for example, increases the risk for low birth weight in the presence of maternal prenatal smoking (Wang et al., 2002). Similarly, a polymorphism in the dopamine transporter gene (*DAT*) has been found to increase the risk for preschoolers' impulsive and oppositional behavior when mothers smoke during pregnancy (Kahn et al., 2003) and to increase children's attention-deficit/hyperactivity disorder (ADHD) when they have prenatal alcohol exposure (Brookes et al., 2006; Kahn et al., 2003; Wang et al., 2002). Pro-gram impacts on children's behavioral dysregulation are thus likely to be greatest among those who are both genetically vulnerable and at risk for exposure to these substances during pregnancy, given the nurses' reduction in women's prenatal tobacco use (D. L. Olds, Henderson, Tatelbaum, & Chamberlin, 1986).

Sensitive, Competent Care of the Child

Parents who empathize with and respond sensitively to their infants' cues are more likely to understand their children's competencies, which leads to less maltreatment and fewer unintentional injuries (Cole et al., 2004; Peterson & Gable, 1998). Competent early parenting is associated with better child behavior regulation, language, and cognition (Hart & Risley, 1995). Later demanding, responsive, and positive parenting can provide some protection from the damaging effects of stressful environ-ments and negative peers (Bremner, 1999; Field et al., 1998) on external-izing symptoms and substance use (Baumrind, 1987; Biglan, Duncan, Ary, & Smolkowski, 1995; Cohen, Navaline, & Metzger, 1994; Field et al., 1998; Grant et al., 2000; Johnson & Pandina, 1991). In general, poor parenting is correlated with low child serotonin levels (Pine, 2001, 2003), which, in turn, are implicated in stress-induced delays in neurodevelop-ment (Bremner & Vermetten, 2004). Child abuse and neglect can lead to different behavioral phenotypes, depending on particular functional polymorphisms.

There is now consistent evidence that the *5HTTLPR* polymorphism in the gene encoding for the serotonin transporter interacts with maltreatment and life stress to increase risk for major depression in humans (Caspi et al., 2003; Eley et al., 2004; Taylor et al., 2006; Wilhelm et al., 2006) and alco-hol consumption in primates (Barr et al., 2003). Moreover, social support may moderate the interacting influences of the *5HTTLPR* polymorphism and child maltreatment (Kaufman et al., 2006). Although not as consistent as the evidence for *5HTTLPR*, most studies indicate that a polymorphism in the gene that encodes monoamine oxidase A interacts with child abuse to increase the risk for severe antisocial, violent behavior in adolescent males (Caspi et al., 2002; Kim-Cohen et al., 2006).

As indicated in the following discussions of results, the NFP has reduced child maltreatment and dysfunctional care of the child, environmental conditions that interact with these genotypes. We are now conducting long-term follow-ups of our samples and genotyping of the children in order to understand the extent to which long-term program effects on adolescent psychopathology and substance use disorders (SUDs) do occur and to specify more precisely those groups who benefit from the intervention, those who do not, and why.

Early Parental Life Course

Closely spaced subsequent births undermine unmarried women's educational achievement and workforce participation (Furstenberg, Brooks-Gunn, & Morgan, 1987) and increase the risk for children's injuries (Nathens, Neff, Goss, Maier, & Rivara, 2000), probably because of compromised parental supervision. Married couples are more likely to achieve economic self-sufficiency, and their children are at lower risk for a host of problems (McLanahan & Carlson, 2002). Nurses therefore promote fathers' involvement (D. L. Olds, 1980) and help women make appropriate choices about the timing of subsequent pregnancies and the kinds of men they allow into their lives, given that antisocial men can exert adverse influences on children (Jaffee, Moffitt, Caspi, & Taylor, 2003).

The reduction in prenatal risks, dysfunctional care of the infant, and improvement in family context is thus important in its own right, but is also likely to have long-term effects on youth antisocial behavior that has its roots in early experience.

Program Design

The same basic program design has been used in Elmira, New York; Memphis; and Denver.

Frequency of Visitation

The recommended frequency of home visits changed with the stages of pregnancy and was adapted to parents' needs, with nurses visiting more frequently in times of family crisis. Mothers were enrolled through the end of the second trimester of pregnancy. In Elmira, Memphis, and Denver, the nurses completed an average of 9 (range 0–16), 7 (range 0–18), and 6.5 (range 0–17) visits during pregnancy, respectively; and 23 (range 0–59), 26 (range 0–71), and 21 (range 0–71) visits from birth to the child's second birthday. Paraprofessionals in Denver completed an average of 6 (range 0–21) prenatal visits and 16 (range 0–78) visits during the child's infancy. Each visit lasted approximately 75–90 minutes.

Nurses as Home Visitors

Nurses were selected as home visitors in the Elmira and Memphis trials because of their formal training in women's and children's health and their competence in managing the complex clinical situations often presented by at-risk families. Nurses' abilities to address mothers' and family members' concerns about the complications of pregnancy, labor, and delivery and the physical health of the infant in a competent manner are thought to provide these visitors with increased credibility and persuasive power in the eyes of family members. In any voluntary prevention program, participants must have sufficient confidence and trust in service providers to welcome them into their lives and homes and engage in the preventive intervention. Nurses thus have a special advantage in working with pregnant women and parents of newborns.

Program Content

The nurses had three major goals: (1) to improve the outcomes of pregnancy by helping women improve their prenatal health, (2) to improve the child's subsequent health and development by helping parents provide more competent care, and (3) to improve parents' life course by helping them develop visions for their future and then make smart choices about planning future pregnancies, completing their education, and finding work. In the service of these goals, the nurses helped the women build supportive relationships with family members and friends and linked families with other services.

The nurses followed detailed visit-by-visit guidelines whose content reflected the challenges parents were likely to confront during specific stages of pregnancy and the first 2 years of a child's life. Specific assessments were made of maternal, child, and family functioning that corresponded to those stages, and specific activities were recommended on the basis of the problems and strengths identified through the assessments.

During pregnancy, the nurses helped the women to complete 24-hour diet histories on a regular basis and to plot weight gains at every visit; they assessed the women's cigarette smoking and use of alcohol and illegal drugs and facilitated a reduction in the use of these substances through behavioral change strategies. They taught the women to identify the signs and symptoms of pregnancy complications, encouraged them to inform the office-based providers about those conditions, and facilitated compliance with treatment. They gave particular attention to urinary tract infections, sexually transmitted diseases, and hypertensive disorders of pregnancy (conditions associated with poor birth outcomes). They coordinated care with physicians and nurses in the office and measured blood pressure when needed.

After delivery, the nurses helped the mothers and other caregivers to improve the physical and emotional care of their children. They taught parents to observe the signs of illness, to take temperatures, and to communicate with office staff members about their children's illnesses before seeking care. Curricula were employed to promote parent–child interaction by facilitating the parents' understanding of their infants' and toddlers' communicative signals, enhancing the parents' interest in interacting with their children to promote and protect their health and development.

Research Designs, Methods, and Findings

In each of the three trials, women were randomized to receive either home visitation or comparison services. Although the nature of the home visitation services was essentially the same in each of the trials as described earlier, the comparison services were slightly different. Both studies employed a variety of data sources. The Elmira sample ($n = 400$) was primarily white. The Memphis sample ($n = 1,138$ for pregnancy and 743 for the infancy phase) was primarily black. The Denver trial ($n = 735$) consisted of a large sample of Hispanic women and systematically examined the impact of the program when delivered by paraprofessionals (individuals who shared many of the social characteristics of the families they served) and by nurses. We looked for consistency in program effect across those sources before assigning much importance to any one finding. Unless otherwise stated, all findings reported in the following discussions were significant at the $p \leq .05$ level using two-tailed tests.

Elmira Results

PRENATAL HEALTH BEHAVIORS

During pregnancy, as compared with their counterparts in the control group, nurse-visited women improved the quality of their diets to a greater extent, and those identified as smokers smoked 25% fewer cigarettes by the 34th week of pregnancy (D. L. Olds, Henderson, Tatelbaum, & Chamberlin, 1986). By the end of pregnancy, nurse-visited women experienced greater informal social support and made better use of formal community services.

PREGNANCY AND BIRTH OUTCOMES

By the end of pregnancy, nurse-visited women had fewer kidney infections; among women who smoked, those who were nurse-visited had 75% fewer preterm deliveries; and among very young adolescents (ages 14–16), those who were nurse-visited had babies who were 395 grams heavier than those of their counterparts assigned to the comparison group (D. L. Olds, Henderson, Tatelbaum, & Chamberlin, 1986).

SENSITIVE, COMPETENT CARE OF CHILD

At 10 and 22 months of the children's lives, nurse-visited poor, unmarried teens, in contrast to their counterparts in the control group, exhibited less punishment and restriction of their infants and provided more appropriate play materials than did their counterparts in the control group (D. L. Olds, Henderson, Chamberlin, & Tatelbaum, 1986). At 34 and 46 months of the children's lives, nurse-visited mothers provided home environments that were more conducive to their children's emotional and cognitive development and that were safer (D. L. Olds, Henderson, & Kitzman, 1994).

CHILD ABUSE, NEGLECT, AND INJURIES

During their first 2 years of life, nurse-visited children born to low-income, unmarried teens had 80% fewer verified cases of child abuse and neglect than did their counterparts in the control group (1 case or 4% of the nurse-visited teens, versus 8 cases or 19% of the control group, $p = .07$). During the second year of life, nurse-visited children were seen in the emergency department 32% fewer times than their control-group counterparts, a difference that was explained in part by a 56% reduction in visits for injuries and ingestions (D. L. Olds, Henderson, Chamberlin, & Tatelbaum, 1986).

The effect of the program on child abuse and neglect in the first 2 years of life and on emergency department encounters in the second year of life was greatest among children whose mothers had little belief in their control over their lives when they first registered for the program, an effect that emphasizes the influence of parenting efficacy on caregiving and child well-being (D. L. Olds, Henderson, Chamberlin, & Tatelbaum, 1986).

During the 2 years after the program ended, its impact on health care encounters for injuries endured: Irrespective of risk, children of nurse-visited women were less likely than their control group counterparts to receive emergency room treatment or to visit a physician for injuries and ingestions (D. L. Olds, Henderson, & Kitzman, 1994). The impact of the program on state-verified cases of child abuse and neglect, however, disappeared during that 2-year period (D. L. Olds, Henderson, & Kitzman, 1994), probably because of increased detection of child abuse and neglect in nurse-visited families and the nurses' linkage of families with needed services (including child protective services) at the end of the program (Geene, 2001).

Results from a 15-year follow-up of the Elmira sample (D. L. Olds et al., 1997) indicate that the program effects on state-verified reports of child abuse and neglect grew between the children's 4th and 15th birthdays. During the 15-year period after delivery of their first child, in contrast to women in the comparison group, those visited by nurses during pregnancy and infancy were identified as perpetrators of child abuse and neglect in an average of 0.29 versus 0.54 verified reports per program participant; this effect was more pronounced for women who were poor and unmarried at registration (D. L. Olds et al., 1997). The impact of the program on child abuse and neglect through age 15 of the children was attenuated in the context of moderate to high levels of intimate partner violence (Eckenrode et al., 2000).

CHILD NEURODEVELOPMENTAL IMPAIRMENT

With children at 6 months of age, nurse-visited poor unmarried teens reported that their infants were less irritable and fussy than did their counterparts in the comparison group (D. L. Olds, Henderson, Tatelbaum, & Chamberlin, 1986). Subsequent analyses of the data indicated that these differences were really concentrated among infants born to nurse-visited women who smoked 10 or more cigarettes per day during pregnancy, in contrast to babies born to women who smoked 10 or more cigarettes per day in the comparison group (Olds, Henderson, et al., 1998). Over the first 4 years of life, children born to comparison group women who smoked 10 or more cigarettes per day during pregnancy experienced a 4- to 5-point decline in intellectual functioning, in contrast to comparison group children whose mothers smoked 0–9 cigarettes per day during pregnancy (D. L. Olds et al., 1994a). In the nurse-visited condition, children whose mothers smoked 0–9 cigarettes per day at registration did not experience this decline in intellectual functioning, so that at ages 3 and 4 their IQ scores on the Stanford–Binet test were about 4–5 points higher than those of their counterparts in the comparison group whose mothers smoked 10+ cigarettes per day at registration (D. L. Olds et al., 1994b).

EARLY PARENTAL LIFE COURSE

By the time the first child was 4 years of age, nurse-visited low-income, unmarried women, in contrast to their counterparts in the control group, had fewer subsequent pregnancies, longer intervals between the births of first and second children, and greater participation in the workforce than did their comparison group counterparts (D. L. Olds, Henderson, Tatel-baum, & Chamberlin, 1988).

LATER PARENTAL LIFE COURSE

At the 15-year follow-up, no differences were reported for the full sample on measures of maternal life course, such as subsequent pregnancies or subsequent births, the number of months between first and second births, receipt of welfare assistance, or months of employment. Poor unmarried women, however, showed a number of enduring benefits. In contrast to their counterparts in the comparison condition, those visited by nurses averaged fewer subsequent pregnancies, fewer subsequent births, longer intervals between the birth of their first and second children, fewer months on welfare, fewer months receiving food stamps, fewer behavioral problems due to substance abuse, and fewer arrests (D. L. Olds et al., 1997).

CHILD/ADOLESCENT FUNCTIONING

Among the 15-year-old children of study participants, those visited by nurses had fewer arrests and adjudications as persons in need of supervision (PINS). These effects were greater for children born to mothers who were poor and unmarried at registration. Nurse-visited children, as trends, reported fewer sexual partners and fewer convictions and violations of probation.

Memphis Results

PRENATAL HEALTH BEHAVIORS

There were no program effects on women's use of standard prenatal care or obstetrical emergency services after registration in the study. By the 36th week of pregnancy, nurse-visited women were more likely to use other community services than were women in the control group. There were no program effects on women's cigarette smoking, probably because the rate of cigarette use was only 9% in this sample and the number of cigarettes smoked among tobacco users was lower than among smokers in Elmira.

PREGNANCY AND BIRTH OUTCOMES

In contrast to women in the comparison group, nurse-visited women had fewer instances of pregnancy-induced hypertension, and among those with the diagnosis, the cases were less serious in nurse-visited women (Kitzman et al., 1997).

SENSITIVE, COMPETENT CARE OF CHILD

Nurse-visited mothers reported that they attempted breast-feeding more frequently than did women in the comparison group, although there were no differences in the duration of breast-feeding. By the children's 24th month of life, in contrast to their comparison group counterparts, nurse-visited women held fewer beliefs about childrearing associated with child abuse and neglect. Moreover, the homes of nurse-visited women were rated as more conducive to children's development. Although there was no program effect on observed maternal teaching behavior, children born to nurse-visited mothers with low levels of psychological resources (limited intellectual functioning and mastery and higher rates of psychological distress) were observed to be more communicative and responsive toward their mothers than were their comparison group counterparts (Kitzman et al., 1997).

CHILD ABUSE, NEGLECT, AND INJURIES

The rate of substantiated child abuse and neglect in the population of 2-year-old, low-income children in Memphis was too low (3–4%) to serve as a valid indicator of child maltreatment in this study. We therefore hypothesized that we would see a pattern of program effects on childhood injuries similar to that observed in Elmira—that is, effects concentrated in more psychologically vulnerable mothers (again, defined by mothers having limited intellectual functioning and mastery and higher rates of psychological distress). During their first 2 years, as compared with children in the comparison group, nurse-visited children had 23% fewer healthcare encounters for injuries and ingestions and were hospitalized for 79% fewer days with injuries and/or ingestions, effects that, again, were more pronounced for children born to mothers with few psychological resources. Nurse-visited children tended to be older (and more mobile) when hospitalized and to have less severe conditions, as compared with children in the control group who had been hospitalized. The reasons for hospitalizations suggest that many of the comparison group children suffered from more seriously deficient care than children visited by nurses.

CHILDHOOD MORTALITY

Because infant and childhood mortalities are such infrequently occurring events, we did not hypothesize that we would observe program effects on childhood deaths, but found nevertheless that by age 9 children in the control group were 4.5 times more likely to have died than their counterparts in the nurse-visited group, a difference that was significant at the $p = .08$ level; in other words, this was a trend. There were 10 deaths in the control group;

one of these was not preventable (because of multiple congenital anomalies), three were due to preterm delivery; three were due to sudden infant death syndrome; and three were due to injury, including two by firearms. The one death in the nurse-visited group was due to a chromosomal anomaly (D. L. Olds et al., 2007). These findings are consistent with the earlier findings on childhood injury in the first 2 years of life and reinforce the interpretation that the program reduced the rates of grossly deficient care of children.

CHILD NEURODEVELOPMENTAL IMPAIRMENT

By age 6, as compared with their counterparts in the control group, children visited by nurses had higher intellectual functioning and receptive vocabulary scores and fewer behavior problems in the borderline or clinical range. Nurse-visited children born to mothers with low levels of psychological resources had higher arithmetic achievement test scores and expressed less aggression and incoherence in response to story stems.

EARLY PARENTAL LIFE COURSE

At the 24th month of the first child's life, nurse-visited women reported fewer second pregnancies and fewer subsequent live births than did women in the comparison group. Nurse-visited women and their first-born children relied on welfare for fewer months during the second year of the child's life than did comparison group women and their children (Kitzman et al., 1997). At ages 6 and 9 of their children's lives, nurse-visited women had more stable relationships with their male partners (D. Olds et al., 2004; D. L. Olds et al., 2007).

LATER PARENTAL LIFE COURSE

During the 9-year period following the birth of the first child, in contrast to control group counterparts, women visited by nurses had longer durations between the birth of the first and second child, fewer months of using welfare and food stamps, and more stable relationships with male partners (Kitzman et al., 2000; D. Olds et al., 2004; D. L. Olds et al., 2007).

Denver Results

In the Denver trial, we were unable to use the women's or children's medical records to assess their injury encounters because the healthcare delivery system was too complex to abstract reliably all of their healthcare encounters as we had done in Elmira and Memphis. Moreover, as in Memphis, the rate of state-verified reports of child abuse and neglect was too low in this population (3–4% for low-income children from birth to 2 years of age) to use child protective service records to assess the impact of the program on child maltreatment. We therefore focused more of our measurement resources on the early emotional development of infants and toddlers.

DENVER RESULTS FOR PARAPROFESSIONALS

There were no paraprofessional visitation effects on women's prenatal health behavior (use of tobacco), maternal life course, or child development, although at 24 months, paraprofessional-visited mother–child pairs in which the mother had a low level of psychological resources interacted more responsively than did control group counterparts. Moreover, although paraprofessional-visited women did not have a statistically significant reduction in the rates of subsequent pregnancy, the reduction observed was a trend ($p < .10$) and clinically meaningful. By the time the children were age 4, mothers and children visited by paraprofessionals, as compared with controls, displayed greater sensitivity and responsiveness toward one another and, in those cases in which the mothers had low levels of psychological resources at registration, had home environments that were more supportive of children's early learning. Children of low-resource women visited by paraprofessionals had better behavioral adaptation during testing than their control group counterparts.

DENVER RESULTS FOR NURSES

Nurse visitations produced effects consistent with those achieved in earlier trials of the program.

Prenatal Health Behaviors. In contrast to their control group counterparts, nurse-visited smokers had greater reductions in urine cotinine (the major nicotine metabolite) from intake to the end of pregnancy (D. L. Olds et al., 2002).

Sensitive, Competent Care of Child. During the first 24 months of the child's life, nurse-visited mother–infant dyads interacted more responsively than did control pairs, an effect concentrated in the low-resource group. As a trend ($p < .10$), nurse-visited mothers provided home environments that were more supportive of children's early learning.

Child Neurodevelopmental Impairment. At 6 months of age, nurse-visited infants, in contrast to their control group counterparts, were less likely to exhibit emotional vulnerability in response to fear stimuli, and those born to women with low levels of psychological resources were less likely to display low levels of emotional vitality in response to joy and anger stimuli. At 21 months, nurse-visited children were less likely to exhibit language delays than were children in the control group, an effect again concentrated among children born to mothers with low levels of psychological resources. Nurse-visited children born to women with low levels of psychological resources also had superior language and mental development, in contrast to control group counterparts. At age 4, nurse-visited children whose mothers had low levels of psychological resources at registration, as compared with control group counterparts, had more advanced language, superior executive functioning, and better behavioral adaptation during testing (D. Olds et al., 2004).

Early Maternal Life Course. By 24 months after delivery, nurse-visited women, as compared with controls, were less likely to have had a subsequent pregnancy and birth and had longer intervals until the next conception. Women visited by nurses were employed longer during the second year following the birth of their first child than were controls. By age 4 of their children, nurse-visited women continued to have greater intervals between the birth of their first and second child, less domestic violence, and enrolled their children less frequently in preschool, Head Start, or licensed daycare than did controls (D. Olds et al., 2004).

Cost Savings

The Washington State Institute for Public Policy has conducted a thorough economic analysis of prevention programs from the standpoint of their impact on crime, substance abuse, educational outcomes, teen pregnancy, suicide, child abuse and neglect, and domestic violence (Aos, Lieb, Mayfield, Miller, & Pennucci, 2004). Although this analysis does not cover all outcomes that have cost implications for the NFP (such as the rates and outcomes of subsequent pregnancies, maternal employment), it provides a consistent examination of all programs that have attempted to affect the listed outcomes. This report summed the findings across all three trials of the NFP and estimated that it saves $17,000 per family. This estimate is consistent with a subsequent analysis produced by the Rand Corporation (Karoly, Kilburn, & Cannon, 2005).

Policy Implications and Program Replication

One of the clearest messages that has emerged from this program of research is that the functional and economic benefits of the nurse–home visitation program are greatest for families at greater risk. In Elmira, it was evident that most married women and those in higher socioeconomic-status households managed the care of their children without serious problems and that they were able to avoid lives of welfare dependence, substance abuse, and crime without the assistance of the nurse home visitors. Low-income, unmarried women and their children in the control group, however, were at much greater risk for such problems, and the program was able to avert many of these untoward outcomes for this at-risk population. This pattern of results challenges the position that intensive programs of this type for targeted at-risk groups ought to be made available on a universal basis. Not only is it likely to be wasteful from an economic standpoint, but such an approach may lead to a dilution of services for those families who need them most, because of insufficient resources to serve everyone well.

One of the reasons the NFP has been given attention by policymakers is that it reduced indicated reports of child abuse and neglect in Elmira. By age 15 of children involved, the nurse-visited group had 48% fewer verified reports of maltreatment than did the control group, and 77% fewer verified reports among mothers who were at higher risk, as compared with control group counterparts. The impact of the NFP on indicated cases of child abuse and neglect was limited to Elmira, however, as the rates of maltreatment found in the official records in Memphis and Denver were too low in the first 2 years of the children's lives (3–4%) to serve as valid outcomes. In recent years we have discovered that one of the reasons that child protective service (CPS) records in Tennessee were so low is that the system for managing this information was seriously flawed and data in that system were invalid, an issue addressed by a suit to reform Tennessee's child welfare system (Yellin, 2000). Overall, the rates of indicated cases of maltreatment in the Elmira control group were about three times higher than in Memphis and Denver, and six to seven times higher for families at greater risk. Given that CPS records typically pick up only a small fraction of actual maltreatment, the results in Elmira are even more important. Finally, we need to emphasize that maltreatment is detected at a greater rate in visited families because visitors are mandated reporters; moreover, they are likely to activate awareness of maltreatment among both formal service providers and family members and friends whom they engage in the NFP program (D. L. Olds, 1980), which is likely to lead to more complete detection of maltreatment in the nurse-visited group (D. Olds et al., 1995).

Replication and Scale-Up of the NFP

Even when communities choose to develop programs based on models with good scientific evidence, such programs run the risk of being watered down in the process of being scaled up to serve a larger number of communities. In 1996 our team accepted an invitation by the U.S. Justice Department to set up the NFP in high-crime communities throughout the United States. We had held off on offering it for public investment until we had enduring evidence of program effects on clinically important outcomes from replicated randomized trials. Even then, it was with some apprehension that our team began to make the program available for public investment in new communities, as we were concerned that the program would be watered down and compromised in the process of being scaled up (D. L. Olds et al., 2003). We therefore created the Nurse–Family Partnership National Service Office, a nonprofit organization devoted to helping new communities replicate the NFP in community settings with fidelity to the model tested in the scientifically controlled studies.

Each site choosing to implement the NFP needs certain capacities to operate and sustain the program with high quality. These capacities include having an organization and community that are fully knowledgeable and supportive of the program, a staff that is well trained and supported in the conduct of the program model, and a real-time information system that benchmarks implementation of the program and maternal and child health outcomes. These accountability data guide efforts to improve continuously the quality of program implementation. Staff members at the NFP National Service Office are organized to help create these state and local capacities (*www.nursefamilypartnership.org*).

Since 1996, the NFP national office has helped new communities develop the program outside traditional research contexts, so that today the program is operating in 310 counties nationally. State and local governments are securing financial support for the NFP (about $9,500 per family for 2½ years of services, in 2006 dollars) out of existing sources of funds, such as Temporary Assistance to Needy Families, Medicaid, the Maternal and Child Health Block Grant, and child abuse and crime prevention dollars.

ACKNOWLEDGMENTS

The work reported here was made possible by support from many different sources. These include the Administration for Children and Families (90PD0215/01 and 90PJ0003), Biomedical Research Support (PHS S7RR05403-25), Bureau of Community Health Services, Maternal and Child Health Research Grants Division (MCR-360403-07-0), Carnegie Corporation (B-5492), Colorado Trust (93059), Commonwealth Fund (10443), David and Lucile Packard Foundation (95-1842), Ford Foundation (840-0545, 845-0031, and 875-0559), Maternal and Child Health, U.S. Department of Health and Human Services (MCJ-363378-01-0), National Center for Nursing Research (NR01-01691-05), National Institute of Mental Health (1-K05-MH01382-01 and 1-R01-MH49381-01A1), Pew Charitable Trusts (88-0211-000), Robert Wood Johnson Foundation (179-34, 5263, 6729, 9677, and 35369), U.S. Department of Justice (95-DD-BX-0181), and W. T. Grant Foundation (80072380, 84072380, 86108086, and 88124688). We thank John Shannon for his support of the program and data gathering through Comprehensive Interdisciplinary Developmental Services, Elmira, New York; Robert Chamberlin and Robert Tatelbaum for their contributions to the early phases of this research; Jackie Roberts, Liz Chilson, Lyn Scazafabo, Georgie McGrady, and Diane Farr for their home visitation work with the Elmira families; Geraldine Smith, for her supervision of the nurses in Memphis; Jann Belton and Carol Ballard, for integrating the program into the Memphis/Shelby County Health Department; Kim Arcoleo and Jane Powers for their work on the Elmira and Memphis trials; Ruth O'Brien, JoAnn Robinson, Pilar Baca, and Susan Hiatt, and the many home-visiting nurses in Memphis and Denver; and the participating families who have made this program of research possible.

REFERENCES

Aos, S., Lieb, R., Mayfield, J., Miller, M., & Pennucci, A. (2004). *Benefits and costs of prevention and early intervention programs for youth.* Olympia: Washington State Institute for Public Policy.

Bandura, A. (1977). Self-efficacy: Toward a unifying theory of behavioral change. *Psychological Review, 84*(2), 191–215.

Barr, C. S., Newman, T. K., Becker, M. L., Champoux, M., Lesch, K. P., Suomi, S. J., et al. (2003). Serotonin transporter gene variation is associated with alcohol sensitivity in rhesus macaques exposed to early-life stress. *Alcoholism: Clinical and Experimental Research, 27*(5), 812–817.

Baumrind, D. (1987). Familial antecedents of adolescent drug use: A developmental perspective. *National Institute of Drug Abuse Monographs, 56* (DHHS Publication No. ADM 87-1335). Washington, DC: U.S. Government Printing Office.

Biglan, A., Duncan, T. E., Ary, D. V., & Smolkowski, K. (1995). Peer and parental influences on adolescent tobacco use. *Journal of Behavioral Medicine, 18*(4), 315–330.

Bowlby, J. (1969). *Attachment and loss: Vol. 1. Attachment.* New York: Basic Books.

Bremner, J. D. (1999). Does stress damage the brain? *Biological Psychiatry, 45*(7), 797–805.

Bremner, J. D., & Vermetten, E. (2004). Neuroanatomical changes associated with pharmacotherapy in posttraumatic stress disorder. *Annals of the New York Academy of Sciences, 1032,* 154–157.

Brookes, K. J., Mill, J., Guindalini, C., Curran, S., Xu, X., Knight, J., et al. (2006). A common haplotype of the dopamine transporter gene associated with attention-deficit/hyperactivity disorder and interacting with maternal use of alcohol during pregnancy. *Archives of General Psychiatry, 63*(1), 74–81.

Caspi, A., McClay, J., Moffitt, T. E., Mill, J., Martin, J., Craig, I. W., et al. (2002). Role of genotype in the cycle of violence in maltreated children. *Science, 297,* 851–854.

Caspi, A., Sugden, K., Moffitt, T. E., Taylor, A., Craig, I. W., Harrington, H., et al. (2003). Influence of life stress on depression: Moderation by a polymorphism in the *5-HTT* gene. *Science, 301,* 386–389.

Chaffin, M. (2004). Is it time to rethink Healthy Start/Healthy Families? *Child Abuse and Neglect, 28*(6), 589–595.

Clark, A. S., Soto, S., & Bergholz, T. S. M. (1996). Maternal gestational stress alters adaptive and social behavior in adolescent rhesus monkey offspring. *Infant Behavior and Development, 19*, 453–463.

Coalition for Evidence-Based Policy. (2008) *Social programs that work.* Retrieved March 31, 2008, from *www.evidencebasedprograms.org/Default. aspx?tabid=30.*

Cohen, E., Navaline, H., & Metzger, D. (1994). High-risk behaviors for HIV: A comparison between crack-abusing and opioid-abusing African-American women. *Journal of Psychoactive Drugs, 26*(3), 233–241.

Cole, R., Henderson, C. R. J., Kitzman, H., Anson, E., Eckenrode, J., & Sidora, K. (2004). *Long-term effects of nurse home visitation on maternal employment.* Unpublished manuscript.

Dolezol, S., & Butterfield, P. M. (1994). *Partners in parenting education.* Denver: How to Read Your Baby.

Duggan, A., Rodriguez, K., Burrell, L., Shea, S., Rohde, C., & Caldera, D. (2005). *Evaluation of the Healthy Families Alaska Program.* Retrieved March 31, 2008, from *www.hss.state.ak.us/ocs/Publications/JohnsHopkins_HealthyFamilies.pdf.*

Eckenrode, J., Ganzel, B., Henderson, C. R., Jr., Smith, E., Olds, D. L., Powers, J., et al. (2000). Preventing child abuse and neglect with a program of nurse home visitation: The limiting effects of domestic violence. *Journal of the American Medical Association, 284*(11), 1385–1391.

Eley, T. C., Sugden, K., Corsico, A., Gregory, A. M., Sham, P., McGuffin, P., et al. (2004). Gene–environment interaction analysis of serotonin system markers with adolescent depression. *Molecular Psychiatry, 9*(10), 908–915.

Elster, A. B., & McAnarney, E. R. (1980). Medical and psychosocial risks of pregnancy and childbearing during adolescence. *Pediatric Annals, 9*(3), 89–94.

Field, T. M., Scafidi, F., Pickens, J., Prodromidis, M., Pelaez-Nogueras, M., Torquati, J., et al. (1998). Polydrug-using adolescent mothers and their infants receiving early intervention. *Adolescence, 33*, 117–143.

Fried, P. A., Watkinson, B., Dillon, R. F., & Dulberg, C. S. (1987). Neonatal neurological status in a low-risk population after prenatal exposure to cigarettes, marijuana, and alcohol. *Journal of Developmental and Behavioral Pediatrics, 8*(6), 318–326.

Furstenberg, F. F., Brooks-Gunn, J., & Morgan, S. P. (1987). *Adolescent mothers in later life.* Cambridge, UK: Cambridge University Press.

Geene, J. P. (2001). *High school graduation rates in the United States: Revised.* New York: Manhattan Institute for Policy Research.

Grant, K. E., O'Koon, J. H., Davis, T. H., Roache, N. A., Poindexter, L. M., Armstrong, M. L., et al. (2000). Protective factors affecting low-income urban African American youth exposed to stress. *Journal of Early Adolescence, 20*, 388–417.

Hart, B., & Risley, T. R. (1995). *Meaningful differences in the everyday experience of young American children.* Baltimore: Paul Brookes.

Jaffee, S. R., Moffitt, T. E., Caspi, A., & Taylor, A. (2003). Life with (or without) father: The benefits of living with two biological parents depend on the father's antisocial behavior. *Child Development, 74*(1), 109–126.

Johnson, V., & Pandina, R. J. (1991). Familial and personal drinking histories and measures of competence in youth. *Addictive Behaviors, 16*(6), 453–465.

Kahn, R. S., Khoury, J., Nichols, W. C., & Lanphear, B. P. (2003). Role of dopamine transporter genotype and maternal prenatal smoking in childhood hyperactive-impulsive, inattentive, and oppositional behaviors. *Journal of Pediatrics, 143*(1), 104–110.

Karoly, L. A., Kilburn, M. R., & Cannon, J. S. (2005). *Early childhood interventions: Proven results, future promise.* Santa Monica, CA: Rand.

Kaufman, J., Yang, B. Z., Douglas-Palumberi, H., Grasso, D., Lipschitz, D., Houshyar, S., et al. (2006). Brain-derived neurotrophic factor-*5-HTTLPR* gene interactions and environmental modifiers of depression in children. *Biological Psychiatry, 59*(8), 673–680.

Kim-Cohen, J., Caspi, A., Taylor, A., Williams, B., Newcombe, R., Craig, I. W., et al. (2006). MAOA, maltreatment, and gene–environment interaction predicting children's mental health: New evidence and a meta-analysis. *Molecular Psychiatry, 11*(10), 903–913.

Kitzman, H., Olds, D. L., Henderson, C. R., Jr., Hanks, C., Cole, R., Tatelbaum, R., et al. (1997). Effect of prenatal and infancy home visitation by nurses on pregnancy outcomes, childhood injuries, and repeated childbearing: A randomized controlled trial. *Journal of the American Medical Association, 278*(8), 644–652.

Kitzman, H., Olds, D. L., Sidora, K., Henderson, C. R., Jr., Hanks, C., Cole, R., et al. (2000). Enduring effects of nurse home visitation on maternal life course: A 3-year follow-up of a randomized trial. *Journal of the American Medical Association, 283*(15), 1983–1989.

Kitzman, H., Yoos, L., Cole, R., Korfrmacher, J., & Hanks, C. (1997). Prenatal and early childhood home-visitation program processes: A case illustration. *Journal of Community Psychology, 25*(1), 27–45.

Kramer, M. S. (1987). Intrauterine growth and gestational duration determinants. *Pediatrics, 80*(4), 502–511.

Landsverk, J., Carrilio, T., Connelly, C. D., Ganger, W. C., Slymen, D. J., Newton, R. R., et al. (2002). *Healthy Families San Diego clinical trial technical report.* San Diego, CA: Child and Adolescent Services Research Center, San Diego Children's Hospital and Health Center.

MacMillan, H. L., Thomas, B. H., Jamieson, E., Walsh, C. A., Boyle, M. H., Shannon, H. S., et al. (2005). Effectiveness of home visitation by public-health nurses in prevention of the recurrence of child physical abuse and neglect: A randomised controlled trial. *Lancet, 365*, 1786–1793.

Main, M., Kaplan, N., & Cassidy, J. (1985). Security in infancy, childhood, and adulthood: A move to the level of representation. *Monographs of the Society for Research in Child Development, 50*(1–2, Serial No. 209), 66–104.

Mayes, L. C. (1994). Neurobiology of prenatal cocaine exposure: Effect on developing monoamine systems. *Infant Mental Health Journal, 15*, 121–133.

McLanahan, S. S., & Carlson, M. J. (2002). Welfare reform, fertility, and father involvement. *The Future of Children, 12*(1), 146–165.

Milberger, S., Biederman, J., Faraone, S. V., Chen, L., & Jones, J. (1996). Is maternal smoking during pregnancy a risk factor for attention deficit hyperactivity disorder in children? *American Journal of Psychiatry, 153*(9), 1138–1142.

Nathens, A. B., Neff, M. J., Goss, C. H., Maier, R. V., & Rivara, F. P. (2000). Effect of an older sibling and birth interval on the risk of childhood injury. *Injury Prevention, 6*(3), 219–222.

Olds, D., Henderson, C. R., Jr., Cole, R., Eckenrode, J., Kitzman, H., Luckey, D., et al. (1998). Long-term effects of nurse home visitation on children's criminal and antisocial behavior: 15-year follow-up of a randomized controlled trial. *Journal of the American Medical Association, 280*(14), 1238–1244.

Olds, D., Henderson, C. R., Jr., Kitzman, H., & Cole, R. (1995). Effects of prenatal and infancy nurse home visitation on surveillance of child maltreatment. *Pediatrics, 95*(3), 365–372.

Olds, D., Kitzman, H., Cole, R., Robinson, J., Sidora, K., Luckey, D., et al. (2004). Effects of nurse home visiting on maternal life-course and child development: Age-six follow-up of a randomized trial. *Pediatrics, 114*, 1550–1559.

Olds, D. L. (1980). Improving formal services for mothers and children. In J. Garbarino & S. H. Stocking (Eds.), *Protecting children from abuse and neglect: Developing and maintaining effective support systems for families* (pp. 173–197). San Francisco: Jossey-Bass.

Olds, D. L. (1997). Tobacco exposure and impaired development: A review of the evidence. *Mental Retardation and Developmental Disabilities Research Reviews, 3*, 257–269.

Olds, D. L. (2002). Prenatal and infancy home visiting by nurses: From randomized trials to community replication. *Prevention Science, 3*(3), 153–172.

Olds, D. L. (2005). The Nurse–Family Partnership: Foundations in attachment theory and epidemiology. In L. J. Berlin, Y. Ziv, L. Amaya-Jackson, & M. T. Greenburg (Eds.), *Enhancing early attachments: Theory, research, intervention, and policy* (pp. 217–249). New York: Guilford Press.

Olds, D. L. (2006). The Nurse–Family Partnership: An evidence-based preventive intervention. *Infant Mental Health Journal, 27*(1), 5–25.

Olds, D. L. (2007). Preventing crime with prenatal and infancy support of parents: The Nurse–Family Partnership. *Victims and Offenders, 2*, 205–225.

Olds, D. L., Eckenrode, J., Henderson, C. R., Jr., Kitzman, H., Powers, J., Cole, R., et al. (1997). Long-term effects of home visitation on maternal life course and child abuse and neglect: Fifteen-year follow-up of a randomized trial. *Journal of the American Medical Association, 278*(8), 637–643.

Olds, D. L., & Henderson, C. R., Jr. (1989). The prevention of maltreatment. In D. Cicchetti & V. Carlson (Eds.), *Child maltreatment: Theory and research on the causes and consequences of child abuse and neglect* (pp. 722–763). New York: Cambridge University Press.

Olds, D. L., Henderson, C. R., Jr., Chamberlin, R., & Tatelbaum, R. (1986). Preventing child abuse and neglect: A randomized trial of nurse home visitation. *Pediatrics, 78*(1), 65–78.

Olds, D. L., Henderson, C. R., Jr., & Kitzman, H. (1994). Does prenatal and infancy nurse home visitation have enduring effects on qualities of parental caregiving and child health at 25 to 50 months of life? *Pediatrics, 93*(1), 89–98.

Olds, D. L., Henderson, C. R., Jr., Kitzman, H., Eckenrode, J., Cole, R., Tatelbaum, R., et al. (1998). Prenatal and infancy home visitation by nurses: A program of research. In C. Rovee-Collier, L. P. Lipsitt, & H. Hayne (Eds.) *Advances in infancy research* (Vol. 12, pp. 79–130). Stamford, CT: Ablex.

Olds, D. L., Henderson, C. R., Jr., & Tatelbaum, R. (1994a). Intellectual impairment in children of women who smoke cigarettes during pregnancy. *Pediatrics*, 93(2), 221–227.

Olds, D. L., Henderson, C. R., Jr., & Tatelbaum, R. (1994b). Prevention of intellectual impairment in children of women who smoke cigarettes during pregnancy. *Pediatrics*, 93(2), 228–233.

Olds, D. L., Henderson, C. R., Jr., Tatelbaum, R., & Chamberlin, R. (1986). Improving the delivery of prenatal care and outcomes of pregnancy: A randomized trial of nurse home visitation. *Pediatrics*, 77(1), 16–28.

Olds, D. L., Henderson, C. R., Jr., Tatelbaum, R., & Chamberlin, R. (1988). Improving the life-course development of socially disadvantaged mothers: A randomized trial of nurse home visitation. *American Journal of Public Health*, 78(11), 1436–1445.

Olds, D. L., Hill, P. L., O'Brien, R., Racine, D., & Moritz, P. (2003). Taking preventive intervention to scale: The Nurse–Family Partnership. *Cognitive and Behavioral Practice*, 10(4), 278–290.

Olds, D. L., Kitzman, H., Hanks, C., Cole, R., Anson, E., Sidora-Arcoleo, K., et al. (2007). Effects of nurse home visiting on maternal and child functioning: Age-9 follow-up of a randomized trial. *Pediatrics*, 120(4), e832–e845.

Olds, D. L., Luckey, D. W., & Henderson, C. R., Jr. (2005). Can the results be believed?: In reply. *Pediatrics*, 115, 1113–1114.

Olds, D. L., Robinson, J., O'Brien, R., Luckey, D. W., Pettitt, L. M., Henderson, C. R., Jr., et al. (2002). Home visiting by paraprofessionals and by nurses: A randomized, controlled trial. *Pediatrics*, 110(3), 486–496.

Olds, D. L., Robinson, J., Pettitt, L., Luckey, D. W., Holmberg, J., Ng, R. K., et al. (2004). Effects of home visits by paraprofessionals and by nurses: Age-four follow-up of a randomized trial. *Pediatrics*, 114, 1560–1568.

Overpeck, M. D., Brenner, R. A., Trumble, A. C., Trifiletti, L. B., & Berendes, H. W. (1998). Risk factors for infant homicide in the United States. *New England Journal of Medicine*, 339(17), 1211–1216.

Peterson, L., & Gable, S. (1998). Holistic injury prevention. In J. R. Lutzker (Ed.), *Handbook of child abuse research and treatment* (pp. 291–318). New York: Plenum Press.

Pine, D. S. (2001). Affective neuroscience and the development of social anxiety disorder. *Psychiatric Clinics of North America*, 24(4), 689–705.

Pine, D. S. (2003). Developmental psychobiology and response to threats: Relevance to trauma in children and adolescents. *Biological Psychiatry*, 53(9), 796–808.

Plomin, R. (1986). *Development, genetics, and psychology*. Hillsdale, NJ: Erlbaum.

Rutter, M., Moffitt, T. E., & Caspi, A. (2006). Gene–environment interplay and psychopathology: Multiple varieties but real effects. *Journal of Child Psychology and Psychiatry*, 47(3–4), 226–261.

Sanders, M. R. (1999). Triple P—Positive Parenting Program: Towards an empirically validated multilevel parenting and family support strategy for the prevention of behavior and emotional problems in children. *Clinical Child and Family Psychology Review*, 2, 71–90.

Saxon, D. W. (1978). The behavior of infants whose mothers smoke in pregnancy. *Early Human Development*, 2, 363–369.

Sood, B., Delaney-Black, V., Covington, C., Nordstrom-Klee, B., Ager, J., Templin, T., et al. (2001). Prenatal alcohol exposure and childhood behavior at age 6 to 7 years: I. Dose–response effect. *Pediatrics*, 108(2), e34.

Streissguth, A. P., Sampson, P. D., Barr, H. M., Bookstein, F. L., & Olson, H. C. (1994). The effects of prenatal exposure to alcohol and tobacco: Contributions from the Seattle Longitudinal Prospective Study and implications for public policy. In H. L. Needleman & D. Bellinger (Eds.), *Prenatal exposure to toxicants: Developmental consequences* (pp. 148–183). Baltimore: Johns Hopkins University Press.

Taylor, S. E., Way, B. M., Welch, W. T., Hilmert, C. J., Lehman, B. J., & Eisenberger, N. I. (2006). Early family environment, current adversity, the serotonin transporter promoter polymorphism, and depressive symptomatology. *Biological Psychiatry*, 60(7), 671–676.

Theodore, A. D., Chang, J. J., Runyan, D. K., Hunter, W. M., Bangdiwala, S. I., & Agans, R. (2005). Epidemiologic features of the physical and sexual maltreatment of children in the Carolinas. *Pediatrics*, 115(3), e331–e337.

U.S. Advisory Board on Child Abuse and Neglect. (1991). *Creating caring communities: Blueprint for an effective federal policy on child abuse and neglect.* Washington, DC: U.S. Government Printing Office.

Wagner, M. M., & Clayton, S. L. (1999). The Parents as Teachers program: Results from two demonstrations. *The Future of Children*, 9(1), 91–115, 179–189.

Wang, X., Zuckerman, B., Pearson, C., Kaufman, G., Chen, C., Wang, G., et al. (2002). Maternal cigarette smoking, metabolic gene polymorphism, and infant birth weight. *Journal of the American Medical Association*, 287(2), 195–202.

Webster-Stratton, C. (1994). Advancing videotape parent training: A comparison study. *Journal of Consulting and Clinical Psychology*, 62, 583–593.

Wilhelm, K., Mitchell, P. B., Niven, H., Finch, A., Wedgwood, L., Scimone, A., et al. (2006). Life events, first depression onset and the serotonin transporter gene. *British Journal of Psychiatry*, 188, 210–215.

Yellin, E. (2000). *Group seeks to overhaul foster care in Tennessee.* Retrieved March 31, 2008, from *query.nytimes.com/gst/fullpage.html?res=9A01E0DD163BF93 2A25756C0A9669C8B63&sec=&spon=&pagewanted=1.*

CHAPTER 3

Toward a Population-Based Paradigm for Parenting Intervention, Prevention of Child Maltreatment, and Promotion of Child Well-Being

Ronald J. Prinz

This chapter discusses a new and emerging paradigm for the prevention of child maltreatment that is based on a public-health-compatible model. A population approach to parenting intervention offers advantages and benefits for the prevention of child maltreatment, particularly given that most families never get into "official" trouble for child maltreatment.

PARENTING PRACTICES AND CHILD MALTREATMENT

Official reports of child maltreatment grossly underestimate its actual prevalence. There is general agreement in the field that this is true, although there is some variance as to the extent of underestimation. In a well-constructed epidemiological study conducted in North and South Carolina, Theodore and colleagues (2005) found that the number of maternal reports of physical abuse via anonymous telephone surveying was 40 times greater than the number of official child physical abuse reports. This study also found that the rate of harsh physical discipline was not significantly different for low- versus high-income households, which flies in the face of the assumption that problematic parenting is only or predominantly associated with poverty.

Several factors might account for the discrepancy between official and actual child maltreatment rates. Some incidents of child maltreatment undoubtedly go undetected, either because no one observes the events or observers choose not to make a report. Another possibility is that some observed child maltreatment might not be severe enough to trigger a child protective services response. Finally, problematic parenting practices might not meet a stringent definition for official child maltreatment but nonetheless are detrimental to healthy child development.

Extrapolating further from the underestimation problem, potentially detrimental parenting practices unfortunately are quite widespread. In a recent random-dialing telephone survey of 3,600 households, Prinz and Sanders (2008) found that 49% of parents reported heavy reliance on discipline strategies for child misbehavior that are mostly coercive in nature and likely to be problematic or at least ineffective. In the same survey 10% of parents reported that they spanked on a frequent or very frequent basis, using an object.

RATIONALE AND DESCRIPTION OF THE PARADIGM

The widespread nature of parenting difficulties presents a dilemma for the field of child maltreatment prevention in terms of two potentially divergent goals: (1) Concentrate intervention with parents at highest risk for child maltreatment, or (2) intervene broadly to address the full range of potentially detrimental parenting and to promote accessibility for parents throughout the population. Both of these goals have inherent challenges. For intervention with the highest-risk families only, attainment of this goal is limited by (1) imperfect prediction of child maltreatment in part because of the low base rate, (2) the danger of overlooking families in which detrimental parenting has already occurred or may occur, and (3) the perceived stigma of participating in an intervention meant for only the most troubled or at-risk segment of the population. Intervening broadly faces the challenges of (1) identifying cost-effective programming strategies that do not try to deliver the highest-intensity intervention to all families, (2) making the intervention truly accessible to the broader population, and (3) possibly running counter to the prevailing belief in the child maltreatment field (Leventhal, 2005).

The broad intervention goal is a central part of the emerging paradigm. This approach has a number of key elements: (1) the coalescing of goals across domains and outcomes; (2) a nonstigmatizing approach; (3) flexibility and accessibility; (4) continuity across settings, situations, and service providers; and (5) cost-efficiency.

Coalescing Goals

Historically, prevention of child maltreatment has developed in a separate sphere from other areas of family-based prevention. The emerging paradigm requires the integration and coalescing of multiple goals for parenting intervention across areas. The same kind of evidence-based parenting intervention that can contribute to the prevention of children's social, emotional, and behavioral problems may contribute to the promotion of school readiness and child well-being. Furthermore, there are many touch points related to the child welfare system where evidence-based parenting interventions would be beneficial, including (1) prevention of child maltreatment and injury (Prinz, 2007); (2) prevention of children's social, emotional, and behavioral problems; (3) family-based treatment of children's mental health problems for those who have endured abuse/neglect; (4) strengthening the parenting competence and confidence of foster parents; (5) treating parents who have engaged in child maltreatment or are at high risk of doing so; and (6) assisting parents who are seeking voluntary services after having been referred for suspected maltreatment that did not rise to the level of substantiation or mandatory action. A coordinated system of parenting interventions that has this kind of broad applicability would be desirable for a population-based approach (Carmona, 2006).

Nonstigmatizing Approach

Parenting interventions need to be delivered in a context that is nonstigmatizing. Currently, parenting interventions are perceived by many parents as being either negative or for ignorant or wayward parents. To be effective, the whole approach to parenting intervention has to emphasize the universal applicability of the parenting assistance so that the larger community of parents embraces such endeavors. An example of such an approach is found in prenatal (birth) classes, which parents across a broad array of economic and cultural groups (and family configurations) find useful and do not perceive as stigmatizing.

Flexibility and Accessibility

A parenting intervention needs to be flexible with respect to delivery formats, ease of administration, and accessibility to meet all of the earlier-noted needs relative to the child welfare system. Having *every* family receive a *long* intervention at a single venue is not only cost-ineffective but also unnecessary and undesirable from a family's perspective.

Continuity across Settings, Situations, and Service Providers

A parent who is exposed to parenting concepts in a preventive intervention should not later (e.g., via child protective services programming) be exposed to conflicting or even contradictory parenting information or interventions. There is considerable benefit to parents and the community when there is a core set of evidence-based parenting information and strategies that is accessible to all parents across service providers and settings.

Cost-Efficiency

Taking a population approach requires cost-efficient strategies, which presumably could lead to demonstrable cost-effectiveness. There are undoubtedly several ways to make such an approach cost-efficient, but two particular strategies may prove helpful. The first is to disseminate services in a manner that makes full use of the existing workforce across many settings. The second is to draw on a continuum of program intensities to find the minimally sufficient but helpful level of intervention for each family's needs.

An Evidence-Based System Designed for Population Dissemination

To address the difficulties of low population reach of evidence-based parenting programs (i.e., reaching a sufficient proportion of the population to alter prevalence rates) requires a public health approach to improving parenting. Reducing the prevalence of coercive parenting in the community requires that a large proportion of the population be reached with effective parenting strategies (Biglan, 1995). Thus, a key assumption of a population-based approach is that parenting intervention strategies should be widely accessible in the community. To achieve this aspiration, a variety of delivery modalities and formats are needed.

A sophisticated example of a public health approach to parenting is the Triple P system developed by Sanders and colleagues (Sanders, 1999; Sanders, Markie-Dadds, & Turner, 2003). The Triple P—Positive Parenting Program was designed as a comprehensive population-level system of parenting and family support. This multilevel system includes five levels of intervention of increasing intensity and narrowing population reach. The entire population is exposed to Universal Triple P (level 1), which is a media and communication strategy designed to reach all parents in a population, and then subsets of families receive increasingly more intense levels of intervention as needed. Selected Triple P (level 2) is a brief one- to two-session intervention; Primary Care Triple P (level 3) is a more intensive but brief four-session primary care intervention; Standard Triple P (level 4) is a more intensive 8- to 10-session active skills training program; and Enhanced Triple P (level 5) is an adjunctive to Standard Triple P for families that need additional programming. The Triple P system was designed to enhance parental competence, prevent dysfunctional parenting practices, and promote better teamwork between partners, thereby reducing an important set of family risk factors associated with child maltreatment and with the development of behavioral and emotional problems in children and adolescents. The full Triple P system, which has been implemented in 15 countries on four continents (North America, Australia, Europe, and Asia), has a well-developed dissemination system for international training and accreditation of service providers.

Various components of the Triple P system have been subjected to a series of controlled evaluations and have consistently shown positive effects on observed and parent-reported child behavior problems, parenting practices, and parents' adjustment (Sanders, 1999; Sanders, Markie-Dadds, Turner, & Ralph, 2004; Sanders, Turner, & Markie-Dadds, 2002). Adequate scientific proof for components of Triple P has been demonstrated by careful randomized controlled trials showing that exposure to the intervention results in better outcomes for children than comparison conditions, such as receiving no treatment, being on a waiting list, or receiving usual care. The strength of the scientific evidence supporting Triple P has been established through systematic replication of findings across sites, investigators, countries, and cultures through many years of research, including more than 40 randomized controlled trials demonstrating its efficacy and effectiveness and many service/field evaluations. An integrated series of controlled outcome studies has provided considerable evidence demonstrating the benefits of the various levels of intervention and modes of delivery in a variety of populations. This program of research has shown successful outcomes with a number of populations and problem areas: preschool-age children and conduct problems (Sanders et al., 2000), children with attention problems (Bor, Sanders, & Markie-Dadds, 2002), children of depressed parents (Sanders & McFarland, 2000), children from maritally discordant homes (Dadds, Schwartz, & Sanders, 1987), children in stepfamilies (Nicholson & Sanders, 1999), children with developmental disabilities (Sanders & Plant, 1989), and children in rural and remote areas where access to services is limited (Connell, Sanders, & Markie-Dadds, 1997). Triple P interventions also have been shown to have an impact on other behavioral and developmental problems, such as persistent feeding difficulties (Turner, Sanders, & Wall, 1994), sleep disorders (Sanders, Bor, & Dadds, 1984), recurrent pain (Devilly & Sanders, 1993; Sanders, Shepherd, Cleghorn, & Woolford, 1994), and habit disorders (Christensen & Sanders, 1987).

Evidence in support of each component of Triple P provides a sound basis for population-level implementation of the whole system, but the evidence favoring population impact requires a different level of evaluation. Research on changing cultural norms, contagion effects, and social support suggests that full-scale implementation may enhance effect sizes for each component. Triple P has been evaluated as a population strategy and shown to reduce the prevalence of conduct problems in preschool-age children from high-risk neighborhoods (Zubrick et al., 2005). Several effectiveness and dissemination studies have been conducted on Triple P demonstrating portability and broad utility in multiple settings (Prinz & Sanders, 2007; Sanders, Murphy-Brennan, & McAuliffe, 2003; Sanders et al., 2005; Sanders, Tully, Turner, Maher, & McAuliffe, 2003; Turner & Sanders, 2006; Zubrick et al., 2005).

A large number of outcome studies have demonstrated collectively that Triple P is effective in strengthening the quality of parenting practices, reducing coercive parenting, and reducing early social, emotional, and behavioral problems in children. Furthermore, there have been several independent replications of Triple P implementation and findings in diverse cultural contexts (Bodenmann, Cina, Ledermann, & Sanders, 2008; Cann, Rogers, & Matthews, 2003; Cann, Rogers, & Worley, 2003; Crisante & Ng, 2003; Dean, Myors, & Evans, 2003; Gallart & Matthey, 2005; Heinrichs, Bertram, Kuschel, & Hahlweg, 2005; Heinrichs, Hahlweg, Bertram, et al., 2006; Heinrichs, Hahlweg, Kuschel, et al., 2006; Heinrichs, Kruger, & Guse, 2006; Rogers, Cann, Cameron, Littlefield, & Lagioia, 2003). The robustness of the main findings for improved child outcomes across diverse cultural groups and contexts is particularly important.

Another characteristic of Triple P is that it was designed specifically to be disseminated broadly in an efficient manner. The tiered levels of intervention matched to families' differing needs work well with the public health principle of minimal sufficiency (i.e., applying the least amount of intervention to solve the problem at hand and prevent future difficulties). Use of the media as a universal tool is an additional public health–compatible feature. In the Triple P system, a media and communication strategy is utilized extensively in a sophisticated and strategic manner to normalize and acknowledge the difficulties of parenting experiences, to break down parents' sense of social isolation regarding parenting, to destigmatize getting help, to impart parenting information directly to parents, and to alter the community context for parenting (Sanders, 1999).

THE U.S. TRIPLE P SYSTEM POPULATION TRIAL

The U.S. Triple P System Population Trial (Prinz & Sanders, 2006, 2007) provides an example of how the paradigm can be operationalized in practice. In this trial, a population-wide implementation of the entire Triple P system for families with children from birth to 7 years of age was conducted using a randomized design. The population trial focused on the prevention of child maltreatment and is the only known controlled trial to date on parenting-intervention prevention of child maltreatment that *randomized geographical areas (in this case counties) to condition*. In this trial, 18 counties in a southeastern state were selected for randomization to condition. These counties range in population from 50,000 to 175,000 individuals. The counties were matched with respect to the prevalence rate of child maltreatment, approximate size (population), and poverty level (proportion of households below the poverty line) and then randomly assigned to (1) the Triple P system or (2) a comparison system (i.e., services as usual). The referent population for the trial consisted of the parents/caregivers in all households with one or more children under the age of 8 years.

Implementation of the Triple P system condition in the population trial involved three major facets: (1) recruitment and training of hundreds of service providers in the delivery of multiple levels and formats of the Triple P system, (2) sustained media and communication strategies (Universal or level 1 Triple P), and (3) ongoing consultation and support to the Triple P–trained providers.

The Triple P training of indigenous service providers who already serve families in the community involves an intensive and systematic regimen that is used around the world. In the population trial, the service providers indicated a high level of satisfaction with Triple P professional training (Shapiro, Prinz, & Sanders, 2008). The racial composition of the service providers mirrored the general population in the participating counties; that is, the proportion of African American service providers participating in Triple P training was similar to the proportion of families who were African American in those communities. The research team examined satisfaction with Triple P and the professional training courses as a function of racial group membership. In a comparison of the satisfaction ratings of 195 African American service providers and 289 European American service providers, both groups rated their satisfaction with the Triple P courses as high. However, the African American providers indicated *higher* satisfaction (on a 7-point scale ranging from 1 = very dissatisfied to 7 = very satisfied):

African American service providers: Mean = 6.52, SD = 1.12, n = 195

European American service providers: Mean = 6.37, SD = 1.15, n = 289

This difference was marginally statistically significant, t (482) = 1.43, p < .10. The statistical test in this situation is not particularly important. The key point is that these data suggest that after participating in fairly intensive exposure and training in Triple P, African American service providers, many of whom were parents themselves, rated the Triple P training and programming as highly or perhaps even more highly than did their European American counterparts.

In a population-based prevention trial of this type, the unit of randomization (in this instance, county) was the unit of analysis. The three main child maltreatment–related indicators for population effects in the population trial were: (1) child out-of-home placements, (2) child injuries related to maltreatment (hospitalizations and emergency room visits), and (3) child maltreatment cases. These three indicators were derived from record-keeping and reporting systems that operated independently from each other. Child out-of-home placements were recorded by the foster care system, child injuries were reported by hospitals and physicians, and child maltreatment cases were reported by the child protective services system. The records for each county were deposited in a central repository.

The results are reported in detail in Prinz, Sanders, Shapiro, Whitaker, and Lutzker (2009) and are summarized here. The 18 counties were grouped into two clusters (Triple P system and comparison). The two clusters of counties did not differ or show time by cluster interactions over the 5 years prior to the start of the population trial for any of the three indicators. After controlling for baseline, significant prevention effects with large effect sizes (i.e., over 1.0 for Cohen's d) following 2 continuous years of implementation were observed for all three population indicators: the Triple P counties showed lower rates of child out-of-home placements, child injuries related to maltreatment, and child maltreatment cases.

Several facets of the population trial make this pattern of results particularly meaningful. First, counties were randomized to condition, while controlling for child maltreatment rate, county population size, and poverty rate in the randomization process. Second, baseline data on the three indicators showed no diverging or biasing trends. Third, there was substantial dissemination of the Triple P system thus far to hundreds of service providers in the intervention counties. Fourth, the three key indicators were each derived from different reporting systems (i.e., foster care system, hospital and medical system, and child protective services system). And fifth, the magnitude of preventive effects was large.

CAVEATS AND CONCLUSIONS

Findings from the U.S. Triple P System Population Trial, combined with the extensive evidence base for Triple P across many settings and circumstances, demonstrate the viability of the population paradigm for strengthening parenting and the utility of Triple P to address multiple child and family outcomes concurrently. The multilevel coordinated system that is Triple P offers efficiencies of programming, interventions that were designed at their inception for broad dissemination, and ways to reach large segments of the population without committing substantial resources to every family. This approach has the potential to destigmatize parental participation or information-seeking regarding parenting improvement because (1) Triple P is presented (and might be perceived) as useful to all parents; (2) though useful for addressing child abuse, the Triple P description and publicity are not couched in terms of child abuse; and (3) there is continuity of parenting principles and strategies across programs and families, which provides a broader appeal that runs counter to the connotation of a highly targeted approach. In addition, tapping multiple systems that impact children is consistent with calls for broad programming (see Wald, Chapter 11, this volume).

The paradigm for population-based parenting interventions does not eliminate the need for policies to improve the economic and environmental conditions in which children and families struggle, support services to address basic needs (e.g., food, shelter, health care, safety), treatment services for adult problems (e.g., substance abuse, posttraumatic stress disorder), and child protective services–triggered interventions. The paradigm also necessitates at least a modest level of cooperation across agencies and organizations in the community. This approach may not work as well if every agency/ organization is strictly out for itself. However, a measure of cooperation or coordination across providers and organizations is possible without organizations having to abandon their main goals. The primary challenge with this paradigm is to coalesce to some degree the goals for the child welfare, health, mental health, and education segments of the professional community to produce population-wide benefits for children and families.

To summarize, the emerging paradigm takes a population perspective, implements parenting interventions that have multiple targets and benefits (i.e., prevention of child maltreatment, prevention of child social, emotional, and behavioral problems, promotion of early childhood preparation for school, and strengthening parental confidence and effectiveness), utilizes the existing workforce across many settings and disciplines, creates efficiencies by making use of a multitiered system of interventions with increasing intensity, and provides continuity of parenting principles and strategies across intervention levels, media, and in-person programming, settings, and providers.

REFERENCES

Biglan, A. (1995). Translating what we know about the context of antisocial behavior into a lower prevalence of such behavior. *Journal of Applied Behavior Analysis, 28,* 479–492.

Bodenmann, G., Cina, A., Ledermann, T., & Sanders, M. R. (2008). The efficacy of the Triple P—Positive Parenting Program in improving parenting and child behavior: A comparison of two other treatment conditions. *Behaviour Research and Therapy, 46,* 411–427.

Bor, W., Sanders, M. R., & Markie-Dadds, C. (2002). The effects of the Triple P—Positive Parenting Program on preschool children with co-occurring disruptive behavior and attentional/hyperactive difficulties. *Journal of Abnormal Child Psychology, 30,* 571–587.

Cann, W., Rogers, H., & Matthews, J. (2003). Family Intervention Service program evaluation: A brief report on initial outcomes for families. *Australian e-Journal for the Advancement of Mental Health, 2,* 1–8.

Cann, W., Rogers, H., & Worley, G. (2003). Report on a program evaluation of a telephone assisted parenting support service for families living in isolated rural areas. *Australian e-Journal for the Advancement of Mental Health, 2,* 9–15.

Carmona, R. H. (2006). *Making prevention of child maltreatment a national priority: Implementing innovations of a public health approach.* Washington, DC: Surgeon General's Workshop.

Christensen, A. P., & Sanders, M. R. (1987). Habit reversal and differential reinforcement of other behavior in the treatment of thumb-sucking: An analysis of generalization and side effects. *Journal of Child Psychology and Psychiatry and Allied Disciplines, 28,* 281–295.

Connell, S., Sanders, M. R., & Markie-Dadds, C. (1997). Self-directed behavioral family intervention for parents of oppositional children in rural and remote areas. *Behavior Modification, 21*(4), 379–408.

Crisante, L., & Ng, S. (2003). Implementation and process issues in using Group Triple P with Chinese parents: Preliminary findings. *Australian e-Journal for the Advancement of Mental Health, 2,* 24–29.

Dadds, M. R., Schwartz, S., & Sanders, M. R. (1987). Marital discord and treatment outcome in behavioral treatment of child conduct disorders. *Journal of Consulting and Clinical Psychology, 55,* 396–403.

Dean, C., Myors, K., & Evans, E. (2003). Community-wide implementation of a parenting program: The South East Sydney Positive Parenting Project. *Australian e-Journal for the Advancement of Mental Health, 2,* 30–38.

Devilly, G. J., & Sanders, M. R. (1993). "Hey Dad, watch me": The effects of training a child to teach pain management skills to a parent with recurrent headaches. *Behaviour Change, 10,* 237–243.

Gallart, S. C., & Matthey, S. (2005). The effectiveness of Group Triple P and the impact of the four telephone contacts. *Behaviour Change, 22,* 71–80.

Heinrichs, N., Bertram, H., Kuschel, A., & Hahlweg, K. (2005). Parent recruitment and retention in a universal prevention program for child behavior and emotional problems: Barriers to research and program participation. *Prevention Science, 6,* 1–12.

Heinrichs, N., Hahlweg, K., Bertram, H., Kuschel, A., Naumann, S., & Harstick, S. (2006). Die langfristige Wirksamkeit eines Elterntrainings zur universellen Prävention kindlicher Verhaltensstörungen: Ergebnisse aus Sicht der Mütter und Väter. *Zeitschrift fuer Klinische Psychologie und Psychotherapie, 35,* 72–86.

Heinrichs, N., Hahlweg, K., Kuschel, A., Bertram, H., Harstick, S., & Naumann, S. (2006). Triple P from parents' perspective: Attendance rates and consumer satisfaction depending on sociodemographic characteristics and migration. *Kindheit und Entwicklung, 15,* 19–26.

Heinrichs, N., Kruger, S., & Guse, U. (in press). Eine experimentelle Studie zum Einfluss von Anreizen auf Rekrutierung und Effecktivitat eines präventiven Elterntrainings. *Zeitschrift fuer Klinische Psychologie und Psychotherapie, 35,* 97–108.

Leventhal, J. (2005). Getting prevention right: Maintaining the status quo is not an option. *Child Abuse and Neglect, 29,* 209–213.

Nicholson, J. M., & Sanders, M. R. (1999). Randomized controlled trial of behavioral family intervention for the treatment of child behavior problems in stepfamilies. *Journal of Divorce and Remarriage, 30,* 1–23.

Prinz, R. J. (2007). Parenting and the prevention of childhood injuries. In L. S. Doll, S. E. Bonzo, J. A. Mercy, & D. A. Sleet (Eds.), *Handbook of injury and violence prevention.* New York: Springer.

Prinz, R. J., & Sanders, M. R. (2006). Testing effects on parenting at a broad scale: The U.S. Triple P System Population Trial. In N. Heinrichs, K. Hahlweg, & M. Doepfner (Eds.), *Strengthening families: Different evidence-based approaches to support child mental health.* Muenster, Germany: Psychotherapie Verlag.

Prinz, R. J., & Sanders, M. R. (2007). Adopting a population-level approach to parenting and family support interventions. *Clinical Psychology Review, 27,* 739–749.

Prinz, R. J., & Sanders, M. R. (2008). *Household survey of parents.* Unpublished manuscript, University of South Carolina.

Prinz, R. J., Sanders, M. R., Shapiro, C. J., Whitaker, D. J., & Lutzker, J. R. (2009). Population-based prevention of child maltreatment: The U.S. Triple P System Population Trial. *Prevention Science, 10,* 1–12.

Rogers, H., Cann, W., Cameron, D., Littlefield, L., & Lagioia, V. (2003). Evaluation of the Family Intervention Service for children presenting with characteristics associated with attention deficit hyperactivity disorder. *Australian e-Journal for the Advancement of Mental Health, 2,* 53–62.

Sanders, M. R. (1999). Triple P—Positive Parenting Program: Towards an empirically validated multilevel parenting and family support strategy for the prevention of behavior and emotional problems in children. *Clinical Child and Family Psychology Review, 2,* 71–90.

Sanders, M. R., Bor, B., & Dadds, M. R. (1984). Modifying bedtime disruptions in children using stimulus control and contingency management techniques. *Behavioural Psychotherapy, 12,* 130–141.

Sanders, M. R., Markie-Dadds, C., Tully, L., & Bor, W. (2000). The Triple P—Positive Parenting Program: A comparison of enhanced, standard and self-directed behavioral family interventions for parents of children with early onset conduct problems. *Journal of Consulting and Clinical Psychology, 68,* 624–640.

Sanders, M. R., Markie-Dadds, C., & Turner, K. M. T. (2003). Theoretical, scientific and clinical foundations of the Triple P—Positive Parenting Program: A population approach to the promotion of parenting competence. *Parenting Research and Practice Monograph, 1,* 1–21.

Sanders, M. R., Markie-Dadds, C., Turner, K. M. T., & Ralph, A. (2004). Using the Triple P system of intervention to prevent behavioural problems in children and adolescents. In P. Barrett & T. H. Ollendick (Eds.), *Handbook of interventions that work with children and adolescents: Prevention and treatment* (pp. 489–516). Chichester, UK: Wiley.

Sanders, M. R., & McFarland, M. (2000). The treatment of depressed mothers with disruptive children: A controlled evaluation of cognitive behavioral family intervention. *Behavior Therapy, 31,* 89–112.

Sanders, M. R., Murphy-Brennan, M., & McAuliffe, C. (2003). The development, evaluation and dissemination of a training program for general practitioners in evidence-based parent consultation skills. *International Journal of Mental Health Promotion, 5,* 13–20.

Sanders, M. R., & Plant, K. (1989). Programming for generalization to high and low risk parenting situations in families with oppositional developmentally disabled preschoolers. *Behavior Modification, 13,* 283–305.

Sanders, M. R., Ralph, A., Thompson, R., Sofronoff, K., Gardiner, P., Bidwell, K., et al. (2005). *Every Family: A public health approach to promoting children's well-being.* Brisbane, Australia: University of Queensland.

Sanders, M. R., Shepherd, R. W., Cleghorn, G., & Woolford, H. (1994). The treatment of recurrent abdominal pain in children: A controlled comparison of cognitive-behavioral family intervention and standard pediatric care. *Journal of Consulting and Clinical Psychology, 62,* 306–314.

Sanders, M. R., Tully, L. A., Turner, K. M. T., Maher, C., & McAuliffe, C. (2003). Training practitioners in parent consultation skills: An evaluation of training for the Triple P—Positive Parenting Program. *Australian Family Physician, 32,* 1–6.

Sanders, M. R., Turner, K. M. T., & Markie-Dadds, C. (2002). The development and dissemination of the Triple P—Positive Parenting Program: A multilevel, evidence-based system of parenting and family support. *Prevention Science, 3,* 173–189.

Shapiro, C. J., Prinz, R. J., & Sanders, M. R. (2008). Population-wide parenting intervention training: Initial feasibility. *Journal of Child and Family Studies, 17,* 457–466.

Theodore, A. D., Chang, J. J., Runyan, D. K., Hunter, W. M., Bangdiwala, S. I., & Agans, R. (2005). Epidemiologic features of the physical and sexual maltreatment of children in the Carolinas. *Pediatrics, 115,* 331–337.

Turner, K. M. T., & Sanders, M. R. (2006). Dissemination of evidence-based parenting and family support strategies: Learning from the Triple P—Positive Parenting Program system approach. *Aggression and Violent Behavior, 11,* 176–193.

Turner, K. M. T., Sanders, M. R., & Wall, C. R. (1994). Behavioural parent training versus dietary education in the treatment of children with persistent feeding difficulties. *Behaviour Change*, *11*, 242–258.

Zubrick, S. R., Northey, K., Silburn, S. R., Lawrence, D., Williams, A. A., Blair, E., et al. (2005). Prevention of child behavior problems through universal implementation of a group behavioral family intervention. *Prevention Science*, *6*, 287–304.

CHAPTER 4

Community-Level Prevention of Child Maltreatment

The Durham Family Initiative

Kenneth A. Dodge, Robert Murphy,
Karen O'Donnell, *and* Christina Christopoulos

Although most American communities support programs and policies that are intended to reduce the community-wide rate of child maltreatment, very few of these efforts are based in the science of how maltreatment occurs or of service-delivery systems (Repucci, Woolard, & Fried, 1999). Even fewer programs are rigorously evaluated for impact, and those programs that have been evaluated have limited the evaluation to clinical trials of small groups. Rarely has a program been evaluated for population-level impact. The goal of the Durham Family Initiative (DFI) is to translate a science-based social-ecological model of how within-home child maltreatment develops, along with knowledge of public policy and practice, into a preventive system of care to reduce the population rate of child maltreatment in Durham County, North Carolina. According to the U.S. Department of Health and Human Services' Administration for Children and Families, because the highest rates of maltreatment are known to occur among children in the first 4 years of life (13.9 per 1,000 population) and the highest proportion of maltreatment fatalities (43% of all deaths) occurs in the first year of life, the DFI focuses on prevention in the earliest years. This chapter describes the DFI's rationale, its initial implementation, empirical outcomes to date, and plans for the future.

RATIONALE

The Context of Durham, North Carolina

In 2000–2001 the population rate of substantiated maltreatment of children birth to age 6 years in Durham County, North Carolina, was 28 per 1,000 population. This figure was substantially higher than the state rate, which was higher than the national rate reported in the preceding paragraph. That year, the Center for Child and Family Policy at Duke University (the Duke Center) collaborated with community leaders to publish a report called *The State of Durham's Children 2000*, based on a review of child well-being statistics. The report targeted child maltreatment as one of the three most important priorities for the community. A year later, a private foundation, The Duke Endowment, made a decade-long commitment to lowering the population rate of maltreatment in Durham County by funding the Duke Center and the Durham community to create, implement, and rigorously evaluate a science-based comprehensive effort based on a public health model of maltreatment. The first step was to develop a plan based on an understanding of how child maltreatment occurs and how it might be prevented.

How Maltreatment of a Child Occurs

Developmental epidemiological findings indicate that child maltreatment (physical abuse or neglect) is relatively likely to develop in a context in which the parent–child relationship has gone awry (Kolko, 2002). The human species has evolved such that the human infant is among the most helpless of all living creatures at birth (Dodge, 2002). For survival, parents are biologically wired to meet the infant's physical and emotional needs through a process of attachment. Both attachment theory and social-cognitive theory describe this process. According to attachment theory (Cicchetti & Toth, 1995), the parent–infant dyad normally develops a symbiotic, mutually rewarding, reciprocal relationship that leads to felt security in the infant. The infant's cries and signals of distress are met with responses by the parent, which tend to the source of distress, and the result is satisfaction and growing affection within the dyad. In cases in which the attachment relationship is characterized by insecurity, the infant is at risk for abnormal development and the parent is at risk for neglecting the infant's needs or even physically maltreating the infant.

According to social-cognitive theory (Azar, 1997; Dix & Lochman, 1990; Dodge, 2006), the parent's behavior toward the infant in a challenging situation (such as the infant crying) is a function of how the parent selectively attends to the infant's cues, interprets those cues, experiences emotion about the infant, accesses problem-solving responses, and evaluates the value of those responses when making decisions about parenting. Parents are competent and effective when they attend to the infant's real needs, interpret the infant's behavior accurately, experience sufficient desire to help, access competent problem-solving responses from a repertoire in memory, and evaluate competent responses as most effective. Empirical studies (Bugental & Johnston, 2000; Nix et al., 1999) indicate that parents are at risk for neglecting and abusing their infant when they selectively attend to annoying infant cues, interpret their infant as intentionally and malevolently thwarting them, experience high levels of frustration and anger, have few competent behavioral responses available in their repertoires, and evaluate neglectful and abusive behaviors as acceptable.

How might problems in attachment and social cognition in the parent–infant relationship develop? Bioecological theory (Bronfenbrenner & Morris, 2006) describes how the parent–infant dyad is embedded in a broader network that includes five levels: individual parent, family, neighborhood, community, and public policy (see Figure 4.1). Positive parent–infant relationships grow out of supportive systems at each of these levels, and risk for maltreatment is enhanced when support is limited at any level. The bases for risk for maltreatment can be organized into four domains: (1) the child's poor health and health care (e.g., low birth weight, chronic illness,

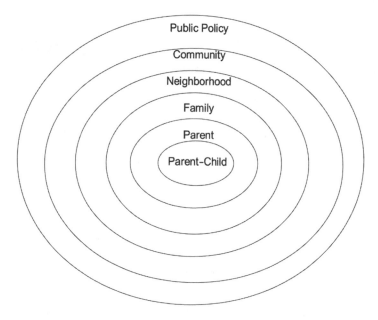

FIGURE 4.1. A social-ecological framework for child maltreatment.

no consistent healthcare), (2) parenting dysfunction (e.g., substance abuse, depression, domestic violence, parenting skill deficits), (3) family financial instability (e.g., unemployment, insufficient public financial benefits, lack of health insurance), and (4) childcare instability (e.g., lack of childcare, lack of backup plans).

At the individual parent level, competence at parenting protects the parent from maltreating the child, beginning with self-care and care for the fetus during the prenatal period and continuing throughout the child's lifespan. Numerous studies indicate that risk is increased for parents who have a history of having been maltreated themselves, who have a diagnosed psychiatric illness, or have substance-use problems (Kolko, 2002).

At the family level, social support buttresses the parent's perseverance in times of frustration, and tangible support offers the parent specific strategies for parenting, resources for solving childcare needs, and financial stability. Family poverty, disorganization, family violence, and marital stress interfere with the parent's ability to grow a secure parent–child relationship (Pinderhughes, Nix, Foster, Jones, & the Conduct Problems Prevention Research Group, 2001), leading to unskilled and harsh parenting. Interventions that are directed toward improving family conditions are predicated on the empirical relation between these conditions and abusive parenting (McLoyd, Aikens, & Burton, 2006). A major premise is that interventions to relieve adverse family conditions can also prevent child neglect and abuse.

At the neighborhood level, social relationships, helpful monitors of parents' behavior, visible models of good parenting, and available childcare provide the parent with supports when needed. Parents who are socially isolated (e.g., have few contacts with others), lacking in social support (e.g., having contact with others but not support), and lacking in social sources of monitoring and feedback on their parenting (e.g., having contact with others but no way to learn from such contact) are most likely to perpetuate erroneous beliefs and to resist intervention (Daro, McCurdy, & Nelson, 2005). In contrast, parents who receive informal respite care from friends and neighbors may be able to defuse volatile parent–child interactions.

At the community level, professional resources are made available, including pediatric care, evidence-based parental mental health and parenting-skill services, and childcare. The community culture also communicates to the parent about norms of acceptable and unacceptable behavior. A community's failure to ameliorate risk factors at all levels raises its maltreatment rate (Coulton, Korbin, & Su, 1999). These risk factors are more common in ineffective communities that lack coordination across social service agencies, lack evidence-based services, lack access to services, and have insufficient social capital.

Finally, at the public policy level, financial resources are made available through food stamp programs, Medicaid, emergency relief, and related services. Parent-support services may be available through government-sponsored efforts. Any lack of coordination among social service agencies may result in the failure of some parents to receive the financial support and mental health services that could help them develop the parenting skills they require (Daro et al., 2005). Without the necessary tangible, social, and cultural resources at each of these levels, parents have a difficult time parenting effectively and are at greater risk for neglect and abuse of their children (McLoyd et al., 2006).

How Communities Can Prevent Maltreatment

Preventive intervention can be directed to any of the levels that contribute to child abuse. Most of the empirically supported maltreatment prevention programs have been derived from basic science in human development and are directed at the individual-parent level to support the parent–infant attachment relationship or to help the parent respond more effectively to the infant's cues. David Olds, who developed the Nurse–Family Partnership intervention (Olds et al., 1997), was a student of Mary Ainsworth, a leading attachment theorist. Daphne Bugental, who developed an effective social-cognitive intervention for maltreating parents (Bugental et al., 2002), is a social-cognitive psychologist. These basic-science roots have served the prevention field well, but they are limited to the individual level.

Relatively few efforts have been directed toward the broader levels of neighborhood, community, and policy, and even fewer of these efforts have been evaluated rigorously (Daro & McCurdy, 2006). Given the empirically based risk factors at these broader levels, we (Dodge et al., 2004) hypothesized that preventive interventions might be more successful if they included one or more of these levels. Furthermore, directing interventions to all of these levels might maximize the likelihood of having a real impact on the community-wide maltreatment rate. At the same time, we required that the program be transportable, that is, have a structure that could be articulated in manuals and defined in writing. These premises formed the basis of the Durham Family Initiative (DFI).

The DFI grew out of the concept of a System of Care (Tolan & Dodge, 2005), which was itself a major reform in the children's mental health service field in the past two decades. This approach is characterized by the identification of the child's individually based needs through a process that includes all stakeholders (i.e., the child, parents, and professionals) and delivery of an integrated system of needed services that are matched to the child. "Needed services" are defined by a joint understanding between the professional's assessment of a child's psychiatric disorder and the family's assessment of its needs. In a System of Care, services are "wrapped around" the child according to the child's and family's needs, not according to external program availability. The community is responsible to provide a continuum of care that stretches from minor to severe cases, from minimal to intensive intervention, and that spans the various domains of a child's life (e.g., school, family, peers). The System of Care concept now pervades practice for children with already identified psychiatric illnesses.

In the DFI, we have framed our effort as a Preventive System of Care (Dodge et al., 2004), in which our focus is to connect families with individually based needed prevention services that could be delivered by the community. To engage in this "connecting" of families, we needed to develop a system that would (1) identify families at risk for maltreatment (that is, those families that need to be connected), (2) make available evidence-based services that the community could deliver, and (3) connect families at risk with community services. This system is depicted in Figure 4.2 as consisting of three steps of screening, matching, and delivery of preventive services.

PROGRAM IMPLEMENTATION

Since July 2002 the DFI has implemented a Preventive System of Care that is based on the following five principles. First, because the goal was community-wide change, *community co-ownership* of every activity was sought, including public agencies, private business, philanthropy, and government leaders. The initial emphasis of the DFI was to coalesce leadership from the major community agencies that serve children by asking the directors to meet monthly to improve their collective impact. These agencies and directors included, not exclusively, the county commissioners, the city manager's office, the public schools, the mental health center, the police department, the juvenile court, the health department, the division of social services, and the daycare council. Early on, this directors group wrote and signed a memorandum of agreement that pledged its constituents to follow System of Care principles in working with each other to align services toward the prevention of child maltreatment. A larger, more public, collaborative group was also formed that included many more community representatives, toward similar goals.

Second, because Duke Endowment intervention funding for the DFI was limited to an average of about $20 per community child per year (still more than $1 million per year in a community of 55,000 children), we sought to *leverage financial resources* whenever possible. Rather than fund an entire program, we negotiated with community agencies to supplement some of their programs in return for their support of programs that were a priority of the DFI. For example, the local Medicaid-supported prenatal care program of social workers was in need of additional social workers

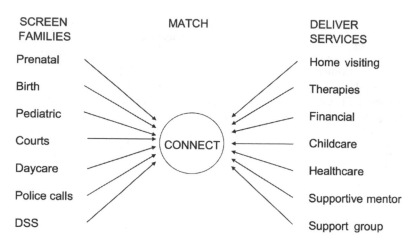

FIGURE 4.2. A Preventive System of Care for reducing child maltreatment.

who could serve non-Medicaid-eligible but low-income pregnant women, including noncitizen Latinas. The DFI funded two extra social worker positions for this purpose on the condition that the entire group of 10 social workers would be trained to administer the empirically based screening instrument that we had developed for pregnant women who might be at risk for maltreatment. The DFI also funded two extra home visitor positions to supplement the five existing government-supported home visitors in return for an agreement to provide the entire team with systematic training and random-assignment evaluation of the program's effectiveness. The randomized controlled trial is under way.

Third, we emphasized *support for evidence-based programs* that have been successful in promoting parenting skills and preventing maltreatment. Directories of programs that meet standards of evidence (such as the Colorado Blueprints) were used to identify programs for funding and implementation by community agencies. When an agency identified a gap in the evidence base, we supported the creation and testing of new services. When an agency already supported an existing program that seemed to be effective, albeit without rigorous evaluation, we supported randomized trials to evaluate program effectiveness. Five randomized trials are currently under way, embedded within the larger DFI program implementation. Even the screening instruments that we developed were based on our own empirical longitudinal study of risk factors for maltreatment among pregnant women within the local community. The larger goal was to instill a culture of rigorous evaluation and accountability.

Fourth, we supported the growth of a *continuum of services* that met diverse needs of families at risk for maltreatment. These services ranged from the professional to the paraprofessional and addressed multiple levels of the social-ecological model. At the individual level, home visiting was supported through an adaptation of the national Healthy Families model (Daro & Cohn-Donnelly, 2002), which is being evaluated through a randomized trial. A novel program of group education and support for pregnant Latinas, called CoMadres, was developed, pilot tested, and implemented through a randomized trial (Flint, 2008).

At the family level, parent–child interaction therapy (Brestan, Eyberg, Boggs, & Algina, 1997) was supported for already maltreating families at risk of recurrence of maltreatment, and domestic violence shelter staff members were trained in attending to the needs of children of abused women. Family events such as festivals were held in high-risk neighborhoods.

At the neighborhood level, social workers were assigned to three of the six highest-risk neighborhoods (by random assignment, for evaluation purposes) and were trained to implement a program to increase neighborhood social capital through leadership development, neighborhood association meetings, and door-to-door recruitment. They initiated English as a second language (ESL) classes in neighborhoods with high concentrations of immigrant Latinos. They started women's groups and a volunteer grandparent mentoring program for new mothers. They watched out for individual families that neighbors identified as being at high risk. The creativity of the social workers matched neighborhood programs with family needs.

At the community level, members of the local police department were trained to screen for child risk factors when they made house calls for domestic violence or for other reasons. The directors' group and community collaboratives are also community-level interventions in that they made funding decisions that affected community programs and advocated for policy changes. Finally, at the public policy level, a variety of reform efforts were initiated, including (but not exclusively) (1) support for legislators and policymakers in bringing an evidence-based approach to funding programs, (2) support for expansion of Medicaid authority to serve pregnant women through prevention programs, (3) encouragement of judges to take into account children's needs when sentencing parents, and (4) support for the public housing authority in allocating resources toward tenant leadership development. Not all of these efforts have been successful in reaching their goals; however, the DFI is still under way.

Finally, we sought to *catalyze areas of potential high impact*. We made decisions about program support that were based on the likelihood that the community rate of maltreatment would be affected, not just on the likelihood of positive outcomes for a small number of families.

EMPIRICAL OUTCOMES

An array of descriptive narratives provide evidence that the DFI has been implemented generally in the way in which it was intended. Funds have indeed been leveraged. Following the formation of the directors group, county commissioners allocated $225,000 per year (to which an additional $60,000 was added in 2006) to support community-wide implementation of System of Care principles, and the city sought and was awarded a state grant to adopt these principles in its mental health service system. Evidence-based programs have been supported by funds in several agencies. It is now standard practice that all Medicaid-supported pregnant women are screened with the instrument we designed so that services can be matched to women in need. The community of Durham has won several national awards, including those for its reform efforts designed to bring better services to families and for being one of America's Promise Alliance's "100 Best Communities" in the nation. Still, the more important evaluation measure concerns the impact on maltreatment outcomes.

The basic design for evaluation is to compare the rate of child maltreatment in Durham County across time, beginning prior to the initiation of the DFI, with the parallel cross-time rate for a group of five other counties in North Carolina that collectively match Durham demographically. Official records were retrieved and coded for this purpose.

For 4 consecutive years beginning in 2002, the official rate of substantiated maltreatment of children in Durham County declined, and the decline was greater than that for the average of the five comparison counties. As shown in Figure 4.3, between 2001–2002 (just before the DFI began) and 2005–2006, the maltreatment rate in Durham declined by 49%, in contrast with 22% for the average of the five comparison counties. For the first time since records became available, the rate of maltreatment in Durham was lower than the statewide average. The official rate among children less than 1 year of age in Durham County has decreased by 45%, in contrast with an average decrease in the five matched counties of 12%. Extrapolating from these figures and the actual numbers of cases of maltreatment in all of the counties over this period, one can estimate that the DFI prevented 468 cases of substantiated maltreatment among children birth to age 6 over these 4½ years.

Of particular interest is the recidivism rate, that is, the rate at which children who have been assessed for possible maltreatment by the Division of Social Services (DSS) receive a reassessment within 6 months. A high rate would indicate a failure of the professional system to respond adequately. Among children birth to age 6, the reassessment rate in Durham County has decreased by 27% since the year prior to the beginning of the DFI (2001–2002). In contrast, the rate for the mean of the five demographi-

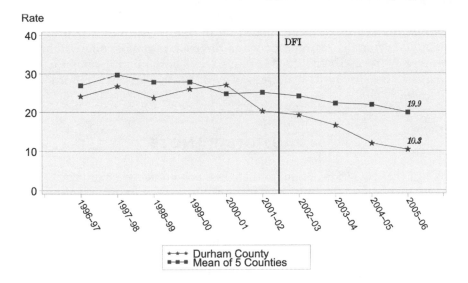

FIGURE 4.3. Official rates of substantiated child maltreatment (per 1,000 population) for children birth to age 6 in Durham County, North Carolina, and a group of five matched comparison counties, across the years 1996–2006.

cally matched comparison counties over the same period has decreased by 17%.

It is plausible that the official rate has decreased because of factors other than the DFI, and so independent sources provide additional information. Anonymous surveys were completed with 1,741 family-serving professionals in Durham County and one of the five comparison counties (Guilford County) in 2004 and 2006. Professionals' estimates of the proportion of children who had been abused decreased by 11% in Durham but increased by 2% in Guilford over the same period. Estimates of the proportion of children who had been neglected decreased by 18% in Durham but decreased by only 3% in Guilford. Estimates of the proportion of children who had been spanked decreased by 11% in Durham but increased by 4% in Guilford. For positive parenting behaviors, professional estimates of the proportion of children shown love, affection, or hugs by parents increased by 5% in Durham but decreased by 2% in Guilford.

It is also plausible that the DFI has changed professionals' perceptions without changing children's actual outcomes, so emergency department and hospital records from local hospitals were scrutinized for evidence regarding child maltreatment. The rate at which children birth to age 6 presented to a hospital or emergency room with a possible maltreatment-related injury decreased in Durham County by 17% between 2001–2002 and 2005–2006, whereas the rate in Guilford County decreased by just 6%. Pediatric hospitalizations for any reason represent a reverse measure of child well being. Between 2001–2002 and 2005–2006, overall hospital visit rates for children ages 0–6 in Durham decreased by 13%, whereas in Guilford rates increased by 8%.

A CAUTIONARY NOTE

Because the evaluation design for the DFI is not a random assignment experiment, numerous alternative explanations for these patterns will always be plausible. Two such explanations must be considered. First, it is possible that the counties have come to differ in the way that maltreatment reports are managed by professionals or how child injuries are coded in emergency rooms. These differences would imply that the DFI's "effect" on maltreatment is artificial. A second possibility is that Durham County has indeed improved in outcomes for its children relative to other counties but the cause of the improvement is some factor other than the DFI, one that co-occurred with the implementation of the DFI. Although statistical tests of changes in county-wide employment rates and in Latino immigration rates revealed that these patterns do not account for changes in maltreatment rates, other differences across time and across counties might account for the patterns observed.

FUTURE PLANS

The DFI, as implemented in the period 2002–2006, was an ambitious effort to prevent maltreatment, but it had many components and some of these components were implemented only partially. Screening was far from universal. Numerous components of intervention occurred simultaneously, so that even if the overall program was indeed successful, it is difficult to conclude which component was most responsible for its effectiveness. To systematize the program to make it ready for dissemination, and to test its effectiveness more rigorously, beginning in 2008 the program evolved into a universal screening and services-matching program called *Durham Connects*. This evolved program aims to (1) engage every family of a newborn infant shortly after the child's birth in one to three home visits; (2) screen for family needs on each of the four empirically based domains of parenting, family financial stability, health and healthcare, and childcare; and (3) match families in need with community services. The County of Durham has been segmented into 20 geographic neighborhoods, and half of these neighborhoods have been randomly assigned to receive the new Durham Connects program immediately. The remaining half will receive it in 2 years. Outcomes for the expected 3,000 children born into intervention neighborhoods will be compared with outcomes for the expected 3,000 children born into control neighborhoods.

CONCLUSIONS

If the results of the evaluation of the Durham Family Initiative are to be believed, then remarkable cost savings have already been achieved for the community of Durham County, North Carolina. The 468 cases of maltreatment that have been prevented over the 4½-year period between July 2002 and December 2006 (or even more if children ages 7–18 are included) could be expected to cost an average of $66,804 per case, according to estimates by Wang and Holton (2007), or a total of $31,264,272. The total funding received by the DFI from The Duke Endowment during the 5-year period from January 2002 through December 2006 was $6,398,248. This amount included 6 months of planning in 2002 and substantial effort devoted to research evaluation across all years. Thus, the total savings could be estimated at $24,866,024. For every dollar invested by the funder, $4.89 was saved in future costs of maltreatment.

Perhaps all or some of these savings would have accrued without the presence of the DFI, and perhaps the estimates are incorrect, owing to assumptions in the calculations by Wang and Holton (2007). Replication and more rigorous analysis will help sort out the robustness of these findings in future years. Nonetheless, the promise of community savings in both human suffering and financial burden is so great that a science-based investment in community-based prevention of child maltreatment seems well worth pursuing.

REFERENCES

Azar, S. T. (1997). A cognitive behavioral approach to understanding and treating parents who physically abuse their children. In D. A. Wolfe, R. J. McMahon, & R. D. Peters (Eds.), *Child abuse: New directions in prevention and treatment across the lifespan* (pp. 198–224). Thousand Oaks, CA: Sage.

Brestan, E. V., Eyberg, S. M., Boggs, S. R., & Algina, J. (1997). Parent–child interaction therapy: Parents' perceptions of untreated siblings. *Child and Family Behavior Therapy, 19*(3), 13–28.

Bronfenbrenner, U., & Morris, P. A. (2006). The bioecological model of human development. In R. Lerner (Ed.), *Handbook of child psychology: Vol. 1. Theoretical models of human development* (pp. 793–828). Hoboken, NJ: Wiley.

Bugental, D. B., Ellerson, P. C., Lin, E. K., Rainey, B., Kokotovic, A., & O'Hara, N. (2002). A cognitive approach to child abuse prevention. *Journal of Family Psychology, 16*, 243–258.

Bugental, D. B., & Johnston, C. (2000). Parental and child cognitions in the context of the family. *Annual Review of Psychology, 51*, 315–344.

Cicchetti, D., & Toth, S. (1995). Developmental psychopathology of child maltreatment. *Journal of the American Academy of Child and Adolescent Psychiatry, 34*, 541–565.

Coulton, C., Korbin, J., & Su, M. (1999). Neighborhoods and child maltreatment: A multi-level analysis. *Child Abuse and Neglect, 23*(11), 1019–1040.

Daro, D., & Cohn-Donnelly, A. (2002). Charting the waves of prevention: Two steps forward, one step back. *Child Abuse and Neglect, 26*, 731–742.

Daro, D. A., & McCurdy, K. P. (2006). Interventions to prevent child maltreatment. In L. S. Doll, S. E. Bronzo, J. A. Mercy, D. A. Sleet, & E. N. Haas (Eds.), *Handbook of injury and violence prevention* (pp. 137–156). New York: Springer.

Daro, D., McCurdy, K., & Nelson, C. (2005). *Engagement and retention in voluntary and new parent support programs: Final report*. Chapin Hall Working Paper. Chicago: Chapin Hall, University of Chicago.

Dix, T., & Lochman, J. (1990). Social cognition and negative reactions to children: A comparison of mothers of aggressive and nonaggressive boys. *Journal of Social and Clinical Psychology, 9*, 418–438.

Dodge, K. A. (2002). Mediation, moderation, and mechanisms in how parenting affects children's aggressive behavior. In J. Borkowski (Ed.), *Parenting and the child's world* (pp. 215–229). Hillsdale, NJ: Erlbaum.

Dodge, K. A. (2006). Translational science in action: Hostile attributional style and the development of aggressive behavior problems. *Development and Psychopathology, 18*, 791–814.

Dodge, K. A., Berlin, L. J., Epstein, M., Spitz Roth, A., O'Donnell, K., Kauffman, M., et al. (2004). The Durham Family Initiative: A preventive system of care. *Child Welfare, 83*(2), 109–128.

Flint, R. C. (2008). *Immediate impact of the CoMADRES Child Maltreatment Prevention trial*. Unpublished manuscript, Duke University, Durham, NC.

Kolko D. J. (2002). Child physical abuse. In J. E. Myers, L. Berliner, J. Briere, T. Hendrix, C. Jenny, & T. A. Reid (Eds.), *The APSAC handbook on child maltreatment* (2nd ed., pp. 21–54). Thousand Oaks, CA: Sage.

McLoyd, V. C., Aikens, N. L., & Burton, L. M. (2006). Childhood poverty, policy, and practice. In K. A. Renninger & I. E. Siegel (Eds.), *Handbook of child psychology: Vol. 4. Child psychology in practice* (pp. 700–775). Hoboken, NJ: Wiley.

Nix, R. L., Pinderhughes, E. E., Dodge, K. A., Bates, J. E., Pettit, G. S., & McFadyen-Ketchum, S. A. (1999). The relation between mothers' hostile attribution tendencies and children's externalizing behavior problems: The mediating role of mothers' harsh discipline practices. *Child Development, 70*(4), 896–909.

Olds, D. L., Eckenrode, J., Henderson, C. R., Jr., Kitzman, H., Powers, J., Cole, R., et al. (1997). Long-term effects of home visitation on maternal life course and child abuse and neglect. Fifteen-year follow-up of a randomized trial. *Journal of the American Medical Association, 278*(8), 637–643.

Pinderhughes, E. E., Nix, R., Foster, E. M., Jones, D., & the Conduct Problems Prevention Research Group. (2001). Parenting in context: Impact of neighborhood poverty, residential stability, public services, social networks, and danger on parental behaviors. *Journal of Marriage and the Family, 63*(4), 941–953.

Repucci, N. D., Woolard, J. L., & Fried, C. S. (1999). Social, community, and preventive interventions. *Annual Review of Psychology, 50,* 387–418.

Tolan, P. H., & Dodge, K. A. (2005). Children's mental health as a primary care and concern: A system for comprehensive support and service. *American Psychologist, 60*(6), 601–614.

Wang, C-T., & Holton, J. (2007). *Total estimated cost of child abuse and neglect in the United States.* Chicago: Prevent Child Abuse America. Retrieved July 29, 2009, from *member.preventchildabuse.org/site/DocServer/cost_analysis. pdf?docID=144.*

CHAPTER 5

How Strong Communities Restored My Faith in Humanity

Children Can Live in Safety

Gary B. Melton

The egocentric title of this chapter may seem odd to readers. That the author has had an existential crisis is of little consequence in itself. Nonetheless, because the source of my anxiety is a matter of considerable social significance (in effect, I suspect, a matter of great personal significance to many readers), I have retained the personal starting point.

For about the past 20 years I have spent most of my professional life worried about a dilemma that has been nearly pervasive across the globe (cf. National Research Council and Institute of Medicine, 2005). On one hand, I (Melton, 1992b, 1995) remain convinced that most people want to do the right thing. Regardless of their cultural and economic background, most people want to participate in an inclusive, democratic community respectful of human rights, including the right to personal security. Most people want their own and others' children to grow up in such a community.

On the other hand, the centrifugal forces in 21st-century life are such that fulfillment of such a vision is (at best) very difficult. I worried whether creation and preservation of community is even possible today. As most famously summarized by Robert Putnam (2000), in the past generation there has been a marked decline in social capital, the "wealth" that people have in relationships. As compared with prior generations, people generally have substantially fewer relationships on which they can count for meaningful assistance (McPherson, Smith-Lovin, & Brashears, 2006), and they are much less trusting of not only their leaders but also their neighbors (Fukuyama, 1996, 2000; Pharr & Putnam, 2000). This disconnection has been accompanied by discontent—a growing malaise marked by increasing alienation, boredom, anxiety, and depression. Unfortunately, this generational trend is most marked among young people (Putnam, 2000; see, e.g., Larson, 2000; Seligman, 1995; Twenge, 2000), presumably including young parents. As starkly demonstrated by the annual survey of U.S. college freshmen conducted for more than 40 years by the University of California, Los Angeles (UCLA) Higher Education Research Institute (HERI) (Pryor, Hurtado, Saenz, Santos, & Korn, 2007), each age cohort is less engaged, less trustful, and more bored than the one that preceded it. Unfortunately, HERI's follow-up survey of college graduates provides an even drearier picture of typical civic engagement (Vogelgesang & Astin, 2005).

My concern about the growing disconnection between parents and children began in the late 1980s and early 1990s, several years before Putnam's (1995) classic article "Bowling Alone" attracted the attention of social scientists and newspaper columnists. Several experiences contributed to my concern. Visiting Eastern Europe and southern Africa during transitions to democracy and the Middle East during a particularly precarious time, I observed the mixture of euphoria, anxiety, and disillusionment associated with those changes (Melton, 1993).

As a Fulbright scholar living in Norway, I experienced the same sense of unease about the well-being of young people and their families that was becoming familiar in the United States (Melton, 1991). In this liberals' Nirvana—a relatively conflict-free, largely homogeneous society with relatively little inequality and with easy access to professional services—parents and policymakers still shared most of the worries of their peers across the North Atlantic.

Most directly on point, I conducted resource assessments in several communities in Greenville County, South Carolina (Melton, 1992a). I was stunned but not surprised by the danger perceived by parents in several inner-city neighborhoods, who often believed (perhaps accurately) that the emergency room was the only resource available to their families. The surprise came in the suburbs where I found that, contrary to similar surveys a generation earlier, parents said that they looked first not to "natural helpers" but instead to professional specialists when their families had problems. Help had become a commodity to *buy*, not what people *do*.

In this context, I was serving as vice-chair of the U.S. Advisory Board on Child Abuse and Neglect. Statutorily charged with assessing the nation's progress in fulfilling the purposes of the Child Abuse Prevention and Treatment Act of 1974 (a statute that at the time actually had no express purposes), the Board perceived its principal mission to be the preparation of a report to Congress and the Secretary of Health and Human Services on the state of child protection in the United States.

The Board's review in preparation of that initial report generated a list of hundreds of problems. The problems were so varied, but also so consistently grave in scope and consequences, and the failures of the system designed to respond were so colossal that the Board declared a national emergency (U.S. Advisory Board on Child Abuse and Neglect, 1990). For a moment (but only a moment), threats to children's security were the center of attention of the nation's media and presumably also its concerned citizens and their leaders (Melton, 2002).

In an article that I wrote at the time (Melton, 1993), these several profound experiences so troubled me that I asked rhetorically in the title, "Is there a place for children in the new world order?" The most positive answer that I could muster in the concluding section was, "I hope so" (Melton, 1993, p. 532).

Experiences that I have had in the past 6 years as director of Strong Communities for Children, an ambitious university-affiliated, foundation-funded, community-wide initiative to prevent child maltreatment, have led me to a happier conclusion. My faith in humanity has been restored. My colleagues and I have learned, to our great pleasure, that we *can* create situations in which whole communities *can* be enabled to help and be helped to protect and preserve children's personal security, parents' and other caregivers' efficacy, and families' integrity and well-being. Furthermore, communities *can* engage in such mutual assistance without being either demeaning or demeaned. The dignity of both children and parents *can* be protected, as community is both achieved and called upon.

After reading a collection of articles about Strong Communities (Melton & Holaday, 2008), one editor gave an apt one-word assessment: The story of Strong Communities is simply "amazing," even at a point then little more than halfway in the planned development of the initiative. Distilling our experience into a relatively brief chapter is a formidable task. I nonetheless try here to describe the conceptual foundation for the initiative, provide a brief sample of the activities therein, summarize the knowledge that has been generated, and indicate some of the questions that remain.

THE CONCEPTUAL FOUNDATION

Strong Communities for Children is the first attempt to apply the U.S. Advisory Board on Child Abuse and Neglect's (1993) proposed strategy for child protection on a large scale. It is useful to begin, therefore, with a brief description of the Board's reasoning and its vision for a new system.

Underfunding is surely the most commonly articulated reason for the failure of the child protection system. At least implicitly, however, the Board disagreed about the primacy of that problem, although it did issue a still unfulfilled recommendation for a federal study of the cost of implementing a national child protection policy and the cost of not doing so (U.S. Advisory Board on Child Abuse and Neglect, 1991, Recommendation B-4).

Looking beyond dollars and cents to more fundamental matters, the Board attributed the emergency to faulty system design—what I have described as "a policy without reason" (Melton, 2005): "The most serious shortcoming of the nation's system of intervention on behalf of children is that it depends upon a reporting and response process that has punitive connotations, and requires massive resources dedicated to the investigation of allegations" (U.S. Advisory Board on Child Abuse and Neglect, 1990, p. 80).

This misdirection of the child protection system resulted from an initially mistaken assessment of the nature and frequency of child maltreatment. When the identification of the battered child syndrome captured the nation's attention in the early 1960s, child maltreatment was believed to affect a few hundred children who were tortured by very deviant parents (Kempe, Silverman, Steele, Droegemueller, & Silver, 1962). Given such assumptions, the logical corollary was to install a system that would enable public authorities to find those children and save them from further abuse.

We know now, however, that even compared with reported cases of suspected child maltreatment—a number that itself is probably a substantial underestimate of the prevalence (Kalichman, 1999; Theodore, Runyan, & Chang, 2007)—the early estimates were low by a factor at least 10^4 (Administration on Children, Youth, and Families, 2007). Whatever else may be said, the most obvious point about the child protection system is that case finding is not the primary problem.

Furthermore, we now know that most cases, even in the formal child protection system, do not involve evil or sick parents. Instead, the modal case is one in which inadequate care occurs because parents are overwhelmed by multiple serious problems in combination with impoverished social and economic resources (U.S. Advisory Board on Child Abuse and Neglect, 1993). Hence, both prevention and treatment logically require a multifaceted approach in the venues of everyday life (cf. Henggeler, Schoenwald, Rowland, & Cunningham, 2002; Swenson, Henggeler, Taylor, & Addison, 2005)—a far cry from the parenting classes or, even more frequently, no services at all other than an investigation (if that can reasonably be called a "service") that child protection system authorities commonly offer families (U.S. Advisory Board on Child Abuse and Neglect, 1993).

Indeed, the U.S. Advisory Board concluded that the ill-designed narrowness of the child protection system leads to tragic results. In language that was frequently cited in the media, the Board noted that "it has become far easier to pick up the telephone to report one's neighbor for child abuse than it is for that neighbor to pick up the telephone to request and receive help before the abuse happens" (U.S. Advisory Board on Child Abuse and Neglect, 1990, p. 80).

Setting the tone for its advocacy of a radically transformed national strategy for child protection, the Board dedicated its second report "to the many thousands of American children and families trapped in the throes of abuse and neglect who are waiting for our society, and its governments, to respond to their plight with *more* than just a report, and *more* than just an investigation" (U.S. Advisory Board on Child Abuse and Neglect, 1991, "Dedication," original emphasis). The Board plaintively added, "For their sake and for the welfare of our nation, we hope they are reached in time" (U.S. Advisory Board on Child Abuse and Neglect, 1991, "Dedication").

For child protection to be effective, the Board concluded, it must be part of everyday life, and for that result to occur, nothing less than a culture change would be sufficient: "The Nation must strive diligently to overcome the isolation created by the demands of modern life and exacerbated by the ravages of poverty. We must tear down the walls that divide us by race, class, and age, and we must create caring communities that support the families and shelter the children within them. We must take the time to see the need and lend a hand" (U.S. Advisory Board on Child Abuse and Neglect, 1993, p. 82). To that end, the Board "challenge[d] all American adults to resolve to be good neighbors—to know, watch, and support their neighbors' children and to offer help when needed to their neighbors' families" (U.S. Advisory Board on Child Abuse and Neglect, 1993, p. 82).

The Board recognized that fulfillment of its strategy would be difficult. Such a neighborhood-based approach "require[d] reversal of powerful social trends," conceptualization of a complex plan, design and implementation of a multitude of elements, fulfillment of such tasks using a 'minimally developed' science and technology of neighborhood development, and changing not just an individual family but also "service providers, the community, and all levels of government—in fact, ... society itself" (U.S. Advisory Board on Child Abuse and Neglect, 1993, p. 81).

In its 1993 report, therefore, the Board did not recommend an immediate wholesale shift in child protection strategies. Instead, the Board's Recommendation #1 was for systematic trials of its neighborhood-based strategy:

> The Federal Government and private foundations should establish a large-scale demonstration program of *Prevention Zones*—comprehensive efforts to improve the social and physical environments in declining neighborhoods with high rates of child maltreatment. These model neighborhoods should be diverse in geography, population density, and

ethnicity. The trials should be closely monitored and rigorously evaluated. Principles learned should be widely disseminated and, with such modifications as suggested by evaluation studies, should lead to a large-scale national effort within five years. (U.S. Advisory Board on Child Abuse and Neglect, 1993, pp. 23, 84; footnote omitted)

THE NATURE OF STRONG COMMUNITIES

The federal government failed to heed the U .S. Advisory Board on Child Abuse and Neglect's (1993) call for the creation of Prevention Zones as the laboratories in which to refine its vision for caring communities. Unfortunately, despite initially intense interest shown by the most pertinent congressional committees (quashed in behind-the-scenes jockeying by the G. H. W. Bush administration and several national child welfare organizations; see Melton, 2002), the federal government also failed to act on a much more detailed blueprint (U.S. Advisory Board on Child Abuse and Neglect, 1991) for a multifaceted national strategy to strengthen communities in order to keep children safe.

There has been greater interest shown by private foundations (see Melton, 2002, for examples). In its support for efforts to reduce the prevalence of child maltreatment through carefully conceptualized and evaluated community initiatives, The Duke Endowment has probably come closer than any other entity to the U.S. Advisory Board on Child Abuse and Neglect's (1993) vision, as embodied in the Board's Recommendation #1.

In that regard, in 2002 The Endowment made two long-term, multimillion-dollar grants. One of the grants went to the Durham Family Initiative, which was undertaken by researchers at Duke University using a strategy described by Dodge, Murphy, O'Donnell, and Christopoulos (Chapter 4, this volume); see also Dodge and colleagues (2004). The other grant was made to the Clemson University (CU) Research Foundation for Strong Communities for Children. Strong Communities is a comprehensive application by the CU Institute on Family and Neighborhood Life (IFNL) of the U.S. Advisory Board on Child Abuse and Neglect's (1993) neighborhood-based strategy in an ethnically and economically diverse urban/suburban/rural area in Greenville and Anderson counties in northwestern South Carolina. (For a detailed description of Strong Communities and its effects in approximately the first 5½ years of the initiative, see Melton & Holaday, 2008.) The total population of the area was 126,000 in 2000; the adult population was 97,000.

The overarching principle guiding IFNL's work is also at the root of Strong Communities. IFNL faculty members believe that both (1) ethical duties to avoid undue intrusion and (2) practical concerns about the effectiveness of distal, clinic-centered services push toward a heavy reliance on primary community institutions (e.g., schools, civic clubs, and places of worship) and the nonprofessional participants within them. They strive to make help "built in"—an expectable part of the routines of everyday life within the settings most central to the community.

Accordingly, IFNL's work always is conceived as increasing the likelihood that *families will be able to obtain help where they are, when they need it, in a form in which they can use it with ease and without stigma.* Stated simply, Strong Communities, like IFNL as a whole, starts from the premise that *people shouldn't have to ask!* In a community in which people are committed to mutual assistance, families should not have to be objectified as patients, clients, or, worse, "cases" before they can receive help. To achieve immediacy and acceptability of help, Strong Communities reaches across the whole community, and it does not distinguish between *helpers* and *clients.*

The ultimate goal of Strong Communities is to *Keep Kids Safe* (prevent child abuse and neglect) across the participating communities. In the spirit of the Golden Rule, however, the penultimate goal is to strengthen community to such a level that *every child and every parent knows that whenever they have reason to celebrate, worry, or grieve, someone will notice, and someone will care.* A corollary goal is that *someone will be available to watch out for (watch over) every family of a child under 6 that wants and needs such support.*

In broad terms, Strong Communities has two components. First, at the heart of the initiative are several community outreach workers (roughly one per town), whose efforts are focused on *mobilization* of the participating communities, which vary in population from about 5,000 to about 50,000. Second, the resulting pool of volunteer labor is used, along with modest redirection of pediatric well care and early childhood education, to make a set of direct services universally available to families of young children in the service area. These services within Strong Communities are known as *Strong Families.*

The outreach workers who are leading the community mobilization have substantial experience in community work (e.g., several themselves had been star volunteers in various local initiatives), but none had been employed before as organizers. Most have relevant graduate education, but their fields of study have been quite varied (e.g., nursing, education, agriculture [a 4-H agent], counseling, and theology).

Hence, the outreach workers are guided not by particular professional education or even specific prescribed techniques, but instead by the following 10 principles (Kimbrough-Melton & Campbell, 2008; for an analogous approach, see Henggeler et al., 2002; Swenson et al., 2005):

1. The specific activities that outreach workers use to engage the community should be logically related to the ultimate outcome of

reducing child abuse and neglect. Specifically, an activity "fits" if it naturally brings people together so that connections among families are enhanced and isolation is reduced.

2. Outreach strategies should be directed toward the transformation of community norms and structures so that residents "naturally" notice and respond to the needs of children and their parents.

3. Outreach activities should continuously "push the envelope." The objective is not necessarily the implementation of discrete programs but instead the continuous creation of settings in which Strong Communities' core message is heard and applied.

4. Outreach should be directed toward volunteer recruitment, mobilization, and retention.

5. Outreach activities should be directed toward the establishment or strengthening of relationships among families or between families and community institutions.

6. Outreach activities should include a focus on the development of widely available, easily accessible, and nonstigmatizing social and material support for families of young children.

7. Although the ultimate goal is the protection of *children*, outreach activities are directed toward *parents*.

8. Outreach activities should be undertaken in a way that enhances parent leadership and community engagement.

9. Whenever possible, outreach activities should facilitate reciprocity of help.

10. Outreach activities should be designed so that they build or rely on the assets (leadership, networks, facilities, and cultures) in and among the primary institutions in the community.

The particular activities that outreach workers initiate or facilitate are remarkably diverse. However, many have used special events to build social capital through stronger community identity, increased collective efficacy, more numerous and strengthened social networks, and greater sensitivity to young families' daily needs (Berman, Murphy-Berman, & Melton, 2008; Murphy-Berman, Berman, & Melton, 2008). For example, Strong Communities activities in one town were jump-started by a community luncheon to celebrate the publication of a community-written book about neighboring (Benson, 2007).

Similarly, through observances of Blue Ribbon Sabbath, scores of religious congregations have spread the Strong Communities message and energized community service to fulfill that message (Melton & Anderson, 2008). Usually observed during April (National Child Abuse Prevention Month), Blue Ribbon Sabbath is a day for special expressions of concern by religious organizations about the safety of children. In 2008, 143 congregations in the service area participated (an increase from about 70 in 2004), of which 25 went beyond the circulation of bulletin inserts and wearing of blue ribbons to undertake other special activities (e.g., special family activities, special worship services, initiation of Strong Families projects, and launching of an e-network for family support). Perhaps most important, however, Blue Ribbon Sabbath has typically been the beginning point for congregational activity. An impressive 95% of the participating congregations have undertaken multiple kinds of activities (as of spring 2008, $M = 7.2$; $SD = 4.1$) within Strong Communities.

Increasing depth and breadth of participation has been typical, regardless of sector. In broad strokes, the initiative has unfolded in four phases (Melton, Holaday, & Kimbrough-Melton, 2008):

1. *Spreading the word* to raise awareness about the nature of the problem and to identify opportunities for enhanced family support.
2. *Mobilizing the community* to become engaged in developing and implementing plans to prevent child maltreatment.
3. *Increasing the resources* for families to obtain nonstigmatizing help whenever and wherever they need it.
4. *Institutionalizing the provision of resources* so that support is sustained over the long term.

In our judgment, most of the recent work in Strong Communities (approximately 6 years after its inception) has been in Phase 3. In this context, "much of the work has been focused on application of the institutional and personal relationships developed in the prior phases to increase resources for families. This phase has required the establishment of new organizational commitments for service and of universal means of enlistment of families of young children" (Melton et al., 2008, p. 87).

As we enter the last years in the projected decade of work, we expect that efforts in Phase 4 will be

> directed towards institutionalizing the resources that result from the mobilization of citizens, organizations and institutions. Institutionalization of resources is described within Strong Communities as *transforming* the norms and structures within the communities, so that residents "naturally" notice and respond to the needs of children and parents. Transformation will occur when action on behalf of families becomes routine and not something that people have to be reminded about or prompted to do. For this reason, outreach workers have been sensitive to creating opportunities for engagement in diverse settings and building permanent structures to support Strong Communities within those organizations. (Melton et al., 2008, pp. 87–88, original emphasis)

The cornerstone of this effort is the creation of Family Activity Centers (FACs), staffed by volunteers or by staff members whose time is contributed by community agencies, located in existing community facilities (e.g., churches, schools, fire stations, and libraries), and offering free or low-fee services. Designed to address factors in the etiology of child maltreatment, the FACs are intended to make help easily available to all families and to build a perception that parents are not alone in their care for their children— in effect, that the community cares about children and voluntarily makes resources available to all. Strengthening relationships among parents, offering general assistance, and facilitating financial security, comprehensive FACs offer at least five core services: (1) family activities, (2) play groups, (3) parents' nights out, (4) chats with a family advocate (generic counseling and advocacy), and (5) financial education, career counseling, and related mentoring. All of the families enrolled in Strong Families also receive a monthly newsletter providing news about developments in Strong Communities and opportunities for family activities. Parents of infants and toddlers also periodically receive *Connections*, parenting tips that are matched to the ordinary schedule for well-child care.

Much of the help in Strong Families is linked to entry points into healthcare and education, the two systems that together include almost all children. Hence, through Extra Care for Caring Families, we are trying to reform pediatric and family healthcare to increase family support. Through both Extra Care and Family Partnerships (an analogous effort based in kindergartens and daycare centers), we are attempting to make chats with a family advocate (a mental-health-trained family support worker), interaction with other parents, and opportunities for parent leadership and community engagement available to all families of our young children in our service area.

In the first year of Strong Families enrollment (March 2006–March 2007), more than 2,000 families signed up. Many more participated in some Strong Families activities during the year, even though they had not formally joined. Of course, the movement continues to grow, so that almost 3,000 families were formally enrolled in Strong Families by the end of 2007. Overall, we estimate that there were more than 20,000 instances of participation in Strong Families during its first 2 years, when about 1,300 activities were sponsored, a number that is rapidly increasing.

THE BREADTH AND DEPTH
OF VOLUNTEER ENGAGEMENT

As the high enrollment and participation in Strong Families indicate, "Strong Communities is a model for broad-based engagement of diverse communities in concerted action to strengthen families and keep kids safe. The initiative has successfully engaged many segments of the community by forming partnerships with important community structures or, when absent or weak, actually creating such structures" (Berman et al., 2008, p. 134).

This general picture of broad and deep community involvement is most vividly illustrated by the involvement of volunteers in Strong Communities. By the end of 2007 (5.75 years from the date when the initiative was formally launched), almost 5,000 individuals (roughly 5% of the adult population in the service area) had contributed about 53,000 hours to the initiative, and the recorded numbers are undoubtedly smaller—perhaps far smaller—than the actual numbers.

Moreover, the volunteers mirror the communities of which they are a part. Indeed, to the extent that the volunteers differ, they tend to be (contrary to typical volunteers in other projects) more disadvantaged (Haski-Leventhal, Ben-Arieh, & Melton, 2008). Almost one-third are minorities, a greater proportion than in the general population of the area. Remarkably, for an initiative focused on children and families, about two-fifths of the volunteers are male.

The age range of volunteers is also diverse; about one-fifth are at least 50, about one-half are between 30 and 49, and more than one-fourth are under 30. Interestingly, given that no special effort has been made to recruit youth volunteers, about one-eighth are under 20. Young people are a part of the initiative because they are respected as part of the community.

Research on volunteering shows that volunteers often have mixed motives. The desire to serve is often accompanied by the desire to strengthen one's résumé and to "network" as part of business or career development. However, volunteers in Strong Communities overwhelmingly reported altruistic motives for participation in the initiative (Haski-Leventhal et al., 2008). At least 80% of volunteers in Strong Communities reported that their contribution is intended "to give back to [the] community" and "to help people in need." Almost one-fifth reported religious motives. Only one self-oriented purpose (personal growth, 16%) was indicated by more than 10% of the sample.

The sources of volunteers are diverse. More than one-fourth have become involved through churches and other religious organizations, and a similar proportion have been recruited through neighborhood associations and civic organizations. The rest (fewer than 10% in each instance) have come, respectively, from schools, businesses, human service agencies, local government, fire departments, police departments, and the media.

The importance of volunteers to the initiative continues to increase. For example, the number of recorded volunteer hours per year almost doubled between 2004 (8,691 hours) and 2007 (16,516 hours). Among those who volunteered at some point during the last quarter of 2007, the total contribution to the initiative through that time averaged 84 hours in 13.6 activities.

THE BREADTH AND DEPTH
OF ORGANIZATIONAL PARTICIPATION

Analogous trends have occurred in organizational involvement in Strong Communities. More organizations are involved, and their participation is both more extensive and more diverse. The number of religious organizations involved grew from 118 in 2004 to 196 in 2007. This number represents about 70% of the churches and other communities of faith in the service area. The number of participating businesses increased from 107 to 168 during the same period.

Seventy-seven other voluntary associations were engaged in Strong Communities in 2007; the increase from 45 in 2004 was the product in part of Strong Communities' own efforts to build civic organizations in communities previously lacking such associations. All of the nationally affiliated civic clubs in the area have participated in the initiative, as have all of the local governments and public safety agencies (local fire departments and law enforcement agencies). Twenty-four voluntary associations have adopted Strong Communities as a central theme of their work.

Most participating organizations have multiple forms of involvement. Through 2007, more than 160 churches used bulletin inserts on Strong Communities (an increase from 100 in 2004). Through 2007, about 70 had held special worship services related to Strong Communities, and almost 60 had conducted special volunteer activities on behalf of the initiative. In both cases, the number of churches reporting such activities increased from 0 in 2004).

Virtually all of the participating businesses made financial contributions, but the majority also joined in volunteer activities. Through 2007, about 60 businesses (three times as many as in 2004) hosted speakers about Strong Communities.

Analyses of journalistic reports derived from biweekly interviews of outreach workers about the activities in their logs in 2003–2005 showed that more than one-fourth of the statements that included a reference to a community sector focused on churches, and one-sixth included references to public safety agencies (Berman et al., 2008). About one-fifth focused on housing complexes and neighborhood associations. Businesses (15.7%), schools (13.6%), and civic organizations (6.9%) were also frequently mentioned. The proportionate involvement of each of these sectors has been steady (hence, growing in absolute terms) across the initiative.

Analysis of the comments in biweekly interviews about special events showed strikingly diverse participation: "for example, neighborhood association leaders, ministers and lay leaders, firefighters, police officers, educators, public officials, Scout leaders, civic club members, ROTC cadets, YMCA leaders, and small business owners" (Murphy-Berman et al., 2008, p. 148). This participation often occurred in ways that went beyond usual professional roles and venues: "For example, a fire department official distributed books to young children in his area, and a business association donated food to a community festival. ... Special events were held in schools, churches, parks, shopping malls, housing developments, fire stations, community buildings, and town squares" (Murphy-Berman et al., 2008, p. 148).

SIGNIFICANCE OF THE INITIATIVE
FOR THE PARTICIPATING COMMUNITIES

Almost all of the volunteers who were randomly selected for interviews about their involvement in Strong Communities have reported that they were satisfied with their experience (Haski-Leventhal et al., 2008). About three-fifths remembered volunteering for Strong Communities—a high proportion, given that Strong Communities typically works through other organizations. All of those respondents were able to describe their involvement in response to an open-ended question, and almost all accurately described the purpose of the initiative. All of them believed that volunteers were important to achieving Strong Communities' goals, and virtually all indicated that the initiative was having an important positive effect on the community (44%, strong impact; 52%, moderate impact). About two-thirds declared that volunteering was "one of the most important things in my life," and almost all of the rest indicated that it had moderate importance to them.

The personal significance of Strong Communities was most vividly illustrated, however, in interviews of 44 exceptional volunteers, those whom outreach staff identified as having played particularly important roles in galvanizing community action within the initiative (Hashima & Melton, 2008). Older on average than other volunteers, the exceptional volunteers commonly had extensive experience in community service, although none were public figures. More than 90% of the exceptional volunteers reported that they attended religious services at least once a week, and more than one-fourth were employed by religious organizations.

Even these highly engaged individuals, however, reported that their experience in Strong Communities had been unique, indeed transforming. Qualitative analysis of interviews of the exceptional volunteers showed that they perceived positive change in the number and diversity of their relationships, their centrality in the community, their understanding of the community, the level of their aspirations and the breadth of their strategies for community change, and their sense of both personal and collective efficacy—all as a result of experiences in Strong Communities.

The following comments by two exceptional volunteers are illustrative:

> With the willingness to serve and the community connections that Strong Communities brings, your face, your name is magnified throughout the city. People know me before I get there. ... [It's] a wonderful thing to have said about you—that people know that you come to help, that it's going to be done, and it's going to be done right. Because if I'm involved, others can get involved because they know it is not some sham. ... My association with Strong Communities has played a part in that.—*Director of a volunteer organization.* (Hashima & Melton, 2008, pp. 167–168)

> I have grown tremendously. I feel that I can conquer a mountain! Like I tell people, when you volunteer, you're not only helping others, you're helping yourself, too, because it helps you to see a lot of things that you wouldn't see. It helps you to know that within yourself you have so much power if you only look for it, search for it, and believe in you[rself]. I get so excited when I'm talking about volunteering. It just gives me [a] sense of strength. ... Since I've been involved with Strong Communities, [I've learned] that anything that I set out to do, I can. I always knew it, but Strong Communities has helped perpetuate it to another level. Each year working with Strong Communities volunteering, I just get more energy. My wife tells me I can't save the world, but I can sure try!—*Apartment manager.* (Hashima & Melton, 2008, p. 169)

There appears to be ample evidence that Strong Communities is in fact transforming the communities it serves. Apart from testimonials of the sort quoted here, the sheer breadth and depth of community participation are strong indicators of community engagement. In light of the isolation and alienation that are rampant, such engagement is an important phenomenon in itself.

There is strong but not yet fully consistent evidence that the community transformation is making a difference in children's safety. On the negative side, the findings on archival data have been inconclusive, but such administrative data are not likely to be sensitive indicators of change. Although local hospital data show a decrease in admissions, including emergency room visits, related to diagnoses associated with neglect among children in the service area and an increase in the comparison area, these changes have not occurred in all pediatric age groups (McDonell, 2008b). Given that most cases of neglect, even if fully investigated, do not result in hospital admissions, stronger effects may be unrealistic to expect.

Referrals to child protective services (CPS) have also not shown consistent changes. However, such rates are highly susceptible to changes in administrative practice. Moreover, the rate of referral in the service area was already so low in absolute terms (and already lower in relation to the comparison area) that there probably is a basement effect. Hence, although we are continuing to monitor CPS data, it is probably unrealistic to expect changes in such referral rates as a result of Strong Communities.

In contrast, on self-report data (usually the most sensitive indicator of socially and legally disapproved behavior) the findings are especially clear and positive, even remarkable. Strong Communities appears to be changing the norms of parental behavior across the community! In a random survey of households with young children, numerous scales directly related to children's well-being and safety showed improvement in the service area but a decline in the comparison area from 2004 to 2007 (McDonell, 2008a). Increases in the service area in relation to the comparison area occurred in the prevalence of nurturing parenting, such as emotional support and parent–child activities, and in the use of household safety devices, such as erection of baby gates. Neglectful, disengaged, and physically assaultive behavior decreased in the service area in relation to the comparison area.

Data collected as part of an annual survey of fifth-graders, their parents, and elementary school teachers by the state Educational Oversight Committee showed significant increases in the service area in the beliefs of parents, teachers, and, especially, children that children are safe at or in transit to school and that parents are taken seriously by school officials (Ben-Arieh & McDonell, 2007). Such beliefs have become less common in matched comparison schools elsewhere in South Carolina.

CAUTION AND CONFIDENCE

The achievements so far in Strong Communities are all the more remarkable because they directly confront the negative social momentum (cf. Garbarino & Kostelny, 1994) that is endemic throughout much of the industrialized world. In that regard, the service area fared better than the comparison area on a number of variables that may be understood as intermediate outcomes, including availability of childcare, parental efficacy, parenting stress, help giving and receiving, social support, and organizational attendance (McDonell, 2008a).

Unfortunately, however, isolation continues to be a problem—even a bigger problem in 2007 than in 2004. "Fared better" on some variables— neighborhood satisfaction, neighboring activities, and organization membership—meant "did less poorly." That is, the service area sample declined less on such variables from 2004 to 2007 than did the comparison area sample. On some other relevant variables (e.g., knowing children in the neighborhood by name), there was a decline in both groups, but the groups did not differ significantly in how much they declined.

Seen in this light, the positive changes in children's safety and in the quality of parenting in the service area are especially impressive. Such changes reflect the power of repeated, multicontext efforts to spread the Strong Communities message and to create new forums for interaction among—and service by and to—young parents. At the same time, with a weakening economy and ever greater financial vulnerability of young adults (Draut, 2006), one must wonder how families will fare in the next 3 years.

The apparently ever stronger forces pushing toward isolation and alienation give stark evidence of the need to be challenging in order to expand and sustain neighbors' support for one another. The communities in which we are working generally have high rates of school suspension and expulsion and of both adult and juvenile incarceration. If families are excluded—or even simply allowed to withdraw—then they cannot be noticed and cared for. Therefore, Strong Communities is increasingly emphasizing the need to *Leave No Families Outside* and, in particular, seeking moral leadership on this point from the religious community.

Thus, the Strong Communities message is less often "feel-good" in tone today than in earlier years, because the time has come to move beyond communities' merely nodding in collective assent to the importance of community for families and of personal security for children. Our message is increasingly one that is explicitly focused on change in community structures and norms. Building on linkages within primary healthcare, elementary schools, and childcare centers, Strong Families is offering programmatic modifications of existing centers of community to achieve universal enrollment and participation in an institutionalized, sustainable, and replicable system of easily available family support.

Creation of a sustainable system requires more than building infrastructure, however. It also requires changes in community norms toward a culture grounded in four values: *caring* (attentiveness and neighborliness toward others), *inclusion* (universality of access and mutuality of respect and caring), *optimism* (the belief, individually and collectively, that action on behalf of families will be effective, because the community is a welcoming and supportive place in which positive things happen for families), and *action* (a norm, individually and collectively, that the possibility of effective action on behalf of families should and will be translated into practical activity).

We believe that our communities are ready to address such a challenge. With neighborhood engagement that is already extraordinary in its breadth and depth, we may be nearing a tipping point at which neighborliness truly becomes a way of life—a culture that is inclusive of families that are now often on or beyond the margins of the community.

When even the most vulnerable children and parents come within the protection of what Archbishop Desmond Tutu (2004) termed "a delicate network of interdependence with our fellow human beings" (p. 25), we will know that they *are* safe and secure. As the late Fred Rogers (known to millions of children and parents as "Mr. Rogers") once said, "All of us, at some time or other, need help. Whether we're giving or receiving help, each one of us has something valuable to bring to this world. That's one of the things that connects us as neighbors—in our own way each one of us is a giver and a receiver" (Rogers, 2003, p. 136). When community institutions are reshaped to make such care for one another easy and natural to do, we will know that children and parents will *remain* safe and secure. The U.S. Advisory Board on Child Abuse and Neglect (1993) envisioned such a society. That vision was truly grand, but Strong Communities is showing that it is not grandiose. It can be achieved!

ACKNOWLEDGMENTS

Strong Communities for Children is supported in substantial part by a long-term grant from The Duke Endowment, but the opinions expressed herein are not necessarily those of The Duke Endowment, its advisors, staff, or trustees. Asher Ben-Arieh and James McDonell have led the research program described herein, Robin Kimbrough-Melton has overseen the community mobilization effort, and Dottie Campbell has coordinated Strong Families. Erica Mabry and Jill McLeigh have maintained the volunteer and organizational databases. As director of the principal host agency (the Center for Community Services in Simpsonville, South Carolina), Linda Smith has also been a leader in the development of Strong Communities. In general, the contributions of a dedicated, creative staff and thousands of volunteers are gratefully and respectfully acknowledged.

REFERENCES

Administration on Children, Youth, and Families. (2007). *Child maltreatment 2005.* Washington, DC: U.S. Government Printing Office.

Ben-Arieh, A., & McDonell, J. R. (2007). *The schools archival data research: Background and initial data analysis.* Clemson, SC: Clemson University, Institute on Family and Neighborhood Life.

Benson, C. (Ed.). (2007). *Neighbors: Stories of Fountain Inn.* Clemson, SC: Clemson University, Institute on Family and Neighborhood Life.

Berman, J. J., Murphy-Berman, V., & Melton, G. B. (2008). Strong Communities: What did participants actually do? *Family and Community Health, 31,* 126–135.

Child Abuse Prevention and Treatment Act of 1974, Pub. L. No. 93-247, 88 Stat. 4, *codified as amended at* 42 U.S.C. §§ 5101-5120.

Dodge, K. A., Berlin, L. J., Epstein, M., Spitz-Roth, A., O'Donnell, K., Kaufman, M., et al. (2004). The Durham Family Initiative: A preventive system of care. *Child Welfare, 83,* 109–128.

Draut, T. (2006). *Strapped: Why America's 20- and 30-somethings can't get ahead.* New York: Doubleday.

Fukuyama, F. (1996). *The social virtues and the creation of prosperity.* New York: Free Press.

Fukuyama, F. (2000). *The great disruption: Human nature and the reconstitution of social order.* New York: Touchstone.

Garbarino, J., & Kostelny, K. (1994). Neighborhood-based programs. In G. B. Melton & F. D. Barry (Eds.), *Protecting children from abuse and neglect: Foundations for a new national strategy* (pp. 304–352). New York: Guilford Press.

Hashima, P. Y., & Melton, G. B. (2008). "I can conquer a mountain": Ordinary people who provide extraordinary community service. *Family and Community Health, 31,* 162–172.

Haski-Leventhal, D., Ben-Arieh, A., & Melton, G. B. (2008). Between neighborliness and volunteerism: Participants in the Strong Communities initiative. *Family and Community Health, 31,* 150–161.

Henggeler, S. W., Schoenwald, S. K., Rowland, M. D., & Cunningham, P. B. (2002). *Serious emotional disturbance in children and adolescents: Multisystemic therapy.* New York: Guilford Press.

Kalichman, S. E. (1999). *Mandated reporting of suspected child abuse: Ethics, law, and policy* (2nd ed.). Washington, DC: American Psychological Association.

Kempe, C. H., Silverman, F. N., Steele, B. F., Droegemueller, W., & Silver, H. K. (1962). The battered child syndrome. *Journal of the American Medical Association, 181,* 17–24.

Kimbrough-Melton, R. J., & Campbell, D. (2008). Strong Communities for Children: A community wide approach to prevention of child abuse and neglect. *Family and Community Health, 31,* 100–112.

Larson, R. W. (2000). Toward a psychology of positive youth development. *American Psychologist, 55,* 170–183.

McDonell, J. R. (2008a). *Strong Communities for Children: The Parents and Neighbors Survey: Analyses of waves 1 and 2 data.* Clemson, SC: Clemson University, Institute on Family and Neighborhood Life.

McDonell, J. R. (2008b). *Summary of findings from ICD-9 child injury study.* Clemson, SC: Clemson University, Institute on Family and Neighborhood Life.

McPherson, M., Smith-Lovin, L., & Brashears, M. E. (2006). Social isolation in America: Changes in core discussion networks over two decades. *American Sociological Review, 71,* 353–375.

Melton, G. B. (1991). Lessons from Norway: The children's ombudsman as a voice for children. *Case Western Reserve Journal of International Law, 23,* 197–254.

Melton, G. B. (1992a). It's time for neighborhood research and action. *Child Abuse and Neglect, 16,* 909–913.

Melton, G. B. (1992b). The law is a good thing (psychology is, too): Human rights in psychological jurisprudence. *Law and Human Behavior, 16*, 381–398.

Melton, G. B. (1993). Is there a place for children in the new world order? *Notre Dame Journal of Law, Ethics, and Public Policy, 7*, 491–532.

Melton, G. B. (1995). Personal satisfaction and the welfare of families, communities, and society. In G. B. Melton (Ed.), *Nebraska Symposium on Motivation: Vol. 42. The individual, the family, and social good: Personal fulfillment in times of change* (pp. ix–xxvii). Lincoln: University of Nebraska Press.

Melton, G. B. (2002). Chronic neglect of family violence: More than a decade of reports to guide U.S. policy. *Child Abuse and Neglect, 26*, 569–586.

Melton, G. B. (2005). Mandated reporting: A policy without reason. *Child Abuse and Neglect, 29*, 9–18.

Melton, G. B., & Anderson, D. (2008). From Safe Sanctuaries to Strong Communities: The role of communities of faith in child protection. *Faith and Community Health, 31*, 173–185.

Melton, G. B., & Holaday, B J. (Eds.). (2008). Strong Communities as safe havens for children [Special issue]. *Family and Community Health, 31*(2).

Melton, G. B., Holaday, B. J., & Kimbrough-Melton, R. J. (2008). Community life, public health, and children's safety. *Family and Community Health, 31*, 84–99.

Murphy-Berman, V., Berman, J. J., & Melton, G. B. (2008). Transformative change: An analysis of the evolution of special events within three communities. *Family and Community Health, 31*, 136–149.

National Research Council and Institute of Medicine, Panel on Transitions to Adulthood in Developing Countries. (2005). *Growing up global: The changing transitions to adulthood in developing countries* (C. B. Lloyd, Ed.). Washington, DC: National Academies Press.

Pharr, S., & Putnam, R. D. (Eds.). (2000). *Disaffected democracies: What's troubling the Trilateral Countries?* Princeton, NJ: Princeton University Press.

Pryor, J. H., Hurtado, S., Saenz, V. B., Santos, J. L., & Korn, W. S. (2007). *The American freshman: Forty year trends.* Los Angeles: University of California, Los Angeles, Higher Education Research Institute.

Putnam, R. D. (1995). Bowling alone: America's declining social capital. *Journal of Democracy, 6*, 65–78.

Putnam, R. D. (2000). *Bowling alone: The collapse and revival of American community.* New York: Simon & Schuster.

Rogers, F. (2003). *The world according to Mister Rogers: Important things to remember.* New York: Hyperion.

Seligman, M. E. P. (1995). *The optimistic child.* New York: Houghton Mifflin.

Swenson, C. C., Henggeler, S. W., Taylor, I. S., & Addison, O. W. (2005). *Multisystemic therapy and neighborhood partnerships: Reducing adolescent violence and substance abuse.* New York: Guilford Press.

Theodore, A., Runyan, D., & Chang, J. J. (2007). Measuring the risk of physical neglect in a population-based sample. *Child Maltreatment, 12*, 96–105.

Tutu, D. (2004). *God has a dream: A vision of hope for our time.* New York: Doubleday.

Twenge, J. M. (2000). The age of anxiety?: The birth cohort change in anxiety and neuroticism, 1952–1993. *Journal of Personality and Social Psychology, 79,* 1007–1021.

U.S. Advisory Board on Child Abuse and Neglect. (1990). *Child abuse and neglect: Critical first steps in response to a national emergency.* Washington, DC: U.S. Government Printing Office.

U.S. Advisory Board on Child Abuse and Neglect. (1991). *Creating caring communities: Blueprint for an effective federal policy on child abuse and neglect.* Washington, DC: U.S. Government Printing Office.

U.S. Advisory Board on Child Abuse and Neglect. (1993). *Neighbors helping neighbors: A new national strategy for the protection of children.* Washington, DC: U.S. Government Printing Office.

Vogelgesang, L. J., & Astin, A. W. (2005, April). *Post-college civic engagement among graduates.* Los Angeles: University of California, Los Angeles, Higher Education Research Institute.

CHAPTER 6

The Period of PURPLE Crying

Keeping Babies Safe in North Carolina

Desmond Runyan *and* Adam Zolotor

More than 60 years ago, John Caffey noted an association between long-bone fractures and subdural hematomas and reported that some children in his case-series had retinal hemorrhages (Caffey, 1946). In 1971, Guthkelch, an English neurosurgeon, described two children with subdural hematoma with no external signs of trauma and postulated the role of rotational forces as the mechanism of injury (Guthkelch, 1971). John Caffey coined the term "shaken baby syndrome" (SBS) in 1972 for children with intracranial hemorrhage without external signs of trauma, inflicted by shaking the child (Caffey, 1972a, 1972b). The mechanism of injury is postulated to be an abrupt acceleration–deceleration injury with rotational forces (Duhaime et al., 1987). These movements cause motion of the brain, within the skull and dura, which tears bridging vessels as they pass through the dural membrane, leading to intracranial hemorrhage. The diagnosis of abusive head trauma (AHT) is suspected when injury is suspected and a head computerized tomograph (CT) reveals either a subdural hematoma or a subarchnoid hematoma, with or without cerebral edema, unexplained by other consistent or witnessed trauma. Eye exams for retinal hemorrhage contribute to the diagnostic evaluation in many cases. Eighty percent of young children who are victims of AHT will have eye findings, as compared with just 6–8% of similar-age children suffering unintentional head trauma (Keenan, Runyan, Marshall, Nocera, & Merten, 2004). In addition, rib, metaphyseal, and femur fractures and multiple fractures in different stages of healing are associated with AHT (Keenan et al., 2004).

This chapter reports progress in a state-wide effort to prevent AHT, a specific form of child maltreatment. The rationale for the effort is described in a summary of the epidemiology. A description of the preparation of materials and piloting follows. Finally, the research design that is being used to evaluate program impact is described.

EPIDEMIOLOGY

The epidemiology of AHT has become clearer in the past 10 years and has paved the way for prevention efforts. In North Carolina the calculated the rate of AHT resulting in intensive care unit admission or death in the first 2 years of life is 17.0/100,000 child years, with a rate of 29.7 in the first year of life (Keenan et al., 2004). A Scottish study produced a very similar estimate, at 24/100,000 infants (Minns, 2005). Dias used a ratio of all AHT in the first 3 years of life as the numerator and live births per year as the denominator to derive a ratio of 41 cases/100,000 live births in western New York State (Dias et al., 2005).

Risk factors for AHT include being a first child, male, part of a multiple birth, from a military family, or having young parents (Keenan et al., 2003). Shaking children for discipline is as much as 10 times more common in developing countries than in the United States and is perpetrated at greater rates by mothers compared to fathers (Runyan et al., 2008). Other risk factors include disability, unstable family situations, prematurity of the child, and lower socioeconomic status (Keenan et al., 2004).

The outcomes resulting from AHT are grim. Twenty-six percent of children in North Carolina with AHT died acutely (Keenan et al., 2003). Several studies note that the majority of survivors have persistent neurological damage at discharge (Duhaime, Christian, Moss, & Seidl, 1996; Gessner & Runyan, 1995; Keenan et al., 2003). Outcomes examined several years later are even worse (Keenan, Hooper, Wetherington, Nocera, & Runyan, 2007). Three years after AHT, 47% of the survivors were more than 3 standard deviations (SDs) below and 60% were more than 1 SD below the mean for IQ (Keenan et al., 2007).

The costs of child maltreatment are enormous. Summarizing available research, Corso and Lutzker (2006) found that medical costs per case of maltreatment varied between $2,400 and $48,000. Cost estimates for AHT are yet higher; acute hospitalization costs an average of $18,000 to $70,000 per child (Dias et al., 2005). Nonmedical costs (e.g., child welfare system and law enforcement) may run as high as $78,000 per case. Lifetime costs of lost productivity by the maltreated child may be as high as $60,000 (Corso & Lutzker, 2006).

PREVENTION

Primary prevention of child abuse among infants has long been of interest, although few successful programs have been reported. At this point, only the Nurse–Family Partnership program and similar home visiting programs have demonstrated success in prevention of child maltreatment in general (Olds et al., 1997). The Children's Bureau has reviewed other "promising approaches," although these are still being studied (U.S. Department of Health and Human Services, 2003) .

Efforts to prevent AHT have included billboards, messages at doctors' offices, teaching in schools, and other modalities. These approaches remain unevaluated (Dias et al., 2005). A program developed by Dias and colleagues in western New York State reported reducing the number of AHT cases by 47% over a 7-year period (Dias et al., 2005). Dias et al. combined a program of nurse education in the newborn nursery, exposure to a video, *Portraits of Promise,* and a signed commitment statement by the new parent(s) stating that they will not shake the baby. The *Portraits of Promise* video graphically portrays the consequences of shaking. Using secular trend data over a 6-year period and comparing the period to a prior 6-year period and to trend data from Pennsylvania, Dias and colleagues reported a 47% reduction in numbers of shaken baby cases in a geographical area of western New York (Dias et al. 2005). Of note, the reported western New York baseline rate was dramatically higher than the rates reported for any other locale, raising a concern about regression to the mean (Dias et al., 2005).

We believe that a strong prevention program can make a difference, but that there were significant limitations to the New York study. Only 69% of the parents signed a commitment statement, and just 23% of the 69% recalled that they saw the video (Dias et al., 2005). In a replication of the New York study, Zeemering-Nelson, Stoiko, Palusci, Bliss, and Combs (2006) used the same approach and reported a 25% reduction in AHT. A less aversive and more positive video may be more successfully delivered and, with repetition, is likely to be better received.

CRYING AND AHT

Crying is pervasive in *normal* infants, even inconsolable crying. The importance of crying in normal infants is indicated by accumulated evidence that the crying properties thought of as "colic" and considered to be a sign of abnormality are actually typical of normally developing infants (Barr, 1990b, 2000, 2006; Barr, Kramer, Boisjoly, McVey-White, & Pless, 1988). Recent studies demonstrate that early crying is the most common stimulus for AHT (and perhaps other forms of infant abuse).

Much of the literature on "colic" is based on the assumption that the crying reflects disease, or something wrong with the infant or the parent–infant interaction (Barr, 1990a, 1990b, 2000; Barr et al., 1988). However, research on the clinical manifestations and normative properties of early crying in the last 25 years has led to a reconceptualization of "excessive" crying and "colic" (Barr, 2006). It has shown that *all normal* babies have "colic-like" crying along a spectrum in the first few months. Some cry more than others, with infants in about the top 20% likely to be diagnosed with "colic" (Barr, 1990b, 2006; Barr et al., 1988). These infants may have weeks to months of inconsolable crying bouts that occur during the first 4 months of life, peaking during the second month (Barr, 1990b; Barr, Paterson, Mac-Martin, Lehtonen, & Young, 2005). Only a small number of infants (< 2%) appear to have abnormal cries that are attributable to sickness or disorder. The reconceptualization is that increased crying is part of normal development rather than due to abnormalities in the infants or their caregivers. Critical to understanding early infant crying is the recognition of (1) large variations among infants in amount of crying, with 25% of infants crying more than 3½ hours per day and 25% crying less than 1¾ hours at the peak (Brazelton, 1962; Hunziker & Barr, 1986), and (2) a spectrum of crying from a little to a lot, with no "cutoff" between normal and abnormal ("colicky") amounts. Figure 6.1 illustrates the large variation in normal infant crying and the natural peak that occurs in the second month of life.

Parent-reported endorsement of shaking as a method of soothing (Reijneveld, van der Wal, Brugman, Hira Sing, & Verloove, 2004) or discipline represents a significant risk for AHT. Although the hypothesis that crying is a stimulus for AHT is reasonable, systematic evidence is difficult to obtain because (1) the diagnosis is relatively infrequent, (2) there is rarely, if ever, a witness, so reports that crying was a stimulus come from perpetrator confessions, (3) confessions may be inaccurate because crying is not a well-accepted defense for harming an infant, (4) records may be missing or incomplete (in one study, most of the records were missing for 20% of substantiated fatal cases (Brewster et al., 1998), and (5) a history of crying obtained at diagnosis may either be a cause or a consequence of trauma.

Barr, Trent, and Cross (2006) examined hospitalization discharge data collected by the California Health and Human Services Agency. Since 1996, these data have included a specific code for SBS. The data reveal an age-related curve of incident cases that begins at the same time and has a similar shape (increase, peak, and decline) as the curve for normal infant crying. This finding provides indirect evidence that crying may be an important stimulus

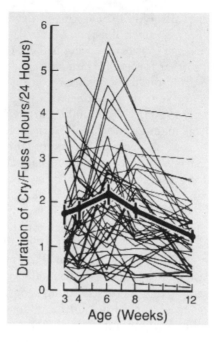

FIGURE 6.1. Crying duration by week of age for 50 infants (mean/standard error in **bold**). From Barr (1990b). Copyright 1990 by MacKeith Press. Reprinted by permission.

for SBS. Further indirect evidence comes from the Edinburgh series, with an identical age-related curve for the incidence of shaken impact syndrome (Barlow & Minns, 2000). Lee, Barr, Catherine, and Wicks (2007) examined the age-specific incidence of publicly reported cases of SBS in the victim database of the National Center on Shaken Baby Syndrome. This study demonstrates that publicly reported cases of AHT, both with and without crying as a reported trigger, peak at 9–12 weeks of age and are similar to the crying curve described by Brazelton in 1962. Furthermore, a similar temporal pattern can be demonstrated with other forms of child abuse and neglect resulting in hospitalization, peaking in the first 5 months of life (Agran et al., 2003), indicating that crying may be an important stimulus for other types of early child physical abuse.

THE PERIOD OF PURPLE CRYING

The National Center on Shaken Baby Syndrome (NCSBS), in collaboration with Dr. Ronald Barr, oversaw the development and testing of prevention materials, referred to as the Period of PURPLE Crying© (PURPLE) materials in 2001–2007. The Doris Duke Charitable Foundation supported much of the developmental work to create parent education materials that address the risk of shaking through understanding early infant crying. See Table 6.1 for a description of the acronym PURPLE. The materials were refined with 28 parent and professional focus groups. Following another round of editing and development, the materials were tested empirically with 4,400 mothers in Seattle and Vancouver to assess their impact on knowledge and behavior change.

Professional researchers led focus groups in Canada and the United States. Focus group participants included mothers and fathers of infants between 4 weeks and 8 months of age. Participants were selected to include differences in backgrounds, including race, economic status, and family makeup. The 28 focus groups included 16 groups of mothers, 2 of fathers, 1 of Native American parents, 2 of Chinese parents, 2 of Punjabi parents, 3 of Spanish-speaking parents, and 2 of Korean parents. The first 19 focus groups were designed to assess the specific content and presentation of the materials in English; the remaining groups were designed to assess meaningfulness and appropriateness of translations of the materials. On the basis of feedback from these participants and others, the initial group of prevention education materials, which included a 12-minute video, a 12-page booklet, a magnet, a bib, and a certificate, was narrowed down to just a 10-minute video and an 11-page full-color booklet. The booklet and video have undergone numerous revisions and retests. The focus groups have revealed that the PURPLE materials helped break down barriers and beliefs about infant crying. Parents, claiming to never being troubled by their infant's

---

TABLE 6.1. The Meaning of PURPLE

P: Peak of crying
- Crying increases and then peaks at 2 months and diminishes between 3 and 5 months.

U: Unexpected
- Bouts of crying begin and end for no apparent reason.

R: Resists soothing
- Some bouts are unsoothable, no matter what the caregiver does.

P: Pain-like face
- The infant looks as if he or she is in pain, even when not.

L: Long lasting
- Bouts can last 1–2 hours.

E: Evening
- Increased crying tends to cluster in the evenings.

cries, would subsequently share personal and emotional struggles with cry-ing. "I thought I was a bad mom or that I was doing something wrong, but this video and booklet have taught me so much," said one Utah mother. "I really relate to these families."

The program components have helped to overcome the challenges of providing programs to parents by ensuring the following elements for the intervention. The materials (1) are educational and attractive to parents of newborns on the first day of life; (2) contain clear, memorable, salient, meaningful, attractive, positive messages; (3) are written at a third-grade reading level; (4) are intended to be multicultural both through transla-tion and the visuals; (5) are designed to be acceptable to public health nurses because it supports their efforts to prevent SIDS and encourage breast-feeding by attending to other issues (i.e., no bottles, blankets, bumper pads, etc.); (6) are economical ($2 for the DVD and the 11-page full-color booklet in an attractive case, for large orders); and (7) are provided so each parent can have a copy, to review when needed and share the materials with temporary caregivers.

Changing behavior in a brief intervention is difficult to do. Most health education campaigns can effect sustained behavior change only through moderate- to high-intensity efforts (Lanza et al., 2001; Rimer et al., 1994). An advantage in the prevention of AHT is that it occurs mostly in the first 6 months of life, so the need for sustained education and behavior change is mitigated. The early occurrence of AHT mandates that we reach parents early to succeed in reducing this form of child abuse.

Preliminary results from a pilot study in Vancouver demonstrated improved knowledge of crying characteristics and increased parent reports of walk-away responses to unsoothable infant crying when parents were frustrated. Overall awareness that shaking is dangerous was high, but the materials further reduced the number of participants who endorsed shak-ing as a means of soothing infants. Furthermore, there was an increased likelihood of parents' sharing information about crying, about walking away when frustrated, and about the dangers of shaking, with tempo-rary caregivers. The program penetration rate was high in Vancouver. Ninety-two percent of the mothers enrolled in the study either saw the video or read the materials (Fujiwara, Barr, Barr, Catherine, & Con-way, 2008).

Two hospitals in North Carolina have served as pilot sites for the implementation of the bedside education component of this project, Mis-sion Memorial Hospital in Asheville and Cape Fear Valley Medical Center in Fayetteville. Both hospitals have followed training procedures developed by the research and implementation teams and the National Center for Shaken Baby Syndrome. Mission Hospital is using a model of bedside nurse discharge teaching, and Cape Fear started with a voluntary discharge education class. Finding low levels of attendance, program administrators at Cape Fear have since switched to a bedside teaching model as well. However, unlike Mission Hospital (and the majority of anticipated hospitals participating in the North Carolina PURPLE effort), Cape Fear Child Advocacy Center has hired two part-time educators to make rounds at the hospital 7 days per week to educate new parents. Both hospitals have achieved penetration rates of greater than 90%. Penetration, for the purposes of this study, includes bedside teaching about the Period of PURPLE Crying and distribution of the DVD and booklet. At the time of this writing, a total of 79 hospitals are at various stages of implementation; we anticipate statewide implementation by February 2009.

NORTH CAROLINA'S INTERVENTION

In concert with the North Carolina Period of PURPLE Crying Leadership Committee, and with support from the Doris Duke Charitable Foundation, The Duke Endowment, and the Centers for Disease Control and Prevention, we plan to deliver information about the Period of PURPLE Crying program to every parent of a newborn in the state on three occasions: (1) in the newborn nursery, (2) in community settings at either a prenatal visit to a health department or a well-child care visit to a health department or primary care provider within 2 weeks of the child's birth, and (3) through a media campaign. An important aim of the media campaign is to help to change the culture by educating everyone about the characteristics of early crying, the frustration it can produce, and the dangers of shaking. It is designed to help to make family, friends, and neighbors more supportive of new parents and knowledgeable about the characteristics of infant crying. The logic model for program implementation and outcome evaluation is shown in Figure 6.2.

In the first instance, nurses in 89 hospitals or birthing centers across North Carolina that provide delivery services will show the mother and father the DVD and discuss options for responding to a crying infant, using prepared scripts. A copy of the DVD and accompanying brochure will be given to the new parents to be shared with other caregivers, including babysitters and daycare providers. At the second occasion, the project team will work with community provider and advocacy systems, including county health departments, the North Carolina Pediatric Society, and the North Carolina Academy of Family Physicians, to deliver the same DVD and educational script to mothers at either prenatal care visits or the first postnatal visits. The Center for Child and Family Health will hire three full-time health educators as outreach workers to train the nursery and office practice staff members, provide program materials, and track

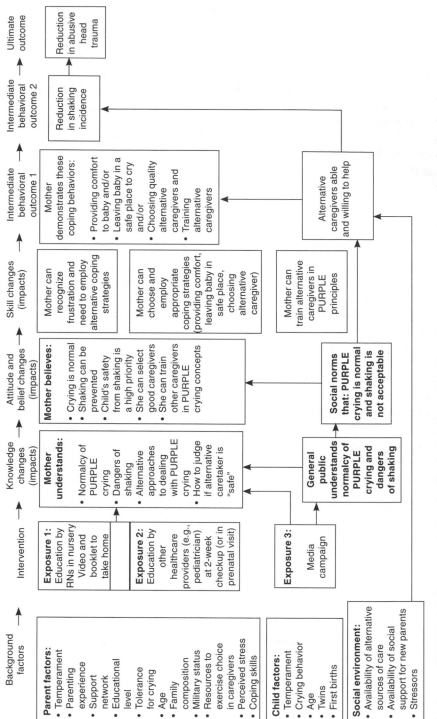

FIGURE 6.2. Logic model for the North Carolina PURPLE Crying intervention study to reduce abusive head trauma.

numbers of materials delivered to each site. In the third instance, the mass media campaign will address infant crying and parental responses to crying.

The media campaign will be developed and supported by the National Center on Shaken Baby Syndrome with the collaboration of faculty of the University of North Carolina School of Journalism and Mass Communication. The primary objective of the campaign is to create awareness of key messages associated with the Period of PURPLE Crying program among key influencers within the general population and to stimulate peer-to-peer transmission of those messages through a variety of social networks. The campaign is to reinforce messages associated with the PURPLE program among parents receiving other components of the intervention.

The integrated media campaign will include both paid placement and earned media initiatives, a combination critical to social diffusion. Paid media initiatives ensure the integrity of campaign messages and generate the critical mass necessary to stimulate peer-to-peer communication. Paid placement materials will include professionally produced ads designed for traditional (radio, television, print) and new media channels. Earned media initiatives are more cost-effective, often perceived as more credible, and play an important role in imparting new, newsworthy knowledge such as breakthroughs in infant crying research. Earned media strategies will be designed to compel the attention of the parents, caregivers, and targeted influencers and to advocate the program's key messages. Media tools and tactics, including staged newsworthy events, news and feature pitch concepts, news releases, advisories, and backgrounders, will be used to attract and sustain media coverage in traditional and new media channels. Outcome measures will include self-reported exposure to the PURPLE campaign as well as recall of key messages associated with the program.

PURPLE will be implemented and evaluated by a research consortium of the University of North Carolina Injury Prevention Research Center, the Center for Child and Family Health (consortium of Duke University, University of North Carolina, and North Carolina Central University), the National Center on Shaken Baby Syndrome in Utah, and the Centre for Community and Child Health Research, Vancouver, British Columbia. This research team has been advised and assisted at all levels of research design and implementation since the inception of this project by a statewide leadership team that includes representatives from the North Carolina Partnership for Children, Prevent Child Abuse North Carolina, the North Carolina State Health Department, North Carolina Pediatrics Society, North Carolina Academy of Family Physicians, North Carolina Healthy Start Foundation, North Carolina Hospital Association, North Carolina Nurses Association, North Carolina Child Advocacy Institute, North Carolina Child Fatality Task Force, North Carolina Area Health Education Centers, and representatives from the Womack Army Hospital, Cape Fear Valley Medical Center, Mission Memorial Hospital, and citizens who have experienced the sequelae of shaking firsthand.

RESEARCH DESIGN

This multipart project involves educating the parents of 125,000 newborns per year for 5 years (a total of about 600,000 births) about crying and SBS, using a carefully developed model curriculum and then examining the reduction in self-reported shaking behavior, the receipt of education by new parents, and the reduction in the number of children hospitalized for AHT. The last mentioned goal will be examined both with active surveillance in the state's pediatric intensive care units and medical examiner's office and through retrospective review of hospital records and hospital discharge data.

In the first 6 months of the program period, baseline data collection has included a telephone survey of nurse directors or charge nurses in all 90 hospitals with maternity care and the one freestanding birth center to identify current practices regarding parent newborn education, particularly as it pertains to infant crying and AHT prevention. This survey also included an assessment of barriers and facilitators to change in practice surrounding newborn education. This survey is essential in that change in practice cannot be assessed without understanding current practice in North Carolina hospitals, and analyses of these data are under way.

An important piece of baseline data is parent-reported shaking of young children. As a follow-up on the previous study in 2002 demonstrating parent-reported shaking of 2.6% (Theodore et al., 2005) of children under age 2, we have fielded an anonymous survey of 2,946 mothers of children under age 2. In addition to a question regarding shaking and other questions about early childhood physical discipline, adopted from the Parent–Child Conflicts Scale (Straus, Hamby, Finkelhor, Moore, & Runyan, 1998), several project-specific questions were designed and included in the survey to identify (1) the potential for injury resulting from shaking, (2) frustration or anger associated with shaking, (3) triggers related to shaking, and (4) shaking observed by others (not mother or partner) of children less than 2 years old. To identify a large sample of mothers of children less than 2, the North Carolina State Center for Health Statistics provided a stratified random sample of mothers' names and addresses. These were sent to a survey research firm for matching with publicly available phone numbers and entered into a computer-assisted survey system by the Survey Research Unit of the University of North Carolina. After assessing the eligibility of potential respondents, the telephone numbers were purged from the computer system to preserve the anonymity of the respondents. This survey will allow us to determine, with a high degree of precision, parent-reported shaking of children under age 2, as well as perceived potential for injury, associated frustration or anger, stimuli for shaking, and shaking of children less than age 2 as observed by other adults. The survey is complete, and data weighting and analysis are ongoing. This survey will be replicated in 2010 to evaluate whether there has been a change over time in parent self-reported shaking behaviors.

After program implementation, we will conduct a telephone survey of new parents to ascertain their exposure to the PURPLE intervention and the media campaign, their recollection and understanding of the messages, their self-reported behaviors in caring for their children during the period of PURPLE crying, and their dissemination of PURPLE materials and messages to other caregivers. A structured telephone interview survey will be conducted with 520 new North Carolina mothers whose babies were born in PURPLE intervention hospitals. The interview will be conducted 4–6 months after the child's birth to allow for the early increased crying period (between 2 and 4 months of age) to have occurred. Each infant will be identified by using birth certificate data to identify the mother's name and address. This information will be matched with publicly available phone numbers to maximize the sample size and minimize cost.

The content of the interview will include the parent's recollection of the hospital-based intervention, as well as the media campaign and its messages; the parent's use and dissemination of the intervention materials after leaving the hospital, practice of the recommended coping skills for dealing with increased crying, advocating the practice of these skills by others who have contact with the baby, and the extent to which the mother reports the baby experienced PURPLE crying.

A critical component of impact evaluation will be active surveillance for AHT beginning in April 2009. We will repeat the prospective surveillance of every serious AHT resulting in hospital admission or death occurring to North Carolina residents in the first 2 years of life, this time for a 3-year period in order to have sufficient statistical power to document a change in rate and a change in the proportion of unintentional to intentional head injury. Every admission to any of North Carolina's pediatric intensive care units for traumatic brain injury or any child who dies prior to his or her second birthday with a traumatic brain injury will be included. In addition, we will retrospectively conduct an interrupted time series analysis of hospital discharge data for North Carolina over 10-year period of time. Finally, we will compare North Carolina's rates to those of surrounding states in the Agency for Healthcare Research and Quality Kids' inpatient database to assess changes in the incidence of AHT for the entire period from 2000 to 2010.

This study will assess the occurrence of, and risk factors for, AHT in North Carolina's children and examine differences in outcome between children experiencing AHT and same-age children experiencing nonabusive traumatic brain injury. The study reprises one conducted in 2000–2002 on the epidemiology of AHT (Keenan et al., 2003). We plan to collect data prospectively on all children less than 2 years of age with traumatic brain injury serious enough to merit observation in a pediatric intensive care unit or monitored step-down unit for a period of 3 years. Standard practice at these institutions involves monitoring all children with newly diagnosed intracranial hemorrhage in the intensive care setting. We expect that all surviving children under age 2 with an intracranial hemorrhage will be referred to one of the nine institutions with a pediatric intensive care unit (PICU) both because of the serious nature of the injuries and because of the potential for medicolegal involvement. Nearly universal PICU admission for living children with AHT was confirmed in our earlier study through a review of state hospital discharge records. The hospital courses of the infants will be monitored until death or discharge. Because nearly all children with AHT have traumatic brain injury, a study of all traumatic brain injury experienced by children under age 2 will provide access to the children of interest and permit comparison with the epidemiology and presentation of AHT.

We will also conduct a case–control study to ascertain the relative risk of a child with AHT having been born in a hospital with a lower rate of delivery and/or lower fidelity of the intervention. At the completion of the data collection for the prospective surveillance for all traumatic brain injury in the state over the 3 years, a case–control analysis nested within the PICU cohort study will be conducted using two different control populations: children hospitalized or dying from unintentional injury and the state birth cohort. The second set of controls will be a set of three infants randomly selected to match each case by the same birthday, using the North Carolina State Center for Health Statistics.

The final component of the evaluation plan will be to estimate the economic impact of the intervention from the perspectives of the healthcare sector, taxpayers in the state, and society as a whole. We will estimate the costs of the intervention according to the principles of economic evaluation (Drummond, O'Brien, Stoddart, & Torrance, 1997; Gold, Russell, Siegel, & Weinstein, 1996). Most of the program costs will be direct and explicit and involve resources closely tied to intervention delivery. We will value those resources using an estimate of their per-unit costs. In most cases, we will assume those costs are effectively represented by market prices for the resources involved. We expect to identify the costs of "contributed services" such as nursing time used in newborn nurseries and physician or nurse time at prenatal and postnatal checkups. A key issue in a study like this involves separating the costs of research from those of intervention delivery (Foster, Jones, & the Conduct Problems Prevention Research Group, 2006).

SUMMARY

AHT is a rare but serious and often fatal form of child physical abuse. Previous work has shown some promise in the prevention of AHT despite methodological limitations and limited program penetration (Dias et al., 2005). The Period of PURPLE Crying is a program that is attractive, salient to all parents, palatable for nurses, and based on empirical evidence demonstrating that crying is the most common trigger for shaking and that crying is a developmentally normal phenomenon that peaks at 2 months and diminishes by 3–5 months. Large pilot studies have shown that this program changes knowledge and attitudes with regard to crying and shaking. However, it will take a much larger trial, a state-wide trial, to demonstrate a population-wide reduction in shaking by parents and of AHT in children under age 2. The Keeping Babies Safe in North Carolina grant can provide such an opportunity.

ACKNOWLEDGMENTS

This work would not be possible without the generous support of the Doris Duke Charitable Foundation, the Duke Endowment, and the Centers for Disease Control and Prevention (Grant No. CDC U49 CE001275-01).

REFERENCES

Agran, P. F., Anderson, C., Winn, D., Trent, R., Walton-Haynes, L., & Thayer, S. (2003). Rates of pediatric injuries by 3-month intervals for children 0 to 3 years of age. *Pediatrics, 111*(6, Pt. 1), e683–e692.

Barlow, K. M., & Minns, R. A. (2000). Annual incidence of shaken impact syndrome in young children. *Lancet, 356,* 1571–1572.

Barr, R. G. (1990a). The "colic" enigma: Prolonged episodes of a normal predisposition to cry. *Infant Mental Health Journal, 11,* 340–348.

Barr, R. G. (1990b). The normal crying curve: What do we really know? *Developmental Medicine and Child Neurology, 32*(4), 356–362.

Barr, R. G. (2000). Excessive crying. In A. J. Sameroff, M. Lewis, & S. M. Miller (Eds.), *Handbook of developmental psychopathology* (2nd ed.). New York: Kluwer Academic/Plenum Press.

Barr, R. G. (2006). Crying behavior and its importance for psychosocial development in children. In R. E. Tremblay, R. G. Barr, & R. D. Peters (Eds.), *Ency-*

clopedia on early childhood development. Montreal: Centre of Excellence for Early Childhood Development.

Barr, R. G., Kramer, M. S., Boisjoly, C., McVey-White, L., & Pless, I. B. (1988). Parental diary of infant cry and fuss behaviour. *Archives of Disease in Childhood, 63*(4), 380–387.

Barr, R. G., Paterson, J. A., MacMartin, L. M., Lehtonen, L., & Young, S. N. (2005). Prolonged and unsoothable crying bouts in infants with and without colic. *Journal of Developmental and Behavioral Pediatrics, 26*(1), 14–23.

Barr, R. G., Trent, R. B., & Cross, J. (2006). Age-related incidence curve of hospitalized shaken baby syndrome cases: Convergent evidence for crying as a trigger to shaking. *Child Abuse and Neglect, 30*(1), 7–16.

Brazelton, T. B. (1962). Crying in infancy. *Pediatrics, 29*, 579–588.

Brewster, A. L., Nelson, J. P., Hymel, K. P., Colby, D. R., Lucas, D. R., McCanne, T. R., et al. (1998). Victim, perpetrator, family, and incident characteristics of 32 infant maltreatment deaths in the United States Air Force. *Child Abuse and Neglect, 22*(2), 91–101.

Caffey, J. (1946). Multiple fractures in the long bones of infants suffering from chronic subdural hematoma. *American Journal of Roentgenology, 56*(2), 163–173.

Caffey, J. (1972a). On the theory and practice of shaking infants. Its potential residual effects of permanent brain damage and mental retardation. *American Journal of Diseases of Children, 124*(2), 161–169.

Caffey, J. (1972b). The parent–infant traumatic stress syndrome; (Caffey–Kempe syndrome), (battered babe syndrome). *American Journal of Roentgenology, Radium Therapy, and Nuclear Medicine, 114*(2), 218–229.

Corso, P. S., & Lutzker, J. R. (2006). The need for economic analysis in research on child maltreatment. *Child Abuse and Neglect, 30*(7), 727–738.

Dias, M. S., Smith, K., DeGuehery, K., Mazur, P., Li, V., & Shaffer, M. L. (2005). Preventing abusive head trauma among infants and young children: A hospital-based, parent education program. *Pediatrics, 115*(4), e470–e477.

Drummond, M. F., O'Brien, B., Stoddart, G. L., & Torrance, G. L. (1997). *Methods for the economic evaluation of health care programmes* (2nd ed.). Oxford, UK: Oxford University Press.

Duhaime, A. C., Christian, C., Moss, E., & Seidl, T. (1996). Long-term outcome in infants with the shaking-impact syndrome. *Pediatric Neurosurgery, 24*(6), 292–298.

Duhaime, A. C., Gennarelli, T. A., Thibault, L. E., Bruce, D. A., Margulies, S. S., & Wiser, R. (1987). The shaken baby syndrome: A clinical, pathological, and biomechanical study. *Journal of Neurosurgery, 66*(3), 409–415.

Foster, E. M., Jones, D., & the Conduct Problems Prevention Research Group. (2006). Can a costly intervention be cost-effective?: An analysis of violence prevention. *Archives of General Psychiatry, 63*, 1284–1291.

Fujiwara, T., Barr, R. G., Barr, M., Catherine, N., & Conway, J. (2008, March). *Changing knowledge and behavior concerning infant crying and shaken baby syndrome: A randomized controlled trial.* Paper presented at the International Conference on Infant Studies, Vancouver, BC.

Gessner, R. R., & Runyan, D. K. (1995). The shaken infant: A military connection? *Archives of Pediatrics and Adolescent Medicine, 149*(4), 467–469.

Gold, M. R., Russell, L. B., Siegel, J. E., & Weinstein, M. C. (1996). *Cost-effectiveness in health and medicine.* New York: Oxford University Press.

Guthkelch, A. N. (1971). Infantile subdural haematoma and its relationship to whiplash injuries. *British Medical Journal, 2*(5759), 430–431.

Hunziker, U. A., & Barr, R. G. (1986). Increased carrying reduces infant crying: A randomized controlled trial. *Pediatrics, 77*(5), 641–648.

Keenan, H. T., Hooper, S. R., Wetherington, C. E., Nocera, M., & Runyan, D. K. (2007). Neurodevelopmental consequences of early traumatic brain injury in 3-year-old children. *Pediatrics, 119*(3), e616–e623.

Keenan, H. T., Runyan, D. K., Marshall, S. W., Nocera, M. A., & Merten, D. F. (2004). A population-based comparison of clinical and outcome characteristics of young children with serious inflicted and noninflicted traumatic brain injury. *Pediatrics, 114*(3), 633–639.

Keenan, H. T., Runyan, D. K., Marshall, S. W., Nocera, M. A., Merten, D. F., & Sinal, S. H. (2003). A population-based study of inflicted traumatic brain injury in young children. *Journal of the American Medical Association, 290*(5), 621–626.

Lanza, E., Schatzkin, A., Daston, C., Corle, D., Freedman, L., Ballard-Barbash, R., et al. (2001). Implementation of a 4-y, high-fiber, high-fruit-and-vegetable, low-fat dietary intervention: Results of dietary changes in the Polyp Prevention Trial. *American Journal of Clinical Nutrition, 74*(3), 387–401.

Lee, C., Barr, R. G., Catherine, N., & Wicks, A. (2007). Age-related incidence of publicly reported shaken baby syndrome cases: Is crying a trigger for shaking? *Journal of Developmental and Behavioral Pediatrics, 28*(4), 288–293.

Minns, R. A. (2005). Subdural haemorrhages, haematomas, and effusions in infancy. *Archives of Disease in Childhood, 90*(9), 883–884.

Olds, D. L., Eckenrode, J., Henderson, C. R., Jr., Kitzman, H., Powers, J., Cole, R., et al. (1997). Long-term effects of home visitation on maternal life course and child abuse and neglect: Fifteen-year follow-up of a randomized trial. *Journal of the American Medical Association, 278*(8), 637–643.

Reijneveld, S. A., van der Wal, M. F., Brugman, E., Hira Sing, R. A., & Verloove, S. P. (2004). Infant crying and abuse. *Lancet, 364,* 1340–1342.

Rimer, B. K., Orleans, C. T., Fleisher, L., Cristinzio, S., Resch, N., Telepchak, J., et al. (1994). Does tailoring matter?: The impact of a tailored guide on ratings and short-term smoking-related outcomes for older smokers. *Health Education Research, 9*(1), 69–84.

Runyan, D. K., Shankar, V., Hassan, F., Hunter, W., Jain, D., Paula, C., et al. (2009). International variations in harsh child discipline. *Pediatrics.* Manuscript accepted for publication.

Straus, M. A., Hamby, S. L., Finkelhor, D., Moore, D. W., & Runyan, D. (1998). Identification of child maltreatment with the Parent–Child Conflict Tactics Scales: Development and psychometric data for a national sample of American parents. *Child Abuse and Neglect, 22*(4), 249–270.

Theodore, A. D., Chang, J. J., Runyan, D. K., Hunter, W. M., Bangdiwala, S. I., & Agans, R. (2005). Epidemiologic features of the physical and sexual maltreatment of children in the Carolinas. *Pediatrics*, *115*(3), e331–e337.

U.S. Department of Health and Human Services. (2003). *Emerging practices in the prevention of child abuse and neglect*. Washington, DC: U.S. Government Printing Office.

Zeemering-Nelson, W., Stoiko, M. A., Palusci, V. J., Bliss, R. C., & Combs, A. (2006, September). *Preventing shaken baby syndrome using a directed parent approach*. Paper presented at the sixth North American Conference on Shaken Baby Syndrome, Park City, UT.

PART III

POLICY AND PRACTICE ISSUES

CHAPTER 7

Quality Improvement in Child Abuse Prevention Programs

Robert T. Ammerman, Frank W. Putnam,
Peter A. Margolis, *and* Judith B. Van Ginkel

Evidence-based community prevention of child maltreatment, mental health treatment, and related public health programs are increasingly being disseminated on larger and larger scales. There are a number of dissemination strategies for scaling up such programs, but most involve the replication of the core program model at multiple sites to provide wider community coverage. Typically, the different sites are located within, and serve distinct, local subcommunities as part of the larger program. The service boundaries of these local sites often reflect geographic, political, racial/ethnic, and socioeconomic divisions within the larger community. Thus, although all of the sites providing services are nominally delivering the same core program, they are nonetheless doing so in very different local environments.

Variation in program implementation has been documented in child abuse prevention programs (Duggan et al., 2000), as well as other prevention initiatives (e.g., Morehouse & Tobler, 2000). Indeed, variability within and between sites is the rule rather than the exception for scaled-up, multisite prevention programs. Such variability has been attributed to differences between sites in their ability to adhere to core elements of program models. Indeed, the behavioral sciences have seen a strong push to create and follow prescriptive treatment manuals, under the assumption that lack of a clear directive has been the primary source of inadequate implementation of evidence-based interventions (Carroll & Nuro, 2002). Yet applying models of care by individuals is different from applying such models by organizations.

Implementation of models at the organizational level is complicated by the number and unique elements of those forces and influences that impact service delivery.

Features of the environments in which programs are undertaken contribute to the variability in how they are delivered across the different sites. The site-specific context in which programs take place has an important influence on their ability to provide effective service delivery. Contextual factors operate at the level of the individual organization as well as in the policy environment. Site-specific contextual features include (1) the site's overall resources; (2) personnel capacity, training, and backgrounds; (3) leadership commitment, management, and supervision; and (4) the characteristics and culture of the populations. Features of the local environment include (1) the extent of local stakeholder support and expectations and (2) the policy environment, such as legislative or funding eligibility and service requirements. Data-driven quality improvement approaches can be used to help local programs adapt to their own local contexts while maintaining those program elements essential to effectiveness.

Programs typically focus on intended variability or adaptations made to services that meet the unique needs of clients or settings. Yet contextual factors introduce variability that is unintended, often undesirable, and challenging to manage. Business and industry have recognized the need to identify and target these factors in order to create uniformly high-quality products and services. Recently, these quality improvement (QI) approaches have been applied to the delivery of healthcare in hospital and group practice settings (Committee on Quality of Health Care in America, Institute of Medicine, 2001; Madon, Hofman, Kupfer, & Glass, 2007). With some exceptions (e.g., Margolis et al., 2001), the application of quality improvement to large-scale community-based prevention and public health programs has lagged considerably behind its application in other healthcare settings.

A number of reasons have been offered for the failure of programs to apply process improvement approaches to reducing costs and improving service. Initial infrastructure costs, lack of expertise, and the fact that most of the organizations providing community prevention services such as home visitation desperately lack resources to meet even current service demands, have impeded the adoption of these practices in community programs. Yet, there are compelling reasons for child abuse prevention programs to adopt quality improvement approaches. First, QI provides a systematic and data-driven approach to adapting programs to the real, specific contextual features of sites or localities. Second, as new practice standards emerge from the research literature, QI methods provide a means to evolve the process of care to support new evidence about how to improve program effectiveness. Third, QI creates an environment focused on maximizing efficiencies, optimizing outcomes, and controlling costs. And fourth, QI can be used to test, on a small scale and in a relatively short time frame, the impacts of procedural or content changes on processes and outcomes that may justify expanded dissemination to other sites within a program or to the field as a whole.

The purpose of this chapter is to describe the applicability of QI methods to child abuse prevention. Illustrative examples are provided from Every Child Succeeds, a home visitation program for first-time at-risk mothers and their children (Ammerman et al., 2007). Because the scientific foundation of quality improvement is large and complex, a comprehensive examination is beyond the scope of this chapter. Rather, we seek to elucidate the potential benefits of QI methods to child abuse prevention programs, identify key elements of QI that are essential to its application, and describe the implementation of QI approaches in a real-world, scaled-up prevention program.

KEY ELEMENTS OF QI

QI in healthcare and public health has been defined as "systematic, data-guided activities designed to bring about immediate, positive changes in the delivery of health care in particular settings" (Baily, Bottrell, Lynn, & Jennings, 2006, p. S5). Deming (1982) conceptualized QI as bringing together four areas of study to achieve improvement in complex organizational systems: (1) system thinking, (2) understanding variation, (3) theory of knowledge, and (4) understanding human psychology. Deming defined a system as "a network of interdependent components that work together to accomplish a shared aim." The aim of programs described here is the prevention of child abuse. *System thinking* refers to appreciating and understanding the many interrelated processes (e.g., referral, enrollment, curriculum, and parenting education) that drive the outcomes produced by these programs. Systems are complex, comprise influences that interact synergistically, and may change over time as new elements are introduced (Senge, 1990). *Understanding variation* refers to the use of statistical methods, most often statistical process control, to learn from variation in processes and outcomes observed in program implementation. These methods are predicated on an appreciation that variability is a characteristic of all processes, and that understanding sources of variation creates opportunities for implementing changes in care processes that result in improved knowledge. *Theory of knowledge* reflects the fact that management of a system requires a structured, scientific approach to building knowledge that involves the efficient and effective use of data to assess relationships between individual processes and outcomes. This leads to the ability of program managers and staff to predict client outcomes reliably. Building knowledge involves planned experimentation within the system in order to understand

and address unexpected variability in outcomes. Finally, an *appreciation of human psychology* addresses the importance of understanding motivation and reactions to change in leading improvement efforts. QI methods can be used to support the development of organizational approaches and service cultures that emphasize (1) the use of measurement to understand the performance of care delivery and outcomes, (2) the importance of transparency of outcome measures to motivate action and learning within and across programs, and (3) the need to change procedures in response to this information so as to maximize results.

Historically, QI methods were developed in the context of manufacturing and industry. Standardization of manufacturing processes created the need for technologies to measure, describe, and track the quantities and quality of manufactured goods. Shewhart (1931) developed approaches to graphing and tracking processes (control charts) along with statistical procedures for describing systems, identifying meaningful patterns in data presentations, and defining significant changes over time. Many of these approaches continue to be widely used in industry, although they have been extensively expanded and refined. The seminal contributions of Deming (1982) and others (Juran, 1992) solidified the discipline of QI and have formed the basis of QI programs in industry, particularly in manufacturing (Maani, Putterill, & Sluti, 1994). In the last two decades, these approaches have been adapted for application in healthcare settings (Committee on Quality of Health Care in America, Institute of Medicine, 2001). QI procedures are now widely used in healthcare, and their growth in this area is exemplified by the emergence of national organizations devoted to QI (e.g., the American Health Quality Organization) and the founding of professional journals for QI research (e.g., *Quality and Safety in Health Care*). Although research on QI in healthcare is still in an early stage, recent meta-analyses (e.g., Boonyasai et al., 2007) document the potential of QI to promote best practices, decrease intersite variability, and enhance outcomes.

Although QI methods were developed for application in industry, their use is now more common in healthcare and public health (Committee on Quality of Health Care in America, Institute of Medicine, 2001). All share common elements that have important implications for child abuse prevention programs. Some of these QI features represent significant departures from the ways in which quality has been typically conceptualized, measured, and addressed in such programs. Others are highly consistent with current practice and require only modest adjustment and refinement for adoption. We now describe these key elements of QI and provide selected examples of their use. More comprehensive general descriptions of improvement science approaches can be found in Langley, Nolan, Nolan, Norman, and Provost (1996).

Components of QI

Successful QI programs are built around specific principles, features, and procedures. These include the following:

How Would We Know That a Change Is an Improvement?

Processes and outcomes are systematically and regularly measured. Measurement is useful, efficient, and reliable. Data are shared across the organization, and transparency is valued.

Human Psychology

All members of the organization are committed to and participate in QI efforts. Service providers and "frontline" staff members are acknowledged as contributing knowledge critical in understanding causes of variation and information needed to drive improvement. They are core members of the QI team.

What Changes Can Be Made That Would Result in an Improvement?

Forums are available to review data, identify areas targeted for change, delineate best practices guided by the empirical literature, generate changes in practice that will be tested and analyzed, and determine if changes in practice are warranted, as based on testing. Changes in procedures are implemented in a systematic and planned manner, with data collected to determine impact. Such tests may be carried out initially on a small scale, proceeding through an iterative process that enables the organization to build knowledge about the process of care prior to full-scale implementation.

Building Knowledge

On the basis of tests of change and improvements in processes derived from findings in the literature, dissemination of new learning and practices to other staff and sites may occur. Dissemination is conducted systematically and monitored over time to ensure successful adoption and continued improvement.

Understanding Processes and Contributing Factors

Data Collection and Management

QI depends on effective and timely data collection. Programs must have a standardized approach to data collection, with measures administered multiple times over the course of service. The selection of measures is challenging, in that programs typically have a number of domains about which they need or want information. There are limits to both the quantity and types of data collection that are feasible. Because data collection is woven into ongoing service provision, a careful balance is needed to avoid sacrificing important program elements in order to gather data. Measures should reflect those processes and outcomes that are primary objectives of programs. For home visiting programs, measures of processes might include the number of visits each family receives, the time between referral to first contact, and the length of time each family participates in the program. Outcome measures might include parenting beliefs, caregiver–child attachment, and number of repeat pregnancies. Provider staff members must be trained in the reliable and accurate gathering of information, which, depending on their previous training and educational backgrounds, may require a considerable amount of time and effort. Ongoing support is needed to ensure consistent accuracy of measurement.

Equally important is a system to store and manage data. In multisite programs, centralized data management may be useful to collect common data. Ammerman and colleagues (2007) describe a web-based data collection system for a multisite home visitation program (i.e., Every Child Succeeds), allowing for multiple agencies to upload data and retrieve standardized summary reports about performance and outcomes. Other home visitation programs use centralized (Olds, 2002) or on-site (Prevent Child Abuse America, 2003) data storage and management systems. Such data systems should permit the adding of measures that are important to specific programs and should be readily changeable as new measures are added or dropped, according to shifting needs and developments in the field. "Out of the box" software packages typically fail to meet these needs fully, often requiring programs to build their own systems.

Data systems are used to provide regular and frequent (monthly or, at a minimum, quarterly) reports on performance indicators. Giving providers such information is an important foundational step for QI. In and of itself it does not improve quality, but it engages providers directly in the process of using data to describe program parameters and outcomes. Where possible, data should be presented over time, allowing for the identification of patterns and trends.

Run Charts, Control Charts, and Measurement Systems

Data are typically graphed on run or control charts (see Moen, Nolan, & Provost, 1999), essential tools in statistical process control. Run charts and control charts reflect a process or outcome based on time or some characteristic (for example, agency, home visitor, or family demographic). One of the most useful features of a control chart is the use of "control limits" to detect when improvements have been made and whether performance is statistically stable over time. These limits are calculated on the basis of the variability of the order of the data points (Shewhart, 1931). Variations between data points within the control limits are due to common cause or random variation in performance. Introducing changes in practice (to all agencies in the system, for example) would be expected to alter performance of all members of the system. Performance outside of the control limits is likely due to special cause or unique features that led to results substantially above or below what would be expected within the system. Changing those entities that are underperforming requires specialized or individualized interventions. Likewise, for those special cause entities that perform at a level greater than does the system, there is an opportunity to identify particularly effective processes or features that might be transportable to other sites.

Figure 7.1 presents an example of a control chart from a multisite home visitation program serving first-time at-risk mothers who are eligible for enrollment during pregnancy and until the child reaches 3 months of age.

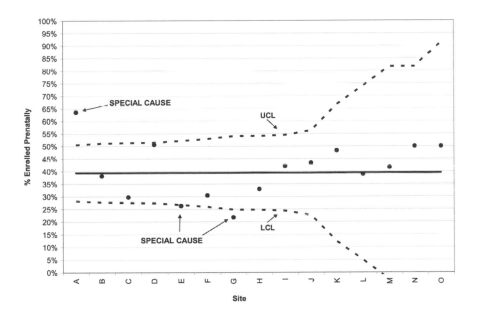

FIGURE 7.1. Control chart showing proportion of new enrollments by site over 1 year. Sites are ordered by size from largest to smallest in terms of caseload. Upper (UCL) and lower (LCL) control limits define the system. Variability within the control limits is attributable to common cause, while variability outside the control limits likely reflects special cause.

The program seeks to maximize enrollment prenatally. This chart shows the percentage of mothers who enroll prenatally in each of the 15 sites over a 1-year period. The middle bar shows the median (39%) for all the sites, reflecting the overall performance of the program, and the dashed lines indicate the upper and lower control limits. Performance of the 12 sites falling within the control limits suggests that current performance is a feature of the operation of the program (see Oakland, 2003). This chart suggests that changes in procedures designed to increase the proportion of enrollees who join prenatally and that are introduced to these sites would be expected to impact each member of the system, improving outcomes for all of them if the changes are effective. Three sites fall outside the system. Two sites (E and G) are below the lower control limit and therefore likely have unique features or practices that impeded their efforts to enroll mothers prenatally. Site A is above the upper control limit, indicating that it has unique features or practices that make it particularly effective at enrolling mothers prenatally. Perhaps these features and practices can be identified and transferred to other sites, thereby increasing prenatal enrollment for the program as a whole. Thus, this control chart contains a good deal of useful information—it shows that (1) there is considerable variability between sites in the system, (2) most of the agencies operate as part of a common system of performance, and (3) two sites are having particular difficulty whereas one site is particularly effective in enrolling mothers prenatally, and this is likely due to causes unique to their sites. Understanding this variation may be extremely important in the development of changes that might improve overall program performance.

Establishing Targets and Identifying Contributing Factors

QI begins with the identification of aims or targeted procedural levels and outcomes sought by the program. For example, procedural targets might include delivering a certain number of home visits over the first year of service, having 100% of referred mothers receive their first home visit within 5 days of initial contact, or having a home visitor deliver a certain number of home visits each month across a caseload. Illustrative outcome targets include the percentage of children fully immunized by age 2, the percentage obtaining a low-risk score on a behavioral inventory, or the percentage developing normally at a particular time point. Measurement of these variables usually reveals that not all targets are met by an individual family, home visitor, agency, or program as a whole. Closing the gaps between actual performances and targets is the subsequent focus of QI.

All QI approaches include the use of conceptual diagrams to describe the relationships between program components and outcomes. These visually represent contributors to a procedure or outcome. The goal of such diagrams is to help participants in the system understand how their work relates to the outcome, to provide a framework for reviewing different aspects of the program, and to identify potential areas where changes might result in improved outcome. Together, the QI team members can consult the empirical literature, as well as their understanding of how services are implemented in their program, in an effort to identify changes that may be needed. Sometimes problems are found in the core features of a process or outcome. An example is the provision of insufficient information to mothers about immunizations, when providing *sufficient* information is an essential component of successfully reaching targeted immunization levels. At other times, problems may be unique to a provider or agency. For example, a community may have inadequate access to pediatric services, making immunizations more difficult to obtain. Resolution of these discrete problems is essential to reaching targets, regardless of the overall efficacy of a particular home visitation approach. Conceptual diagrams are used to develop alternative strategies that will subsequently be implemented, tested, and monitored.

Progress toward reaching targets is reflected in regularly produced reports. These reports show results on measured variables, past performance and change, and predetermined target levels. An example of these reports is a red/green chart, in which green denotes having reached targeted levels and red indicates not having reached targets. Figure 7.2 shows a hypothetical red/green chart for a six-site program. In this example there are six variables reflecting home visitation processes (time to first visit, frequency of visits in the first year as per model directives, and referrals of families to community resources) and outcomes (well-baby visits to the pediatrician in first year, having a regular source of healthcare—that is, medical home—and immunizations) labeled as indicators. The percentages of families who have met the criteria on each of these variables are indicated by site. The target level for each variable is also presented. Shaded boxes indicate "red" performance, which is below the targets. Unshaded boxes indicate "green" performance, which has met or exceeded the targets. In addition, the percentage for all six sites for each variable is displayed. At a glance, it is evident that all sites have both met and failed to meet some of the targets—suggesting potential areas that can be addressed using QI methods. Moreover, one site (site B) is mostly shaded, suggesting that it is struggling in a number of areas and may need close attention to rectify unique problems or needs. One variable (well-baby visits) is mostly shaded, suggesting that the target may be too high or that all of the sites need additional training, support, or resources to move to the "green" level of performance. Another variable (medical home) is all unshaded, suggesting that the target may be too low and that it needs to be adjusted to a higher level. The value of the red/green chart is clear—it pro-

Indicator	Target	Sites						Program Total
		A	B	C	D	E	F	
Time to First Visit	70%	90.9%	61.8%	54.0%	80.0%	76.5%	76.5%	73.3%
Visit Frequency	50%	51.7%	42.2%	56.8%	72.3%	46.8%	54.4%	54.0%
Referrals	50%	31.7%	41.4%	69.2%	60.8%	66.8%	13.6%	47.3%
Well-Baby Visits	75%	70.3%	49.1%	42.3%	79.2%	14.7%	44.8%	50.1%
Medical Home	85%	90.0%	92.6%	100.0%	98.0%	95.8%	96.6%	95.5%
Immunizations	80%	100.0%	67.6%	83.2%	78.2%	87.2%	92.9%	84.8%

FIGURE 7.2. A hypothetical red/green chart indicating performance above and below predetermined targets for six sites (labeled A–F) and for the program as a whole. Shaded boxes reflect performance below the target (red), and unshaded boxes reflect performance above the target (green). Time to First Visit = percentage of families receiving first home visit within a predetermined time period; Visit Frequency = percentage of families receiving number of visits provided during a specified period as per model directives; Referrals = percentage of families referred to other community resources; Well-Baby Visits = percentage of children receiving predetermined number of well-baby visits with pediatricians during first year; Medical Home = percentage of children with regular and consistent source of pediatric care; Immunizations = percentage of children up-to-date on immunizations.

vides a snapshot of performance across variables and domains, allows for comparisons within and between sites, permits assessment of performance relative to predetermined targets, and identifies sites that may be especially effective or struggling. An additional feature of the red/green chart that can be used is the display of midway points reflecting partial progress toward targets. These map out a series of intermediate steps toward reaching targets and permit monitoring of progress over time.

Using Improvement Methods

Improvement focuses on specific processes or outcomes in which change is desired. The variable may be one that is problematic for multiple sites or a single site. Even if the underperformance is widespread, improvement can begin with a focused and circumscribed application with a single site or even a few home visitors within a site. Through the creation of a conceptual diagram, and with input and active involvement from frontline staff, changes in processes and/or service content emerge that warrant testing. Baseline measurement establishes current performance and, ideally, reflects a stable system using statistical process control charting. In contrast, unstable systems are poorly controlled and unpredictable, requiring that work instead be directed toward bringing stability to the system.

Improvement follows the Plan-Do-Study-Act (PDSA) approach to implementing and studying the impacts of changes in processes or content (Deming, 1994; Langley et al., 1996). Applied sequentially, PDSA cycles provide a systematic framework to drive improvement. In the first "Plan" phase, specific change options are considered and selected. The goal of the test of change is determined and parameters of monitoring the test are selected. In child abuse prevention, parameters include how many home visitors will be involved, how long the test will be conducted, how many families will be examined, and what the unit of measurement will be. In the second "Do" phase, the change plan is implemented. Continual measurement provides information about the relative success or failure of the strategy. In the third "Study" phase, data are examined and the test is evaluated. Although fully meeting targets may be the result of a test, more often it is found that the test yielded partial success. The next step is determined in the fourth "Act" phase. Partial success may warrant adjustment to the change strategy, or perhaps new elements need to be added. A second cycle is carried out, following the steps outlined earlier. Over a period of time, successive applications of PDSA cycles should lead to successive incremental improvements, approaching and then reaching targets. This iterative approach is the foundation of QI. Identification of effective strategies leads to consideration of replication with other home visitors and sites and dissemination to all practitioners if needed.

Figure 7.3 presents an example of changes in performance over time after implementation of procedures designed to improve a process. Specifically, the chart shows the percentage of families enrolled within 1 month following referral for 10 home visitation sites by month over a 30-month period. After 14 months, an improvement phase was initiated in which a series of procedural changes were implemented through discrete PDSA cycles. Changes in procedures were selected on the basis of an examination of current practices, identification of barriers and facilitators to rapid providing of the first home visit, and development of best practices for optimizing the transition from referral to visit. The monitoring of data over the next 16 months revealed substantial improvement. Recalculating the control limits from baseline to the improvement phase provides the statistical basis for the inference that changes in performance resulted from the improvement efforts. In addition, over this time period there is a narrowing of the control limits, reflecting a decrease in the overall variability of the system. Furthermore, examination of the means demonstrates the magnitude of the change,

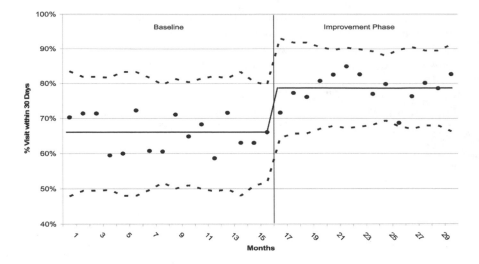

FIGURE 7.3. Control chart showing changes in percentage of families seen for their first home visit within 1 month after referral. Data are from 10 sites reflected by month. Medians and control limits are calculated separately for baseline and improvement phases, revealing changes brought about following implementation of new procedures.

in that the mean percentage of families seen for their first home visit within 30 days was 66% in months 1–14 and 78% in months 15–30.

Improvement initiatives may also require controlled comparisons of two or more strategies or the application of new strategies under multiple and divergent conditions. Experimental designs are applied in these efforts, and statistical approaches to contrasting alternative strategies or parameters have been developed (see Moen et al., 1999). More complicated factorial designs often require considerable expertise and support, although they have the advantage of accelerating improvement work and increasing the quantity of information derived from PDSA cycles.

APPLICATION OF QI:
EVERY CHILD SUCCEEDS AS AN EXAMPLE

Every Child Succeeds (ECS) is a large-scale, community-based home visitation program that serves at-risk first-time mothers in southwestern Ohio and northern Kentucky. Serving a broad area covering seven counties, ECS implements its program through 16 agencies. These agencies use two national models of home visitation, Healthy Families America (Daro & Harding, 1999) and the Nurse–Family Partnership (Olds, 2002), overlaid by supports and augmentations designed to enhance efficiency and optimize outcomes. ECS has many of the features of such scaled-up prevention programs that require a QI system. First, services are decentralized and delivered by multiple agencies and sites, thereby increasing the likelihood of variability and drift in implementation. Second, agencies are under the jurisdiction of multiple government entities and are funded by several funders, creating differential demands and requirements that can interfere with a focused, tightly controlled application of services. And third, the geographical dispersion of agencies complicates efforts to communicate regularly with home visitors and to efficiently disseminate information regarding best practices and changes in procedures.

The foundation of the QI Program in ECS is eECS, a Web-based data management system (Ammerman et al., 2007). Using, eECS, home visitors and agencies upload information about participants, service parameters, and outcomes. These in turn are accessed by administration to monitor program implementation and effectiveness. Summary reports are automatically available to service providers. These are used to guide the supervision of home visitors and to identify areas in need of improvement for individual participants, home visitors, agencies, or ECS as a whole. Control charts are prepared that show changes over time, permitting identification of shifts in performance or outcomes that may require rapid response. Red/green charts are produced and distributed to all agencies, indicating targets for ECS generally and showing whether or not agencies have reached targets on multiple quality indicators reflecting process and outcome variables. Transparency in the reporting of performance across agencies and home visitors is integral to creating a culture of quality, such that striving to deliver the highest-quality services is embraced as part of daily work rather than perceived as a separate, burdensome addition (Juran, 1992). An important feature is that home visitors and agencies contribute to all levels of the QI Program. Teams are formed around specific quality indicators, consisting of agency and administration representatives, and they are responsible for establishing targets, changing targets as needed, and identifying best practices that warrant dissemination.

Agencies and home visitors who are struggling to reach targets participate in separate improvement projects. Working with a Quality Improvement Consultant (QIC), agencies and home visitors create a conceptual diagram that displays influences on performance that may drive improvement or undermine quality. Potential changes are generated, and these are systematically tested through PDSA cycles. Reviews of findings may lead to adoption of new procedures if they are found to be effective, or reconsideration of potential influences necessitating a new round of PDSA cycles. Although some of the procedural changes that emerge from improvement projects may be idiosyncratic to a specific agency, others may have broad applicability and lead to changes in best practices. These in turn are disseminated to other agencies through training and distribution of new materials.

Creating and maintaining the QI Program in ECS has been a challenging undertaking. It is labor intensive, requires increased staffing, and must be closely monitored to ensure consistent application. Offsetting these requirements are the rewards of focusing on issues that are of greatest interest to home visitors, namely, the day-to-day work of providing home visits and addressing the needs of families.

QI AND TRADITIONAL RESEARCH METHODS

Child abuse prevention has progressed through traditional research methods (for example, clinical trials) in which controlled studies are conducted to identify optimal interventions and document their impacts or theoretical constructs are examined using experimental designs. Such approaches are essential to further development of the field and will continue to be the foundation of new knowledge in prevention science. Indeed, QI shares several features with traditional research practices, including reliance on measurement and data for analysis and decision making and the use of controlled designs. However, there are several distinctive differences between the two methods that underscore the unique contributions of QI to an empirical approach to prevention.

Table 7.1 presents contrasting features of traditional research methods and QI. Whereas traditional research methods are primarily idiographic in their focus, QI approaches operate at the systems level. Traditional research methods use probability theory to analyze statistically samples that are drawn from a population in order to generalize to similar populations. In contrast, QI is less concerned with sampling and generalizability, emphasizing instead planned experimentation to determine if changes in specific systems are associated with improvements. Traditional research requires large samples to optimize statistical power. In QI, samples may be small. Hierarchical oversight, in which a study is overseen by a team of investigators and implemented by a research staff, is typical in traditional research. In contrast, QI requires participation by "frontline" practitioners who are most proximal to the processes and outcomes that are targeted for improvement. Trained QI professionals are equally important members of the QI team, although their role is often that of facilitator. Traditional research often takes a considerable amount of time and is expensive, particularly in the use of clinical trials. QI is a more rapid process (sometimes yielding information in a matter of days) and typically relies on fewer resources. Tra-

TABLE 7.1. Contrast between Traditional Research Methods and QI

Traditional research	Quality improvement
• Primarily idiographic.	• Primarily systems.
• Sampling to make generalizations to larger population.	• Focus is on specific unit of interest within an organization.
• Large n.	• Small n.
• Hierarchical oversight.	• Involves all participants.
• Takes a long time and is expensive.	• Takes a short time and is less expensive.
• Discrete length, time limited, size predetermined.	• Iterative, changes made in response to observed effects.
• Goal is to understand causal relationships, confirm and develop theory.	• Goal is to reach preset targets by understanding and changing systems.
• Provider and site differences are problematic, complicate interpretation, are assumed to represent flawed implementation.	• Provider and site differences are expected, distinctions between common cause and special cause, opportunities for learning.

ditional research studies have distinct start and end points, involving a predetermined number of subjects or measurements and a fixed duration. QI is ongoing, and although there are specific start points in PDSA cycles, the end points can vary, depending on the magnitude and pattern of change. QI is an iterative process, in which a series of changes are implemented sequentially, sometimes over a short time period. Traditional research is theory-driven, and experimental methods are used to test hypotheses derived from theory and elucidate causal relationships between variables. Although theory may be used to select possible changes in procedures, QI is not concerned with testing theoretical constructs or necessarily demonstrating causal relationships. Rather, QI is focused on changing procedures to increase impact and efficiency and on optimizing outcomes. Finally, although multisite studies are increasingly common, in traditional research site differences are considered a nuisance that should be eliminated. In QI, site variability is expected and provides an opportunity for learning (through examination of common and special causes) and improvement of practices (Moen et al., 1999).

QI and traditional research methods are complementary. Whereas traditional research methods are primary sources of critical and essential content for programs, QI is important in determining the ways in which programs should implement services. Although in its infancy, research on QI has demonstrated the effectiveness of QI procedures in reducing between-site variability and improving outcomes, at least in healthcare settings (Margolis et al., 2004). Continued research on QI and the development of standard ways to integrate learnings from QI and traditional research approaches constitute a priority for future efforts (Forum on the Science of Health Care Quality Improvement and Implementation, Institute of Medicine, 2007).

NEXT STEPS AND FUTURE DIRECTIONS

QI has only recently been introduced to the child abuse prevention field. Statistical process control methods, as described in this chapter, are novel and hold great potential to provide a systematic approach to using data to improve the implementation of scaled-up programs. Although much work remains to be done to identify how best to create QI infrastructures in prevention programs, effective models are available in healthcare and business (Shojania & Grimshaw, 2005). In this chapter, we describe the key features of a QI system and provide selected examples from a home visitation program to highlight application of QI principles in a prevention context. The behavioral sciences, in general, have struggled with how best to move interventions developed in the laboratory or highly controlled settings into the field. The disappointing results that are sometimes obtained in this transition are potentially addressed using QI. Future research should focus on studying the impact of QI on child abuse prevention outcomes.

ACKNOWLEDGMENTS

We acknowledge the support of the United Way of Greater Cincinnati, Help Me Grow Program (Ohio), and Kentucky H.A.N.D.S.

REFERENCES

Ammerman, R. T., Putnam, F. W., Kopke, J. E., Gannon, T. A., Short, J. A., Van Ginkel, J. B., et al. (2007). Development and implementation of a quality assurance infrastructure in a multisite home visitation program in Ohio and Kentucky. *Journal of Prevention and Intervention in the Community, 34,* 89–107.

Baily, M. A., Bottrell, M., Lynn, J., & Jennings, B. (2006, July–August). The ethics of using QI methods to improve health care quality and safety. *Hastings Center Special Report,* S1–S40. Garrison, NY: Hastings Center.

Boonyasai, R. T., Windish, D. M., Chakraborti, C., Feldman, L. S., Rubin, H. R., & Bass, E. B. (2007). Effectiveness of teaching quality improvement to clinicians: A systematic review. *Journal of the American Medical Association, 298,* 1023–1037.

Carroll, K. M., & Nuro, K. F. (2002). One size cannot fit all: A stage model for psychotherapy manual development. *Clinical Psychology: Science and Practice*, *9*, 396–406.

Committee on Quality of Health Care in America, Institute of Medicine. (2001). *Crossing the quality chasm: A new health system for the 21st century*. Washington, DC: Author.

Daro, D., & Harding, K. (1999). Healthy Families America: Using research to enhance practice. *The Future of Children*, *9*, 152–178.

Deming, W. E. (1982). *Out of the crisis*. Cambridge: Massachusetts Institute of Technology, Center for Advanced Engineering Study.

Deming, W. E. (1994). *The new economics for industry, government, education* (2nd ed.). Cambridge: Massachusetts Institute of Technology, Center for Advanced Engineering Study.

Duggan, A., Windham, A., McFarlane, E., Fuddy, L., Rohde, C., Buchbinder, S., et al. (2000). Hawaii's Healthy Start Program of home visiting for at-risk families: Evaluation of family identification, family engagement, and service delivery. *Pediatrics*, *105*, 250–259.

Forum on the Science of Health Care Quality Improvement and Implementation, Institute of Medicine. (2007). *Advancing quality improvement research: Challenges and opportunities*. Washington, DC: Author.

Juran, J. M. (1992). *Juran on quality by design*. New York: Free Press.

Langley G. J., Nolan, K. M., Nolan, T. W., Norman, C. L., & Provost, L. P. (1996). *The improvement guide: A practical approach to enhancing organizational performance*. San Francisco: Jossey-Bass.

Maani, K. E., Putterill, M. S., & Sluti, D. G. (1994). Empirical analysis of quality improvement in manufacturing. *International Journal of Quality and Reliability Management*, *11*, 19–37.

Madon, T., Hofman, K. J., Kupfer, L., & Glass, R. I. (2007). Implementation science. *Science*, *318*, 1728–1729.

Margolis, P. A., Lannon, C. M., Stuart, J. M., Fried, B. J., Keyes-Elstein, L., & Moore, D. F. (2004). Practice based education to improve delivery systems for prevention in primary care: Randomised trial. *British Medical Journal*, *328*, 388.

Margolis, P. A., Stevens, R., Bordley, W. C., Stuart, J., Harlan, C., Keyes-Elstein, L., et al. (2001). From concept to application: The impact of a community-wide intervention to improve the delivery of preventive services to children. *Pediatrics*, *108*, e42.

Moen, R. D., Nolan, T. W., & Provost, L. P. (1999). *Quality improvement through planned experimentation* (2nd ed.). New York: McGraw-Hill.

Morehouse, E., & Tobler, N. (2000). Preventing and reducing substance use among institutionalized adolescents. *Adolescence*, *35*, 1–28.

Oakland, J. (2003). *Statistical process control* (5th ed.). Oxford, U.K.: Butterworth-Heinemann.

Olds, D. L. (2002). Prenatal and infancy home visiting by nurses: From randomized trials to community replication. *Prevention Science*, *3*, 153–172.

Prevent Child Abuse America. (2003). *Program information management system (PIMS)*. Retrieved March 2, 2009, from *www.healthyfamiliesamerica.org/research/pims.shtml*.

Senge, P. M. (1990). *The fifth discipline: The art and practice of the learning organization.* New York: Doubleday Currency.

Shewhart, W. A. (1931). *Economic control of quality of manufactured product.* New York: Van Nostrand.

Shojania, K. G., & Grimshaw, J. M. (2005). Evidence-based quality improvement: The state of the science. *Health Affairs, 24,* 138–150.

CHAPTER 8

Differential Response

Jane Waldfogel

As other chapters in this volume document, there is a growing interest on the part of policymakers and agency staff in identifying and developing programs to prevent child maltreatment. In addition to efforts to prevent child maltreatment among the general population, there is also a good deal of interest in programs to prevent maltreatment among families who come to the attention of child protective services. The high recidivism rate among such families (see overview in Waldfogel, 1998a) suggests the potential benefits that could accrue in terms of child safety if the child welfare system were more successful in its prevention efforts.

In the past decade an increasing number of states have begun experimenting with differential response as a way to prevent maltreatment by better engaging families referred to child protective services (CPS) (see overviews in Merkel-Holguin, Kaplan, & Kwak, 2006; U.S. Department of Health and Human Services, 2003b; Waldfogel, 2008). The basic premise of differential response is simple: Rather than responding to all reports in the same way, CPS agencies should distinguish between those that warrant a traditional, adversarial investigation and those that could benefit from an alternative, more assessment-oriented response. In principle, providing lower-risk families with an alternative response could prevent future maltreatment by engaging families in a more helpful way, providing a more nuanced assessment of their needs, and increasing the likelihood that families receive needed services. In the long run, offering an alternative response might also increase the willingness of reporters to refer families to CPS, as well as the willingness of families and community members to cooperate with the agency. In addition, targeting investigative resources to high-risk families might better prevent future maltreatment in those families.

A national survey carried out by the American Humane Association (AHA) and the Child Welfare League of America (CWLA) (Merkel-Holguin et al., 2006) identified 15 states with differential response programs—programs that provide two or more discrete responses to screened-in CPS reports, based on the level of risk in the case, and with the assessment-oriented response providing services to families on a voluntary basis and without perpetrators and victims being listed on a central registry.[1] Focusing on the evidence from these states, in this chapter I consider what we know about differential response and, in particular, the role it might play in the prevention of child maltreatment.

BACKGROUND: CPS AND THE CASE FOR DIFFERENTIAL RESPONSE

Child protective services refers to a set of public policies, funding mechanisms, agencies, and services that represent society's response to child abuse and neglect. Although exact legislation, funding mechanisms, and services differ across states (and even more substantially across countries), most CPS systems operate on the assumption that child maltreatment is a distinct condition that requires intervention by the state.

CPS tends to encompass three broad areas: reporting, screening/investigation, and disposition/service provision. In the area of reporting, all 50 states in the United States have laws that stipulate when a report of abuse or neglect should be filed and who may be required to file such a report. Although all states have reporting laws that require certain individuals (e.g., doctors and teachers) to report suspected child maltreatment, voluntary reports from concerned citizens are almost always accepted. Once a report is made, there are a variety of possible responses, but, typically, the next stage is a screening process in which a decision is made as to whether the state has both a mandate and sufficient information to investigate the reported family. When both these factors hold, an investigation or assessment is undertaken to determine if a child has been maltreated, whether services are needed to prevent further maltreatment, and whether the child

---

[1]In addition to the states that have implemented differential response in accordance with this definition, several states have implemented other reforms designed to better engage families and prevent future maltreatment (Merkel-Holguin et al., 2006). Examples include programs that refer screened-out cases for services (California, New Jersey, and New Mexico) or provide services to cases that were investigated but unsubstantiated (Massachusetts). A few states (Iowa, North Dakota, and South Dakota) provide a more assessment-focused initial response to all screened-in cases. As discussed later, other sources have used slightly differently coding schemes or identified different states as involved in differential response reforms. Table 8.1 summarizes the data from the various sources.

can remain safely at home or should be removed to foster care or another out-of-home setting.

The operation of child protective services in the United States has been criticized on several counts. In particular, five major problems with CPS have been identified (Waldfogel, 1998a):

1. *Overinclusion.* Some families who are in the system should not be, whereas others who are at low risk receive an unnecessarily adversarial response from CPS.
2. *Underinclusion.* At the same time, some families that should be involved with CPS are not (this group includes families missed by the system, families not reported, and families who ask for services voluntarily but are not provided them).
3. *Capacity.* The number of families involved with CPS at any one time far exceeds the capacity of the system to serve them.
4. *Service delivery.* Many families do not receive needed services, and for many others service delivery is fragmented and lacks coherence.
5. *Service orientation.* The dual mandate of CPS—to protect children and preserve families—creates tensions and makes it difficult to provide services appropriately tailored to individual families' needs. Instead, agencies tend to adopt a one-size-fits-all response, which, depending on the case may be unduly oriented toward child protection and insufficiently oriented toward family preservation or vice versa.

These fundamental problems and tensions within CPS point to the need for a new approach to child protection, one that I and others have called "differential response." The key element of a differential response to child protection is a more customized approach to families at the point of intake. Providing a gentler, more assessment-oriented response to lower-risk families—while reserving the more adversarial investigative response for high risk-families—should engage lower-risk families in a more helpful way. The long-run goal is that changing the response to lower-risk families will also foster the development of a more community-based system of child protection, with greater involvement by informal and natural helpers.

THE MODEL: WHAT DOES DIFFERENTIAL RESPONSE LOOK LIKE?

The distinguishing feature of a differential response system is the provision of more than one type of response at the point of intake. Prior to the introduction of differential response, CPS agencies typically offered a narrowly prescribed response to reports of abuse or neglect, with reports that are screened-in investigated in accordance with strict rules and regulations that specify who must be seen and in what time frame. With differential response, CPS agencies continue to provide an investigative response to high-risk cases, but offer an alternative response to lower-risk cases.

An alternative response differs from an investigation in a number of ways (see also Merkel-Holguin et al., 2006). The focus of a traditional investigation is to determine whether a child has been abused or neglected and by whom, and what services, including removal, might be needed on an emergency basis to guarantee the child's safety. An investigation concludes with a determination as to whether the child was abused or neglected, as well as a determination as to the identity of the perpetrator, who typically is listed on a central registry. A CPS investigation bears some similarity to a police investigation, and in some jurisdictions police investigators actually carry out CPS investigations, or accompany CPS investigators, on at least some cases.

There are good reasons for the investigative orientation of the traditional CPS response. In the highest-risk cases, in which a child is at risk of serious injury or harm by a caregiver, a quick and authoritative response is necessary. And contacts with the alleged perpetrator necessarily will be adversarial. Many of these cases, after all, will result in court involvement, involuntary removal of the child, and possibly criminal charges against the perpetrator.

Differential response allows for an alternative, more assessment-oriented response to lower-risk cases. Consider a 9-year-old child who is missing school because she is being kept home to help care for her 4-year-old brother when her mother is not feeling well. A case of this kind is often screened-in by CPS but arguably does not need a heavy-handed and adversarial response, which might only serve to alienate the family. Rather, it could benefit from a less threatening and more assessment-oriented response that asks parents how they are doing and what services might help them better meet their children's needs.

In a lower-risk case like this, the challenge is not so much to determine whether the child is missing school, but rather why it is happening and what might be done to remedy the situation. In such a case, removal of the child, or long-term involvement with CPS, is unlikely. Rather, the most that is likely to be offered is short-term services by CPS or a referral for services from another provider in the community. For this reason, engaging with the family in a constructive way and enlisting the help and resources of community partners or informal helping networks is crucial. Not to engage in this way is to miss an opportunity for prevention, as cases such as this may deteriorate and return with more serious problems if initial referrals are not responded to appropriately. Yet if approached in a low-key and nonthreatening way, many low-risk families may be willing to accept help on a voluntary basis.

Clearly, moving to a differential response system poses many challenges. There is the challenge of distinguishing which cases need a traditional investigation versus which ones could safely benefit from a more assessment-oriented response. A case that at the time of the report appears to be just a benign instance of a child missing school from time to time may actually involve serious maltreatment (and a case that initially presents as serious and criminal abuse may not be so serious after all). Agencies that use a differential response approach must have a very good system for distinguishing high-risk and low-risk cases and a fail-safe system for transferring cases between the two tracks should the need arise (if a high-risk case was inappropriately placed on the assessment track, or vice versa).

A differential response system must have the capacity to deliver both types of response—a police-oriented investigation that determines whether a child has been abused or neglected, and by whom, and that can take immediate steps to assure his or her protection, as well as a service-oriented assessment that engages families and identifies service needs and that has the capacity to meet those needs. Thus, a differential response system must have, in addition to trained investigators, workers who know how to engage families. It must also have links with community-based partners and informal helping networks, links that traditional CPS agencies have not typically had. With limited resources and the need to give priority to investigative and protective activities, CPS agencies cannot provide long-term services to low-risk families. The involvement of other partners, not traditionally involved with CPS, is crucial. So too is the capacity to engage families and to work with them to make lasting changes. If children are going to be protected in the long term, families and communities will have to take the lead role.

HOW WIDELY HAS DIFFERENTIAL RESPONSE BEEN ADOPTED?

Florida and Missouri were the first states to experiment with differential response, starting in 1993 and 1994, respectively (Waldfogel, 1998a, 1998b). Florida's initial differential response program was relatively short-lived, as subsequent reforms (pursuant to a privatization initiative as well as a renewed emphasis on police-oriented investigations) ended that program in 1998 (although the state is now beginning a new differential response initiative; see Merkel-Holguin et al., 2006). Missouri's reforms, after being piloted and closely evaluated, were subsequently extended statewide, serving as a model for other states to follow.

By 2003 a national study conducted by Walter R. McDonald and Associates for the federal Department of Health and Human Services identified 20 states that were offering an alternative response at intake in at least some jurisdictions, with an alternative response defined as "a formal response of [the] agency that assesses the needs of the child or family without requiring a determination that maltreatment has occurred or that the child is at risk of maltreatment" (U.S. Department of Health and Human Services, 2003b, p. 5-1). (Note that this definition is different from the definition of differential response that I use here, and that Merkel-Holguin et al., 2006, use in their study—that is, two or more discrete responses to screened-in CPS reports, based on the level of risk in the case, and with the assessment-oriented response providing services to families on a voluntary basis and without perpetrators and victims being listed on a central registry). Subsequent to the review, several other states began experimenting with alternative response or differential response systems. North Carolina began a pilot in 2002, which was implemented statewide in 2006; also as of 2006, California, Connecticut, Maryland, Wisconsin, and New Jersey also had at least some counties experimenting with alternative or differential response (Waldfogel, 2008).

The alternative responses in the 20 states included in the national study had in common that they were intended for lower-risk families and designed to be more assessment- and service-oriented and less threatening and intimidating to families (U.S. Department of Health and Human Services, 2003c). However, in the states that offered multiple tracks, it was not always clear just how different the assessment and investigation tracks were in practice (U.S. Department of Health and Human Services, 2003a, 2003c). In many jurisdictions, the same workers carried out both assessments and investigations and some reported that many of their activities were similar regardless of the track. The main difference seemed to be that the workers had more discretion when carrying out an assessment; that is, the list of activities that they had to carry out was shorter, consisting mainly of having to review prior CPS records, interviewing or observing the children, interviewing the caregivers, and consulting with involved professionals as needed. In addition, as noted earlier, the overall goal of the alternative response was different, focused less on whether maltreatment had occurred and who had committed it, and more on what services might be necessary. In line with this approach, families receiving an alternative response were less likely to be listed on a central registry tracking victims and perpetrators of child abuse and neglect than families who had been investigated.

Agencies that had implemented an alternative response also commented on the challenges they faced and the need they saw to improve their systems (U.S. Department of Health and Human Services, 2003c). Several of the challenges they mentioned resonate with those identified earlier: the need to establish mechanisms to move cases from one track to another if necessary, to better integrate CPS services with community-based services, and to train workers in how to engage families. Other challenges were unexpected: the need to review workloads and to establish specific and limited goals for intervention. Agencies also pointed to the specific challenge posed by domestic violence cases, which required attention to both family needs and safety and thus did not fit neatly into either the standard investigative or assessment model.

A later national study, carried out jointly by the American Humane Association and the Child Welfare League of America, documented differential response reforms in 15 states (Alaska; Florida; Hawaii; Kentucky; Louisiana; Minnesota; Missouri; North Carolina; Oklahoma; Pennsylvania; Tennessee; Virginia; Washington; West Virginia; Wyoming; and Washoe County, Nevada) (Merkel-Holguin et al., 2006). Several other states were identified that had defunct differential response reforms (Arizona, Delaware, and Texas) or other reforms that provided some form of alternative response (California, Iowa, Massachusetts, Michigan, New Jersey, New Mexico, North Dakota, South Dakota, Wisconsin, and Westchester County, New York) not meeting their definition of differential response (i.e., two or more discrete responses to screened-in CPS reports, based on the level of risk in the case, and with the assessment-oriented response providing services to families on a voluntary basis and without perpetrators and victims being listed on a central registry).

EVALUATION OF THE IMPACT OF DIFFERENTIAL RESPONSE

Evaluations conducted in several states provide some information about the impact of differential response to date (see overviews in Merkel-Holguin et al., 2006; Waldfogel, 2008). Missouri, one of the earliest adopters, has been most extensively studied. The initial stage of Missouri's reform, begun in 1994, had a quasi-experimental design, with the reform implemented in 14 small and medium-sized counties across the state, as well as in selected zip codes in St. Louis County and the city of St. Louis, and then evaluated against a control group drawn from similar areas (from around the state, St. Louis County, and the city of St. Louis). The evaluation of the initial pilot (Siegel & Loman, 2000) found that child safety was as good or better in the reform areas, that recurrence of abuse/neglect reports was lower, and that families received services sooner, were more cooperative, and were more satisfied. The findings on child safety—in particular, the lower recurrence rate of reports—were echoed in the findings of an evaluation of community partnerships for child protection, which also found reductions in repeat reports in their Missouri site (St. Louis) (Daro, Budde, Baker, Nesmith, & Harden, 2005). However, the magnitude of the effects was relatively modest, a finding that the evaluators attributed to high caseloads and limited resources to fund services for low-risk families. The Missouri legislature stipulated that the reform had to be cost-neutral and did not allocate any new funding for additional caseworkers, nor did it fund additional services for families on the assessment track, instead counting on community-based agencies to provide these.

A 5-year follow-up (Loman & Siegel, 2004a) found that re-report rates for families in the reform areas continued to be lower 5 years' postreferral. However, the 5-year follow-up also found that out-of-home placement rates were slightly higher for families in the reform areas, a finding that seemed to be linked to a lack of services for low-risk families, in particular those with teenagers. A later follow-up (Loman, 2005) found that cases investigated in reform areas were more likely to have a perpetrator arrested for severe physical or sexual abuse than cases investigated in the nonreform areas, confirming the prediction that reserving an investigative response for high-risk cases would lead to a more intensive response to those cases.

In 1998 differential response in Missouri was converted from a pilot into a statewide policy, and by 1999 it had been implemented in every county in the state. An evaluation using data up to 2002 (Loman & Siegel, 2004a) found varied opinions among staff members about the new approach; some endorsed the underlying philosophy and felt that families were better served, whereas others did not agree with or understand the rationale or saw other challenges to implementing the new approach.

North Carolina is another state whose differential response reform has been extensively studied. Begun as a pilot demonstration in 2002 in 10 counties, North Carolina's multiple-response system was expanded to an additional 42 counties in 2003 and implemented statewide (to the remaining 48 counties) in January 2006. North Carolina's reform is a system-wide effort to make practice more family-responsive, and the differential response at intake is only one component of a wider set of reforms. A quasi-experimental evaluation compared outcomes for families in the original pilot counties to outcomes for families in matched comparison counties not involved in the original pilot, and also gathered data from families and workers in the pilot counties using interviews, surveys, and focus groups (Center for Child and Family Policy, 2004). This evaluation found that the multiple-response system reform led to better coordination and communication across agencies and was viewed positively by both family members and workers, without any difference in re-report rates between pilot and control counties. Pilot county families did receive more services.

Only one state—Minnesota—has evaluated differential response using an experimental, random-assignment design (see Loman & Siegel, 2004b, 2005, 2006). Minnesota began its experiment with differential response in 2001 by randomly assigning families who had been determined eligible for an alternative response to receive either an alternative response or a traditional investigative response. Because of the random assignment, families who were assessed were comparable to those who were investigated in terms of their level of risk at referral and, presumably, their risk of recurrence.

The results as of 2004 indicated that families randomly assigned to the alternative response received more services and were less likely to have a repeat report and less likely to have a child placed in care than similar families randomly assigned to the investigative track (Loman & Siegel, 2004b, 2005). A process study (that included families in the experimental study as well as some families who had received the alternative response in nonexperimental counties) found that both families and workers liked the assessment approach better, and families were more likely to say that they had been involved in decision making and had benefited from their involvement with CPS (Loman & Siegel, 2004b). In addition, although handling a case on the assessment track cost more money in the short run (because of increased worker time and services costs), it saved money in the long run, owing to the reduction in subsequent costs associated with the lower recurrence rates (Loman & Siegel, 2005). An extended follow-up, conducted in 2006, confirmed this overall pattern of results (Loman & Siegel, 2006).

Does Differential Response Increase Families' Engagement with Services?

If differential response is to enhance community prevention of maltreatment, a key question is whether it is able to increase families' engagement with services. In thinking about this question, it is important to recall that there are a range of differential response models in place. In some models, there is a very sharp distinction between an investigative response and an alternative assessment-oriented response, but in other instances, the distinction is fuzzier. For example, in a qualitative study carried out by the Urban Institute, drawing on interviews with workers and families about their perceptions of the two tracks in Kentucky and Oklahoma, a striking finding was that community workers and family members often did not know which track the family had been served on at CPS (Zielewski, Macomber, Bess, & Murray, 2006). In particular, although family members agreed in principle with the idea that families would respond better to a less coercive response, those who themselves had received an alternative response did not know that. Other material on Kentucky and Oklahoma confirms the impression that the reforms in those states did not, at least in the initial years, lead to a sharp distinction between the traditional investigative response and the new assessment response (Merkel-Holguin et al., 2006). And even when there is a sharp distinction between the investigative and assessment response, workers may need additional training in engaging families in order for families to experience the encounter more favorably (see, e.g., Merkel-Holguin et al., 2006; State of Washington Department of Social and Health Services, 2005; Virginia Department of Social Services, 2004).

But other studies provide a more positive view, supporting the conclusion that "parents are much more likely to engage in services" if they received a differential response (Schene, 2005, p. 7). In particular, the random assignment evaluation (and accompanying process study) in Minnesota provides a number of indications that families were more engaged (Loman & Siegel, 2005). The process study found that workers delivering an alternative response reported the caregiver was uncooperative at initial contact only 2% of the time, as compared with 44% of the time in control group cases. Families receiving an alternative response were more likely to report being very satisfied with the way they were treated by workers (58 vs. 45%), more likely to describe the worker as very friendly (53 vs. 41%), and more likely to say they were involved a great deal in decisions about their children (68 vs. 45%). They were also more likely to report being relieved, hopeful, satisfied, helped, pleased, reassured, and encouraged, and less likely to report being angry, afraid, irritated, worried, negative, pessimistic, or discouraged. The alternative response also did a better job of engaging spouses: Among married couples, the share saying the spouse had been present during the assessment was 82% in the alternative response group versus 65% in the traditional investigation group.

The quasi-experimental study in Missouri—comparing reform to non-reform areas—found that families receiving an alternative response were less likely to be rated as noncooperative than those receiving a traditional response (14 vs. 28%) and were less likely to flee (9 vs. 12%) (Siegel & Loman, 2000). They were also more likely to say they were satisfied with how their case was handled and that they had a great deal of involvement in decisions that affected them and their children.

Evidence from North Carolina also is indicative of a positive response from workers and family members (Center for Child and Family Policy, 2004, 2006). Families in the pilot counties reported very high levels of satisfaction with the way the worker had treated them and with the help they received; they also reported very high levels of participation in decisions involving their children and families. Focus groups with workers confirmed that they felt they were approaching families in a more family-centered way and finding families more open and less resistant to their intervention.

Does Differential Response Increase the Availability and Receipt of Services for Lower-Risk Families?

If differential response is to contribute to community prevention of maltreatment, a second key question is whether it increases the availability and receipt of services for lower-risk families. A perhaps obvious, but important, point is that providing services to more low-risk families, whether this is to be done by CPS agencies themselves or by community-based agencies, has resource implications. For differential response to succeed in increasing families' receipt of services, communications between CPS and service providers need to be strengthened and more services must be available for low-risk families (Schene, 2001).

DePanfilis (2004) likens the CPS system to a funnel. Of every 100 cases that enter the funnel, on average 33 are screened out. In a traditional CPS system, of the 67 that are screened in, 47 are unsubstantiated (and often receive no further services), 8 are substantiated but receive no further services, and only 12 of the original 100 remain open for services. Under a differential response model, many more cases could potentially be referred for services. If all low-risk screened-in families needed services and decided to take up the offer of services, an additional 55 families would be in the service pipeline (the 47 who otherwise would have been unsubstantiated and the 8 who would have been substantiated and closed). Even if only a quarter of these families ended up receiving services, they would constitute a larger group than the group receiving services currently.

Yet, often differential response reforms focus mainly on the provision of the initial response and little, if at all, on how services for the families are to be obtained. Most implementation of differential response has been cost-neutral, meaning that few dollars can be devoted to long-term services. The Urban Institute's study of Kentucky and Oklahoma, for example, found that for the most part, the differential response systems in those two states relied on existing service networks and providers, which in some instances were adequate, but in others were not (Zielewski et al., 2006). States such as Virginia have also identified the lack of sufficient funding for services as a challenge (Merkel-Holguin et al., 2006; Virginia Department of Social Services, 2004).

Minnesota is exceptional in that the state obtained funding from the McKnight Foundation, which allowed it to expand service provision to low-risk families. The experimental evaluation and accompanying process study found that not only were families more engaged (as detailed earlier), but also that families received more services (Loman & Siegel, 2004b, 2005, 2006). Families receiving the alternative response were more likely to have their cases opened for services (36 vs. 15%). In addition to being more likely to receive the types of services traditionally prescribed by CPS (services such as counseling), families in the alternative response group were also more likely to receive less traditional services. According to worker reports, these families were more likely to receive employment assistance, vocational training, transportation, Temporary Assistance to Needy Families and food stamps, emergency food assistance, housing, rent payments, and childcare assistance. Family member reports reinforced this view, indicating that families that were provided an alternative response were more likely to receive food and clothing; help with utilities, appliances, and furniture; home repair; financial help; counseling for a child; respite care; and help with employment and job searches. Alternative response families received more services, not just from CPS and providers paid by CPS, but also from unpaid community resources such as emergency food providers, mental health providers, support groups, recreational facilities, youth organizations, childcare providers, schools, and employment and training providers.

In addition, the Minnesota evaluation and process study found that families receiving the alternative response were more positive about the services they received (Logan & Siegel, 2004b, 2005). Alternative response group families were more likely to say the services they received were what they needed (48 vs. 33%) and more likely to say they received enough services to be really helpful (44 vs. 27%). At the 1-year follow-up these families reported lower levels of financial stress or stress associated with relationships with other adults, as well as lower levels of drug abuse problems and domestic violence (Logan & Siegel, 2004b). However, impacts on other outcomes for the children and families were few. In particular, the evaluation found no consistent differences between the alternative response and control groups on measures of child well-being such as child health, behavior, and school achievement, or on measures of parenting such as parents' reports of their relationships with their children, their use of discipline, and their ability to care for their children (Logan & Siegel, 2005).

We do not know which of the Minnesota results would have occurred in the absence of the additional funding. Most states implementing differential response have not had access to the kinds of resources that Minnesota had. And the reforms in those other states have not been subject to a random assignment evaluation.

The quasi-experimental study in Missouri—that compared reform areas to nonreform areas—found that families in the reform areas received services more quickly than families in the nonreform areas and also received more services; as in Minnesota, the most pronounced difference concerned services having to do with basic necessities such as food, clothing, shelter, and medical care (Siegel & Loman, 2000). Also like the findings for Minnesota, the evidence from Missouri indicated that the reform was associated with increased receipt of services from community providers, most of whom were not paid by CPS. The evaluators attributed this to greater knowledge on the part of workers in the reform areas as to what resources were available, as well as to improved communication between the CPS workers and community-based agencies (Siegel & Loman, 2000). This latter result is encouraging, given that the Missouri reform was explicitly cost-neutral and therefore did not benefit from the infusion of funds that Minnesota's reform did.

In North Carolina too, evaluators found that families in the reform counties received services more quickly than in comparable nonreform counties and that this front-loading of services reduced the likelihood of children reentering CPS over the next 6 months (Center for Child and Family Policy, 2006). Parents in the reform counties said in focus groups that the services they received helped improve their parenting skills and their knowledge about community resources (Center for Child and Family Policy, 2006).

CONCLUSION: WHAT ROLE MIGHT DIFFERENTIAL RESPONSE PLAY IN PREVENTING FUTURE MALTREATMENT?

In the long term, we would like to know if differential response is effective in preventing future maltreatment among families provided an alternative response, among families provided an investigative response, and among families in the community more generally. However, the evaluations to date, although promising, cannot definitively answer these questions. As discussed earlier, there is mounting evidence from several states that providing an alternative response to lower-risk families may lower the risk of recurrence for those families. There is also some evidence from Missouri that reserving the investigative response to the highest-risk cases results in more criminal prosecutions in those cases. And the results regarding the impact of differential response on family engagement and service provision are promising. But we do not yet know the extent to which services in the community are changing. For instance, we do not yet know whether differential response is increasing the willingness of reporters, community members, and family members to cooperate with CPS or increasing the supply of services for families.

A decade ago differential response was a new approach that had been implemented in just two pilot states, Florida and Missouri. Today it is becoming a more widely accepted form of CPS practice. Only 13 states at this point have *not* experimented with differential response, alternative response, or something similar (Table 8.1). Is differential response making a difference for families? Are families who are offered an alternative response faring better than they would have under a more investigation-oriented system—that is, are children better protected and are children and families more engaged and more likely to receive services they need? The evidence thus far suggests that the answer may well be yes. To the extent that child safety and repeat maltreatment can be measured, children seem to be as well, or better, off on these indicators under differential response. And families seem to be more engaged, receiving more services, and more satisfied with them.

But the evidence also points to challenges. Differential response is not a panacea. Even with a more assessment-oriented response for the lower-risk cases, the challenges of working with families referred to CPS remain—

TABLE 8.1. Diffusion of Differential Response Reforms

State	DR	Defunct DR	AR	Other	New	No DR or AR
Alabama						No
Alaska	DR		AR			
Arizona		[DR]	AR			
Arkansas						No
California				Other		
Colorado						No
Connecticut					New	
Delaware		[DR]				
Florida	DR					
Georgia			AR			
Hawaii	DR					
Idaho			AR			
Illinois						No
Indiana						No
Iowa				Other		
Kansas			AR			
Kentucky	DR		AR			
Louisiana	DR		AR			
Maine			AR			
Maryland					New	
Massachusetts				Other		
Michigan				Other		
Minnesota	DR		AR			
Mississippi						No
Missouri	DR		AR			
Montana						No
Nebraska						No

TABLE 8.1. (continued)

State	DR	Defunct DR	AR	Other	New	No DR or AR
Nevada	DR		AR			
New Hampshire						No
New Jersey				Other		
New Mexico				Other		
New York				Other		
North Carolina	DR					
North Dakota				Other		
Ohio						No
Oklahoma	DR		AR			
Oregon						No
Pennsylvania	DR		AR			
Rhode Island						No
South Carolina						No
South Dakota			AR	Other		
Tennessee	DR					
Texas		[DR]				
Utah			AR			
Vermont			AR			
Virginia	DR		AR			
Washington	DR		AR			
West Virginia	DR		AR			
Wisconsin				Other		
Wyoming	DR		AR			
Total	15	3	20	9	2	13

Note. States can appear in more than one category. DR indicates the state was coded as differential response by Merkel-Holguin et al. (2006); [DR] indicates the state was coded as defunct differential response by Merkel-Holguin et al. (2006); AR indicates the state was coded as alternative response by the U.S. Department of Health and Human Services (2003a); Other indicates the state was coded as other innovative child welfare reform by Merkel-Holguin et al. (2006). New indicates the state was not coded DR or AR by other sources but was coded as experimenting with alternative or differential response by Waldfogel (2008); No indicates state was not coded as DR, [DR], AR, New, or Other by any of the given sources.

engaging families and connecting them to services while assessing risk and walking that fine line between protecting children and preserving families. Differential response requires well-trained staff, good relations with community-based agencies, and adequate funding for services for low-risk as well as higher-risk families. But even with these challenges, the evidence suggests that differential response may offer an improved response for lower-risk families without jeopardizing children's safety in either low- or higher-risk cases. If so, then differential response should contribute to community prevention of maltreatment, at least for those families coming to the attention of CPS. ·

REFERENCES

Center for Child and Family Policy. (2004). *Multiple Response System (MRS) evaluation report to the North Carolina Division of Social Services (NCDSS).* Durham, NC: Duke University, Center for Child and Family Policy.

Center for Child and Family Policy. (2006). *Multiple Response System (MRS) evaluation report to the North Carolina Division of Social Services (NCDSS).* Durham, NC: Duke University, Center for Child and Family Policy.

Daro, D., Budde, S., Baker, S., Nesmith, A., & Harden, A. (2005). *Community partnerships for protecting children: Phase II. Outcome evaluation. Final Report.* Chicago, IL: Chapin Hall Center for Children, University of Chicago.

DePanfilis, D. (2004). *Testimony before the Subcommittee on Human Resources of the House Committee on Ways and Means.* Unpublished manuscript.

Loman, L. A. (2005). *Differential response improves traditional investigations: Criminal arrests for severe physical and sexual abuse.* St. Louis, MO: Institute of Applied Research. Retrieved September 18, 2007, from *www.iarstl.org.*

Loman, L. A., & Siegel, G. L. (2004a). *Differential response in Missouri after five years: Final report.* St. Louis, MO: Institute of Applied Research. Retrieved July 24, 2006, from *www.iarstl.org.*

Loman, L. A., & Siegel, G. L. (2004b). *Minnesota alternative response evaluation: Final report.* St. Louis, MO: Institute of Applied Research. Retrieved July 24, 2006, from *www.iarstl.org.*

Loman, L. A., & Siegel, G. L. (2005). Alternative response in Minnesota: Findings of the program evaluation. *Protecting Children, 20*(2–3), 79–92.

Loman, L. A., & Siegel, G. L. (2006). *Extended follow-up study of Minnesota's Family Assessment Response: Final report.* St. Louis, MO: Institute of Applied Research. Retrieved September 18, 2007, from *www.iastl.org.*

Merkel-Holguin, L., Kaplan, C., & Kwak, A. (2006). *National study on differential response in child welfare.* Washington, DC: American Humane Association and Child Welfare League of America.

Schene, P. (2001). Making differential response work: Lessons learned. *Best Practice/Next Practice, 2*(1), 15–19.

Schene, P. (2005). The emergence of differential response. *Protecting Children, 20*(2/3), 4–7.

Siegel, G. L., & Loman, L. A. (2000). *The Missouri Family Assessment and Response Demonstration Impact Evaluation: Digest of findings and conclusions.* St. Louis, MO: Institute of Applied Research. Retrieved July 24, 2006, from *www.iarstl.org.*

State of Washington Department of Social and Health Services. (2005). *Alternative Response Systems Program: Progress report, July 1, 2003–June 30, 2004.*

Retrieved September 11, 2007, from *www.americanhumane.org/site/Doc-Server/AltResponseReport_WA.pdf?docID=4523*.

U.S. Department of Health and Human Services. (2003a). *National study of child protective services systems and reform efforts: Findings on local CPS practices.* Retrieved June 6, 2006, from *aspe.hhs.gov/cps-status03*.   ˋ

U.S. Department of Health and Human Services. (2003b). *National study of child protective services systems and reform efforts: Review of state CPS policy.* Retrieved June 6, 2006, from *aspe.hhs.gov/cps-status03*.

U.S. Department of Health and Human Services. (2003c). *National study of child protective services systems and reform efforts: A summary report.* Retrieved June 6, 2006, from *aspe.hhs.gov/cps-status03*.

Virginia Department of Social Services. (2004). *Evaluation of the differential response system.* Retrieved July 26, 2006, from *www.dss.state.va.us/files/division/dfs/cps/reports/eval_drs.pdf*.

Waldfogel, J. (1998a). *The future of child protection: How to break the cycle of abuse and neglect.* Cambridge, MA: Harvard University Press.

Waldfogel, J. (1998b). Rethinking the paradigm for child protection. *The Future of Children, 8*(1), 104–120.

Waldfogel, J. (2008). The future of child protection revisited. In D. Lindsey & A. Shlonsky (Eds.), *Child welfare research: Advances for practice and policy* (pp. 235–241). Oxford, UK: Oxford University Press.

Zielewski, E., Macomber, J., Bess, R., & Murray, J. (2006). *Families' connections to services in an alternative response system.* Washington, DC: Urban Institute.

CHAPTER 9

Innovations in Child Maltreatment Prevention

Resolving the Tension between Effective Assistance and Violations of Privacy

Doriane Lambelet Coleman

Many promising innovations in child maltreatment prevention contemplate direct interventions in the lives of children and their families. To the extent that agents and agencies of the government would be involved in such initiatives, it is important to consider whether they implicate constitutional rights of privacy, and if so, how these rights might be accommodated without sacrificing reductions in the incidence of child maltreatment. In any event, because privacy is both a strong cultural value and an important component of children's healthy development and families' well-being, it is essential that even nongovernmental initiatives designed to reduce the incidence of child maltreatment reflect a real (as opposed to a merely rhetorical) respect for this principle. Often, efforts to build relationships between families and their communities are operating against the cultural and political grain that privileges individual and family privacy and that correspondingly finds intrusive even well-meaning efforts to "meddle in family business." Innovative programs that fail to respect individual and family privacy run the risk of violating constitutional rights and of losing (or never establishing) families' cooperation.

This chapter develops these ideas and suggests that the success of innovations involving prophylactic interventions in the lives of children and families is tied in part to the inclusion of strategies designed to secure the "buy-in" and consent of target individuals and communities. Both practically and metaphorically, success depends on whether families are willing to open their doors and then to engage the interventions. Throughout, the chapter is specifically attentive to the fact that the maltreatment problem historically has been addressed differently by different disciplines, including in the definition of the problem itself and in the conception of the proper bounds of outsider intervention in the family. And it takes the position that a multidisciplinary approach is ultimately necessary to its resolution.

INNOVATIONS IN CHILD MALTREATMENT PREVENTION INVOLVING DIRECT INTERVENTIONS IN THE LIVES OF CHILDREN AND FAMILIES

In addition to educational measures and community outreach programs, innovations in child maltreatment prevention most frequently contemplate direct intervention by relevant professionals in the lives of at-risk children and families. On the basis of the view that this focus has been insufficiently effective, some recent initiatives reflect a universal public health approach, contemplating either direct intervention in the lives of all children and families within a community or voluntary universal access.

Examples of such initiatives include the State of North Carolina's school-based child and family support teams, each of which includes a school nurse and school social worker whose job it is to "coordinate services among education, health and social service agencies" so that individual at-risk "children receive the help they need so they can focus on learning," and the Durham Family Initiative's plan to send nurses to visit the homes of all new parents in Durham County to celebrate the birth of their children and to provide education and services relevant to increasing the likelihood of child well-being and minimizing the incidence of child maltreatment (Dodge, Murphy, O'Donnell, & Christopoulos, Chapter 4, this volume; Easley, 2006).

By definition, efforts designed to prevent child maltreatment involve addressing the causes of the problem at either or both its macro and micro levels before maltreatment (ever or again) occurs. Although direct intervention in the lives of children and families is first and foremost a tool for those who work to investigate allegations of maltreatment and to address its effects in substantiated cases, it is also potentially powerful as a tool for those who work to prevent it. For example, to the extent that stress and a lack of relevant education and services contribute to causing maltreatment, one-on-one assistance from an effective professional with relevant resources may make a real difference. Incidentally, including direct intervention in the lives of children and families as part of the project to increase child well-being also provides an opportunity for the development of information about the likelihood that particular children are either at risk for or victims of maltreatment, and thus a better opportunity to protect those children from future harm.

Historical perspectives and practice are insufficient standing alone as a justification for present policy. This is particularly true where the relevant perspectives and practice have been largely discredited on the grounds that they reflected stereotypical views about the capacities, inadequacies, and tendencies of certain minority subgroups within society. For example, the practice in the late 1800s of effecting the permanent removal of poor, southern European immigrant children from their parents and families based on the belief that these families lacked virtue and the necessary work ethic to raise successful American children, has been discredited, as has the practice that existed through at least the mid-1900s of doing the same to Native American children because of the view that their culture, language, housekeeping, and childrearing practices were both inconsistent with raising children who could eventually assimilate into mainstream American society and inherently harmful to their health and welfare (Hong, 2003).

Nevertheless, it is important to recognize that the social work community has a long history of thinking about itself as engaged in the business of "child saving" and particularly about its prophylactic interventions in the lives of children and families as "helping." Indeed, efforts to "broaden the scope of [the] definition" of maltreatment within some disciplines was seen as "a means of expanding the arena where [this] help can be given" (Giovannoni & Becerra, 1979, p. 70). As one commentator explained early in the 20th century, where the legal definition of maltreatment would disallow particular helping interventions, child protective services nevertheless "has a duty toward the children whose circumstances are, each week that the family is left to itself, becoming worse, but which are not yet so bad that court action is advisable or possible. ... It must avail itself of every reasonable opportunity to reconstruct such families as are moving on to inevitable shipwreck" (Giovannoni & Becera, 1979, pp. 68–69).

THE PRIVACY IMPLICATIONS OF PROPHYLACTIC INITIATIVES INVOLVING DIRECT INTERVENTION IN THE LIVES OF CHILDREN AND FAMILIES

Whether or not they are intended and implemented in this self-described tradition of "helping," innovations in child maltreatment prevention involving direct intervention in the lives of children and families necessarily implicate privacy concerns. That is, regardless of the good intentions of those who would intervene, where they are successful, they will necessarily breach the physical, psychological, and political boundaries that ordinarily exist between the family and outsiders, and between the individual and others. (Families understand this intuitively, just as they understand that those who would come to help them can also cause enormous disruptions.) From this perspective, preventive interventions in the lives of children and families are possibly different only in degree from interventions resulting from reports of maltreatment or those that are part of family reunification efforts following substantiated maltreatment.

For example, in pairing a school nurse with a social worker to reach out to high-risk families, North Carolina's school-based child and family support teams recognize the fact that children are more likely to succeed in school and thus in life if they are healthy, both physically and emotionally. Treating only the child's most immediate physical needs is insufficient if overall well-being is the goal. At the same time—and this was certainly not lost on those who conceived the program—it capitalizes on the physical separation of the children from their parents, providing an opportunity for the state to identify the possibility of maltreatment, something that it could not otherwise accomplish systematically, that is, in the absence of a report of maltreatment. As a result, this program is simultaneously well intentioned, relevant, and potentially invasive.

School-based programs like this one are invasive in that they require the state to breach the boundaries of the child's physical and psychological privacy. The extent of the intrusion, and thus of its potential implications for the child emotionally and for the state legally, depends on the nature of the investigation. A cursory physical examination not involving a strip search or genital examination will obviously be less intrusive, and thus less problematic, than one that includes such scrutiny. So too, open-ended questions designed to elucidate the child's sense of well-being within the boundaries of his or her own comfort level will be less intrusive, and thus less problematic, than questions directed at particular parenting practices (Coleman, 2005, pp. 518–521).

There is no indication that North Carolina's program affords its nurse-social worker teams the discretion to conduct examinations and interviews of the most invasive sorts just described. Indeed, all indications are to the contrary. For example, consistent with the state's commitment to a multiple-response approach to triaging child protection cases, the program strongly encourages the nurse-social worker team's prompt establishment of a relationship with the target child's parents to maximize the likelihood that any assistance offered will be helpful both to the child and to the family. Moreover, formal team training emphasizes the program's intention that any suspicions of maltreatment be referred to child protective services and that once maltreatment is suspected, even the most cursory investigations designed to develop evidence about maltreatment be conducted exclusively by that agency. Although certain permitted lines of inquiry potentially tread on investigatory grounds—questions about sleeping arrangements and food are illustrative in this regard—compliance with the program's requirements will generally minimize its intrusiveness (J. Rosch, personal communication, 2008).

Nevertheless, particularly invasive examinations and interviews are discussed here to make clear that invasiveness occurs along a continuum, with resulting harms and liability tracking that continuum, and because strip searches, genital examinations, and probing personal interviews have been conducted as part of well-child examinations at school. In other words, they are by no means unheard of, and well-intentioned policymakers have sought (thus far unsuccessfully) to defend their inclusion in analogous programs. For example, in 2003, the United States Court of Appeals for the Tenth Circuit ruled against one such program established in the state of Washington. The program required that children enrolled in the state's Head Start program who had not had private pediatric examinations receive complete physicals, including genital examinations, at school. The children were examined on desks in an open classroom designated for this purpose. Their parents were not given the opportunity either to consent or to deny consent to the procedure, and they were not present when the examinations took place. The court ruled that the examinations were unconstitutional violations of both the children's Fourth Amendment right to privacy and their parents' autonomy rights (*Dubbs v. Head Start, Inc.*, 2003).

Like North Carolina's child and family support teams, the Durham Family Initiative's plan to send a nurse to visit the homes of all new parents in Durham County is a very thoughtful approach to the prevention of stress- and education-related maltreatment. Indeed, to the extent that the child and family support teams are school-based, home-based programs like this one might be viewed as complementary: Prospective and new parents are interviewed and their residential environments evaluated with the goal of ensuring (to the extent possible) that those parents and environments are safe and healthy ones for the children. And to the extent that there is a basis for concern, the program endeavors to provide the necessary support and services, for either or both the children and their parents. Undoubtedly, there are instances in which a home visit in this program results in the suspicion or discovery that a child is at risk of maltreatment and thus possibly a referral to child protective services. Because of this possibility, this program, like the school-based child and family support teams, is relevant, well intentioned, and invasive.

In this instance, however, the intrusion (at least initially) involves the adults' privacy interests in the sanctity of their homes, their lifestyles, and their personal histories. These interests are powerful. As I have written elsewhere,

> Although it is no longer true—if it ever was—that a family's home is a castle, it is true that in law and culture, the personal residence is expected to be the individual's principal private sanctuary. Indeed, the law allows even the criminal to retreat into his home carrying with him the knowledge that the government generally may not enter without a particularized warrant and probable cause. Thus, what is in the family's refrigerator, closets, drawers, or even in plain view, is usually subject to its individual members' most reasonable and highest expectations of privacy. (Coleman, 2005, pp. 511–512)

A similar continuum of invasiveness exists for these privacy interests, so that the deeper the home visitor pries physically and/or historically and psychologically, the more problematic the intrusion may be. For example, although both looking into a refrigerator and looking into a diary—or asking questions during an interview that are designed to arrive at the same ends—are troublesome in terms of privacy, the latter is likely to be considered particularly invasive in relation to the former.

Whenever child maltreatment prevention efforts risk intruding on privacy in the ways just described, it is important to consider how the program can accommodate the implicated interests without sacrificing reductions in the incidence of maltreatment. Before this point is considered further, however, it is important to address the views, shared by many in the child welfare community, that privacy does more harm than good where maltreatment is concerned (Coleman, 2005, pp. 415–416) and that individual and family privacy are less meaningful (and thus do not merit serious consideration) in families that are already subject to government oversight—for example, families that receive financial assistance on the condition that they permit caseworkers to monitor their expenditures.

Proponents of low legal barriers to entry into the family have often taken the position that "family privacy is a bad thing ... [which] only protects fringe and abusive parents from the scrutiny they properly deserve; here, mainstream and innocent parents have no stake in family privacy" (Coleman, 2005, p. 536). Even those who would ordinarily reject this view—because they accept that privacy "is valued in general for reasons that have absolutely nothing to do with ... hiding personal flaws and dirty laundry" (Coleman, 2005, p. 536)—may be uncomfortable privileging privacy over intervention in the family at times when the maltreatment problem is considered acute or in circumstances where it appears that more careful efforts have failed to yield the desired results. In other words, just as some people are willing to sacrifice aspects of privacy to secure victory in "the war on terror," so too some are willing to sacrifice aspects of privacy to secure victory in the "war on maltreatment." Particularly vulnerable in this context are the children's own privacy interests, because children may not be thought to have much in the way of privacy interests in any event, and because violating whatever measure of privacy they do have is perceived to be justified under the circumstances. Indeed, in this respect, children's interests are often perceived to be aligned with the interests of those who would investigate them (rather than with their parents') either because they are in fact at risk of maltreatment or because it is believed that "they have a group-based stake" in an all-out assault on the problem" (Coleman, 2005, p. 536).

The view that respect for privacy is less important where the government is already involved in the family is also prevalent. The notion here is that the individuals in such families are accustomed to precisely the sorts of intrusions that would cause others to bristle, so that further intrusions (even if these are based in an unrelated program) are less likely to be perceived by their targets as problematic. One might even imagine that it is possible to delve more deeply into the privacy of these individuals—and thus come to know them and their needs better—because they are so anesthetized. The fact that they are more likely, as a statistical matter, to be involved in maltreatment adds to this sense and to the related sense that their privacy interests are somehow less deserving of protection.

Although these views certainly can be defended, ignoring or at least depreciating privacy is ultimately unhelpful to the child welfare community and to the success of innovative approaches to child maltreatment prevention.

Whatever one's view of the role of the law in this context, ignoring or depreciating privacy is unhelpful because, as against the government and its agents, it is a legally protected interest to which penalties for violations may attach. Most relevant in this context are the legal barriers to state employees' entry into and search of the family home and to the sequestration, examination, and interrogation of family members, including parents and children, both within and outside the home. State employees for this purpose include not only the police and child protective services social workers but also publicly employed teachers and medical personnel to the extent that they seek to gather information in part to build a child maltreatment case. In particular, courts are increasingly rejecting the argument that there is a "special needs" exception to the Fourth Amendment's warrant requirement in child welfare cases, including those in which the privacy rights at issue are those of the child him- or herself to be free from unreasonable physical and oral examinations. Indeed, the United States "Supreme Court and the lower [federal] courts ... have consistently found that children have reasonable expectations [of privacy]" (Coleman, 2005, p. 514). For obvious reasons these expectations are not coterminous with those of adults; nevertheless, it is wrong to presume that they are nonexistent. In jurisdictions where this is clearly established law, state employees who violate it may not claim immunity from liability (Coleman, 2005, pp. 169–181). Notably, this result is not different where the intrusion involves an individual or family that is subject to governmental oversight for a different reason. Although as a practical matter they have less privacy than others who have no existing special ties to the government, legally speaking, they are entitled to have unrelated intrusions judged on their own merits.

Of course, privacy is not exclusively a legal value. Indeed, it would be more accurate to think of the law as privileging privacy because of its status in society as a preeminent cultural and political norm. Indicia of respect for the privacy of the individual as against all others, including family members, and for the privacy of the family as against all outsiders to that group, are ubiquitous, ranging from the interior design of modern houses to the persistence of the historical metaphor of the family as sovereign territory. In this larger context, rather than being a negative, privacy in both its physical and psychological aspects is believed to be necessary to the individual's development of a proper sense of self, dignity, and personal security, and to the family's success as the fundamental unit of liberal democratic society.

Because privacy is a privileged cultural and political value, children are taught both to develop their own sense of privacy and to respect the privacy of others. Indeed, the indoctrination begins early, as

> children from a very young age [it is hoped] develop a sense of attachment to their primary caregiver(s) and conversely a sense of trepidation if not fear of those whom they do not know. These senses are inherently physical in their manifestations, as all it takes to make many babies—particularly those who are not accustomed to being handled by strangers—whimper or cry is to remove them from the arms and places with which they are familiar. And even as they come to understand that authorities other than their parents exist, and thus to mediate their physical responses to strangers, older children—beginning as early as two or three—develop an emotional and intellectual appreciation for personal space and zones of privacy that almost by definition recognizes government officials as the quintessential strangers. The fact that these officials are legally tasked with their care and protection ... is generally a foreign notion even to older children. These children have been taught (including by their parents, pediatricians, and even the government itself in the public schools context) to elevate privacy as a value, and to allow intimate [physical and verbal] contact only within the family or close personal associates. (Coleman, 2005, pp. 515–516)

In other words, in addition to its stature as a legal and cultural norm, privacy also has come to have developmental significance for children.

Understanding the role that privacy plays in the child welfare context thus requires contemplating but then also moving beyond its legal aspects to include its cultural, political, and developmental implications. These implications have and inevitably will continue to complicate but not necessarily to obstruct innovations in child maltreatment prevention involving direct intervention in the lives of children and families. It may be unrealistic to imagine that American culture could shift (or that we would want it to shift) to the point that would allow the village to raise the child. Yet it is probably not unrealistic to believe that it could shift to the point where the village appropriately supports parents when they struggle to raise the child.

RESOLVING THE TENSION BETWEEN EFFECTIVE ASSISTANCE AND VIOLATIONS OF PRIVACY

It is beyond the scope of this chapter to provide a comprehensive blueprint for resolving the tension between effective assistance and violations of privacy. However, it is important to highlight those points of law and policy that are essential to any prevention project that would involve government employees in the interventions and those features of existing or planned projects that appear promising in terms of addressing privacy's cultural, political, and developmental implications. It is hoped that these references can contribute to useful research on and development of effective privacy measures as these would be incorporated into ongoing and future initiatives to prevent child maltreatment.

The essential point of law in this area is familiar to most if not all who work in child welfare, whatever their discipline: If government employees are involved in direct interventions in the lives of children and families, obtaining informed and voluntary consent from the relevant adults is probably critical to the legality of the effort. This is particularly true of programs in which the employee is a mandated reporter or in which at least a part of his or her work involves looking out for and reporting suspicions of maltreatment. In other words, it is no longer safe to assume that there is a "child welfare exception" to the Fourth Amendment (Coleman, 2005, pp. 466–501).

What appears to be less well understood is the fact that children cannot give lawful consent even to intrusions directed at their own persons. Indeed, children are not qualified legal actors in most circumstances (Coleman, 2005, pp. 462–463; 2007, p. 547). Thus, although it is a good idea for psychological reasons to get their assent, this will not validate an examination or interview that otherwise transgresses the established bounds of privacy. This means that school-based programs like North Carolina's child and family support teams are vulnerable to the extent that they do not involve obtaining informed and voluntary parental consent for their children's participation in the related programs. The Head Start program mentioned earlier in this chapter, which involved school-based physicals including genital examinations, failed to pass muster precisely because of the extraordinary intrusiveness of the effort and the failure of the program to obtain parental consent in advance of the exams.

Where state employees are not involved in the interventions, consent is still crucial even though the constitutional implications are absent. In this private context, consent is important to avoiding trespass and offensive touching claims (Dobbs, 2001, pp. 52–63, 95–199) and to securing the trust and buy-in of the family and its members. Assuming that the minimum legal requirements necessary to avoid these claims are met, however, consent is primarily a way to begin to secure trust and buy-in. It will get those administering the program in the door, both physically and metaphorically, but it does not necessarily result in the family's sense that they can be trusted with its privacy. What this means is that initiatives designed to prevent child maltreatment involving direct intervention in the lives of children and their parents should include additional extralegal features that can help to foster this necessary trust.

Policies reflecting such features include multiple-response systems (Waldfogel, Chapter 8, this volume), which assume the possibility of a non-adversarial collaboration between parents and social services, and training programs and protocols designed to sensitize social workers and others to the family's legitimate privacy concerns. In addition, three ideas that have received substantial treatment by other contributors to this book appear to be at least theoretically promising prospects for securing trust and buy-in, and thus for addressing the complications privacy interposes in efforts to connect parents with community-based prevention programs. These are universality, public health models for child maltreatment prevention, and a reexamination of mandatory reporting requirements. The rest of this chapter is devoted to a discussion of the role these concepts might play in the effort to foster trust between target individuals and the modern child welfare community.

Universality

As described elsewhere in this volume (e.g., Prinz, Chapter 3), *universality* refers to the inclusion in preventive efforts of either everyone in a given community or everyone in a given community who desires access to the related services. The goal of such initiatives is precisely to universalize the effort to prevent child maltreatment and as a result to reframe it as an effort to promote child well-being. Unlike traditional child maltreatment prevention efforts, "everyone" has a stake in child well-being and thus "everyone" might properly cooperate in such an initiative.

There are obvious problems with this approach, which also receive attention in this book. Likely most important is that it focuses resources broadly and thus—to the extent that resources are limited as they generally are—risks the programs' relative neglect of those individuals and families who most clearly need help (Olds et al., Chapter 2, this volume). It is for this reason, for example, that the United Kingdom is said to be considering revisions to its long-standing universal home visits program, revisions that would provide for more targeted attention to children and families who have demonstrated the greatest need.

However, to the extent that these problems can be addressed and that there is a commitment at least to a version of universality in a given community, implementation of this idea could potentially contribute to securing the trust and buy-in of families that would otherwise be wary even of obviously well-intentioned interventions. This trust could come about primarily because universal efforts to secure child well-being are likely to contribute to destigmatizing the home visit and related invasions of privacy, which in this country have tended disproportionately to target poor and minority families because they were believed to be led by either bad or at least inadequate parents. To gain the trust and buy-in of those who really need help, the initiatives must be convincing that this generation of "child savers" is not operating in the historical frame that has long considered parents in these groups to be unworthy of raising their own children. Universality, at least in concept, should help to address the distrust that is borne of this history and thus to afford caseworkers a different degree of entry into the family simply because everyone—rich or poor, white or minority—would be "meddled with" to ensure to the extent possible that their children were well cared for. No one would be off-limits for such scrutiny because implicit in universality is the premise that everyone can benefit to a certain degree from participating in community-based efforts to support parents in their work to raise healthy children.

Public Health Models

Public health models designed to foster child well-being or to prevent child maltreatment propose in some way to medicalize the relationships between investigators and providers, on one hand, and children and families in a community on the other (Prinz, Chapter 3, this volume). They conceptualize both child maltreatment prevention and the promotion of child well-being as efforts that are susceptible to both prophylactic and reactive treatment. As such, and like multiple-response systems, public health models effect an important shift in focus away from the traditional adversarial or prosecutorial approach to addressing child maltreatment that continues to prevail in most parts of the country today. Most concretely, instead of being visited by a social worker accompanied by a police officer, a child or family might be visited by a nurse or someone else with relevant medical training. And instead of intrusions designed specifically to determine whether the child needs to be removed from the family and whether the parent has committed a legally relevant offense, the intrusions might be designed to determine the relevant individuals' strengths and weaknesses and the nature and extent of the support that might appropriately be offered in those circumstances.

Public health models do not and should not replace adversarial or prosecutorial approaches in relevant circumstances, including those involving serious child abuse. (Child sexual abuse falls within this category of serious child abuse.) Moreover, these models will generally cost more than those that do not similarly rely on medical professionals to administer the effort. Nevertheless, to the extent that this obstacle is addressed, public health models are promising in a number of respects relevant to privacy.

First, like initiatives based on universality, public health models would likely contribute to destigmatizing the effort to promote child well-being and to prevent child maltreatment (Prinz, Chapter 3, this volume). Most people are invested in public health both *writ large* and as this institution might positively affect private health and thus private outcomes. For this reason, no matter one's race, ethnicity, or socioeconomic status, engaging the medical profession carries relatively little (if any) stigma, perhaps particularly as such engagements are contrasted with interventions in the family by traditional child protective services social workers and affiliated individuals. Moreover, parents who participate in medicalized prevention efforts are more likely to be perceived as good parents seeking to secure their child's best interests than are those who are engaged by traditional child protective services, even if the services provided by the two are otherwise the same.

Second, public health models for child maltreatment prevention and promotion of child well-being are likely to be perceived by most people as less intrusive than the traditional adversarial approaches. In part this perception occurs because of the probable reduction in associated stigma. (Stigmatic interventions are generally perceived by the law to be more intrusive than interventions lacking this quality. For example, suspicion-based investigations are generally found to be more intrusive than suspicionless investigations. And investigations conducted by or whose results will be provided to law enforcement are more intrusive than those that do not fall in this category [Coleman, 2005, pp. 497–498].) But it also occurs because public health models are not similarly adversarial and because, relative to traditional approaches, they do not implicate the same expectations of privacy: Regardless of race, ethnicity, or socioeconomic status, most people at some point consult with the medical profession, often in connection with the most intimate details of their personal histories and conditions. This fact may go a long way in explaining why target individuals in existing programs have tended to trust medical professionals more than they have trusted other home visitors (Olds et al., Chapter 2, this volume) and why public health models may be more successful in diverse communities than volunteer models such as that which Melton has successfully grown in South Carolina. (Melton, Chapter 5, this volume).

Third, public health approaches to child maltreatment prevention are likely to be more convincing as paradigms for child well-being than other approaches, particularly those that continue to involve traditional actors and protocols. Child well-being already has deep associations with private and public health measures. Most important, these associations are generally positive ones, again, particularly in comparison with those that link child maltreatment prevention and child protective services.

New Thinking on Mandated Reporting

Pursuant to federal law, all states have mandatory child abuse and neglect reporting requirements. These requirements provide either that certain categories of individuals—for example, medical personnel, therapists, social workers, teachers, and childcare providers—must report suspected maltreatment to the designated authorities, generally child protective services and/or law enforcement, or that "everyone" is a mandated reporter (Coleman, 2005, p. 427). The requirements were established to ensure to the extent possible that the state has an opportunity to intervene in the family to remove and/or protect children who are victims or at risk of maltreatment.

This reporting system has had both positive and negative effects in a number of areas (Appelbaum, 1999; Lukens, 2007). For present purposes, however, the principal concern has been that family-friendly approaches of the sort described throughout this book are unlikely to be successful where those responsible for gaining the family's consent, trust, and buy-in are simultaneously responsible for reporting all suspected maltreatment to traditional authorities (Olds et al., Chapter 2, this volume). The risk of failure is based on the likelihood that families will be unwilling to permit even well-meaning outsiders to penetrate their privacy when they know that their consent will increase the probability (as a result of the unique access they would permit) that they will be reported to the authorities. It is also based on the likelihood that any progress made toward the prevention of child maltreatment will be thwarted if those who manage to gain the family's trust effectively cause a second, but this time adversarial, intervention in the family as a result of their reporting obligations. This latter issue in particular has received substantial attention from child and family therapists who understand that they need to secure and to keep the family's trust to be able to make real progress toward ameliorating their patients' circumstances (Appelbaum, 1999). The issue has salience beyond the formal therapeutic setting, however.

A comprehensive examination of the benefits and burdens of the mandatory reporting system is thus important to positive outcomes for child maltreatment prevention efforts that contemplate direct intervention in the lives of children and families. Within this structure, particularly close attention should be paid to the effects of mandated reporting on the child welfare community's efforts to secure the consent, trust, and buy-in of its target populations. Although there is always a risk that the failure to report suspected maltreatment will be linked to negative outcomes for particular children, this risk must be balanced against the likelihood that, at least in certain circumstances, trust-based, family-friendly interventions may be more effective in the fight against maltreatment than traditional efforts have been to date.

Among the specific proposals for policy reform that should be considered in this context are the development of laws that would:

1. Permit (or perhaps even require) the establishment of formal (legal) relationships between local child protective services (CPS) and nongovernmental maltreatment prevention programs that involve direct intervention in the lives of children and families.
2. Provide for the possibility within such relationships for home visitors associated with certified programs to (a) bypass child abuse reporting hotlines and the protocols associated with those hotlines when they witness suspected maltreatment and (b) to go directly to the relevant CPS supervisor for consultation and evaluation of the relevant facts.
3. In appropriate cases, permit the CPS supervisor to accept the home visitor's report as the equivalent of an investigation so as to preclude the necessity for a separate and potentially adversarial intervention by strangers (CPS investigators) into the lives of the family and child.

The risks and benefits associated with such reforms would have to be studied and then balanced carefully before any conclusions could be reached about their overall effectiveness in light of the states' long-standing and predominant child welfare goals. Particular issues to consider as part of such an evaluation would include, among other things, the criteria that nongovernmental programs and their home visitors would have to meet to qualify for this streamlined process; the matter of educating nongovernmental actors about the law and CPS administrative policy relevant to establishing legal violations; and CPS's ability financially and logistically to manage such a partnership. Ultimately, the expectation is that public–private partnerships developed along these lines would look a lot like the differential response approaches described by Waldfogel (Chapter 8, this volume), albeit with a complementary private dimension. Although this dimension would add certain complexities to existing, purely public programs, because CPS in many jurisdictions already has relevant experience in working collaboratively with private actors and programs, a partnership in this context should not require fundamental structural changes in the way the agencies do their work. Even if such changes were necessary in particular instances, however, they would be justified to the extent that additional gains toward the communities' child welfare goals could be achieved.

CONCLUSION

Individual and family privacy are highly valued in American culture and law. In these contexts, privacy has a number of meanings, including personal integrity, respect, dignity, and freedom from stigma. Notwithstanding inconsistent historical practices by well-meaning "child savers," the law especially does not discriminate among population subgroups with respect to the kind and degree of privacy to which individuals and families are due. Moreover, the law accords children, including quite young children, privacy rights that are more extensive than many in the child welfare community might expect. Because of these circumstances, it is crucial that community-based child maltreatment prevention efforts include the means to secure the consent, trust, and buy-in of those whose privacy they would disturb. Among the ideas that appear promising in this regard are three that have received serious attention from other contributors to this book, including the notion that the child maltreatment prevention effort be universalized and recast as an effort to promote child well-being, a public health approach to interventions in the family to promote child well-being, and new thinking on mandatory reporting requirements by those who would collaborate with parents to secure their children's best interests. To the extent that these and related ideas are pursued, progress will have been made toward a future in which an increasing number of vulnerable parents and children comfortably partner with their communities to minimize the incidence and nature of child maltreatment.

REFERENCES

Appelbaum, P. S. (1999). Child abuse reporting laws: Time for reform, *Psychiatric Services*, 50, 27–29.

Coleman, D. L. (2005). Storming the castle to save the children: The ironic costs of a child welfare exception to the Fourth Amendment. *William and Mary Law Review*, 47, 413–540.

Coleman, D. L. (2007). The legal ethics of pediatric research. *Duke Law Journal,* *57,* 517–624.

Dobbs, D. B. (2001). *Practitioners treatise series: Vol. 1. The law of torts.* St. Paul, MN: West Group.

Dubbs v. Head Start, Inc., 336 F.3d 1194 (10th Cir. 2003).

Easley, M. (2006). *Governor Easley announces new program to help at-risk school children* [Press release]. Retrieved December 10, 2007, from *www.governor. state.nc.us/News_FullStory.asp?id=3466.*

Giovannoni, J. M., & Becerra, R. M. (1979). *Defining child abuse.* New York: Free Press.

Hong, K. E. (2003). Parens patri[archy]: Adoption, eugenics, and same-sex couples. *California Western Law Review,* p. 40.

Lukens, R. J. (2007). The impact of mandatory reporting requirements on the child welfare system, *Rutgers Journal of Law and Public Policy,* 5, 177 et seq.

CHAPTER 10

Healing in the Place of Last Resort

The Role of the Dependency Court within Community-Based Efforts to Prevent Child Maltreatment

Cindy S. Lederman

I have spent 15 years as a judge in juvenile court, every day handling termination of parental rights cases involving abuse and neglect. I am a field practitioner. I see both the important role that courts currently play in individual maltreatment cases and the potential role they could play as participants in community-based efforts to prevent child maltreatment. However, when community-based prevention efforts are considered by scholars and community leaders, juvenile or dependency courts are usually absent from the discussion: They are absent as possible participants in that effort and they are absent as potential targets of change. This is a mistake. If we are willing to consider modifying the way courts do business, they can function as both, and in the process, contribute to prevention and healing.

This chapter first discusses impediments to the capacity of courts to play a leadership role in innovative efforts to prevent and heal child maltreatment; these impediments largely explain the courts' absence from discussions about community-based prevention efforts. The chapter then focuses on the courts' potential role as agents of change. Specifically, it addresses some of the challenges courts face in acting as agents of change, describes their authority and capacity to forge innovative practices, reports on one example of court-driven innovation, and concludes with prospects for the courts' future role in community-based efforts to prevent and to heal child maltreatment.

COURTS AS AGENTS OF CHANGE

Impediments to the Court's Role as a Leader

The court is not the first institution that one considers as a potential agent of innovation and change in the development of community-based efforts to prevent maltreatment. Several attributes of courts account for this situation.

First, courts administer an adversarial system in which the rights of parents too often trump the well-being of the children at issue. When parties are true adversaries there is little interest in working together to find a resolution to the underlying issue that caused the case to come into court, but rather a desire to prevail regardless of the consequences. The emphasis is not on solving the problem, but on winning the case. Acting in the best interest of the child is not often the priority of the parent, especially at the inception of a dependency case.

Second, judges generally have little or no training in the science of child development or in how to consume relevant research effectively (Osofsky, Maze, Lederman, Grace, & Dicker, 2002). If we judges had a better understanding of science, and of child development in particular, we could do a better job. Judges want to do a good job. Judges want to make the right decisions. But their lack of understanding of child development too often keeps them from being effective. A most significant tragedy, a perfect example of where we have dropped the ball because we don't understand science, is the fact that courts have universally ignored the consequences of maltreatment for infants and toddlers. Judges think, "They are going to be okay, they are resilient, they could not have noticed anything happening anyway, and even if they are harmed, they can't talk, so how could a judge possibly know what's wrong?" A small step toward improvement in court practice is the trend for judges to interview children as young as age 5. These children can talk and engage with us.

Third, we make hundreds of decisions every day in a matter of moments, with the same dignity and pace as traffic court. Unlike traffic court, however, the decisions made in juvenile or dependency court affect human lives in profound ways. In Miami, each dependency judge sees approximately 150 families each week. There are too many cases, each with complex issues and problems, and never enough time to devote the attention that each case deserves.

Fourth, judges assume, mistakenly, that traditional interventions (like parenting classes) always work if the participants really care. The way success is defined in the justice system is how fast one can close the largest number of cases, whether that closure involves family reunification or termination of parental rights. What we fail to realize is that we cannot meet our legal responsibility of making reasonable efforts on behalf of these families if the services we provide are not effective. We cannot prevent re-abuse, and we cannot resolve the underlying problem that caused parents to maltreat their child. We cannot modify human behavior by sending someone to a class that sounds as though it might be helpful. Our blind, even ignorant faith in programs alone, without a requirement of evidence-based services and evaluation, can actually jeopardize the well-being of the very children we are trying to protect.

Fifth, and perhaps most important, as things stand, the court is the place of last resort. When everyone and everything else fails, families involved in maltreatment come to court. These families are, as Daro (Chapter 1, this volume) has noted, "broken families." Judges would love to support "consumer families," but they don't encounter the court. We get the families that will not open their doors; the families that are so limited in their knowledge of parenting that we literally have to explain to them that when their babies cry, they need to pick them up and that they are not spoiling them when they do; the families that need to be taught that it's a really good idea to smile at babies—that it makes them feel good and that it's important for the parent–child relationship (Lederman, Osofsky, & Katz, 2001). Broken families have never heard of the "shaken baby syndrome" that Runyan and Zolotor (Chapter 6, this volume) aim to prevent by making it a part of our common vocabulary. We teach parents in these families not to shake their babies. Sometimes we talk to parents about how important it is to read to their babies, and they are so puzzled because, they tell us, "My baby can't understand what I'm reading." Sometimes young mothers from broken families come to court with their babies dressed up like little dolls because they believe that this will demonstrate to the court that they are good mothers.

Because of these impediments, an enormous change is necessary for courts to assume a leadership role in the development of innovative, community-based approaches to child maltreatment prevention. This change could come about if we begin to look at juvenile courts as laboratories: laboratories of learning about why maltreatment occurs and how it can be prevented.

The Potential Leadership Role of the Court

Is there a way that the court can create a context for studying human behavior and for testing the efficacy of interventions for families? The juvenile court judge's role is (in part) to modify human behavior, which is difficult with only a legal degree. There are many effective, evidence-based intervention alternatives available to judges, but most judges are not aware of them. Judges are also poorly trained to discern the difference between ineffective interventions and evidenced-based interventions. Judges need to work with practitioners and scientists as a team to use relevant expertise in making optimal decisions. If they begin to do this, they have the potential to become leaders in changing practices nationally and even in influencing public policy (Lederman & Osofsky, 2004; Osofsky & Lederman, 2004).

Consider the case of Susie, a girl in our courts in Miami-Dade County, who was sexually abused as a child and is now a young single mother who has, in turn, been alleged to maltreat her own baby daughter. Susie has no experience with positive parenting models and no support systems. In fact, when asked to draw a picture of her mother, she draws her with a black eye. Her case has been thrust upon the court, which cannot relinquish its responsibility. The court's task is daunting: How do we teach Susie to become a good parent? What do we think Susie knows about being a good parent? Why do we assume that just because she has a child she knows what to do? How, in the 12 months the law gives us before we have to terminate her parental rights, can we teach her to make her child feel safe and stable and loved when she has never, ever, felt that security herself? That is the court's role, and it is also why the courts need the expertise of scientists and practitioners.

I believe that the court *can* do a great deal. Indeed, courts can play leadership roles, and they should. There are a number of things that judges can require in a local community. For someone as disadvantaged as Susie, we can throw out those parenting programs that put her in a class for 10 weeks where she gets lectured to and then is given a certificate in "Parenting." We know that such short-term, passive approaches are not going to be effective for someone like Susie whose needs are so great. We can learn about developmental delays. We can provide services for infant mental health. We can introduce evidence-based innovations such as home visitation. We can bring proven programs into our courts.

It's not always easy to teach judges to adopt new approaches. I used to teach judges across the country about domestic violence. That was not a happy job. But judges are much more open to learning about infants, toddlers, and the science of early childhood development because they want to help these maltreated children for whom they have great sympathy—sympathy they do not share for battered women in domestic violence court. What we have learned is that translational research, which has important implications for judges, has to be communicated in a way that judges can understand and appreciate.

One method of education being used to communicate with judges about the importance of the science of child development and evidence-based approaches to family intervention is through brief video presentations of scientific experiments such as the Strange Situation and the Still Face procedure; both were developed and are used by developmental scientists. We created a video that depicts a mother in front of her baby, engaging the baby in a normal manner—that is, with a loving or receptive affect—but with little or no touching. Then the mother is told to turn away, and then to turn back with no affect on her face. The mother is in the same place, right next to the baby. The video depicts the strong reaction of the baby to her mother's unusual lack of affect. The baby becomes confused, anguished, and has gaze aversion. Her behavior deteriorates, she tears at her clothing, and she becomes anxious to the point at which it is difficult to watch, all within 2 minutes. It is hard to believe that babies this young are affected by such a small, simple behavioral change by the mother. And yet they are. We show this video to judges and child welfare professionals, and their perception that a baby does not know what is happening or is unaffected by his or her surroundings is gone forever. Judges come back to us years later and say, "That video is the one thing I remember."

Interventions in Court: Infant–Parent Psychotherapy

Courts may have the authority and resources to prescribe innovative interventions for families and at the same time to require rigorous, scientific evaluations of the impact of these interventions. We are supporting just such an innovative intervention and evaluation in Dade County Court. This is a "court of the future" concept in juvenile court, which has us working very closely with academic researchers and practicing experts.

The infant–parent psychotherapy intervention is directed toward parents of young babies who have low-level parenting skills. With the impediments of the law, funding, and the cumulative disadvantages of the family's context, we cannot always send families to a different place. We know that we cannot change where they live, we can't change their life experience, but *maybe* we can teach them how to parent. We would rather do this work at the beginning of the parent–child relationship than at the end. That is, the challenge of working in the child welfare system with teenagers who are dropping out of school, running away, and engaging in all kinds of dangerous behavior is one that we want to obviate altogether. We should focus on families when the children are young. We can do so in the courts by recognizing high-risk families early in life and directing them to evidence-based interventions before the damage is too great.

Our intervention is based on the research of Alicia Lieberman (Lieberman, Ippen, & Van Horn, 2006) through the collaboration of Joy Osofsky (Appleyard & Osofsky, 2003; Osofsky, 2004), who works intensely with our court (Lederman & Osofsky, 2004). This research indicates that some parenting classes may be ineffective, particularly didactic ones in which someone lectures to parents, with no babies in the room and no observation of a healthy relationship. Years ago, Lieberman generated the idea of taking parents to a childcare center so they could experience a healthy caregiver relationship. This work has grown into Infant–Parent Psychotherapy (IPP), which we now use in our court (Lieberman, Van Horn, & Ippen, 2005; Osofsky, 2004). The guiding concept is one of nurturing a healthy relationship by working with the child and the mother in the relationship. The children have come to us because they have been harmed in that relationship, and we need to try to heal them in the relationship. This is a therapeutic intervention. It enhances the mother's awareness of what her child's needs are, of how to be responsive to the child, and of reciprocity. The therapist addresses some of the emotional-behavioral problems with the child as well, and is there to deal with some of the "ghosts in the nursery" (Fraiberg, Adelson, & Shapiro, 1975) that may be prohibiting the mother from becoming the parent she needs to be.

Goals

The goal of this psychotherapy is to "heal" the wound in the relationship between the child and the parent. The therapeutic work incorporates a broad range of techniques to enhance the mother's awareness of and responsiveness to her child's needs. The emotional and behavioral problems of the child are also addressed, because they may be both consequences of past maltreatment and risk factors for future maltreatment. In the therapy, the therapist models appropriate parenting behavior; promotes empathy and the restoration of trust and reciprocity in the infant–parent relationship; examines the mother's cognitive concerns, based in her own upbringing, about her parenting competence; and otherwise generally promotes healthy parent–infant interactions.

What the therapist does looks almost like play therapy or even sometimes home visitation, because the mother (or sometimes the father) comes in and sits on the floor in our baby room with an infant mental health therapist. What is so fascinating is that almost always when a mother comes into the room with her baby for the first time and is asked to sit on the floor and play with her baby, she looks at us and says, "I don't understand. You want me to sit on the floor with my baby?" Each time this happens our appreciation for the depth of the problem is renewed. Quite often, the child sits against the wall, afraid to be with the mother. But this is a long intervention—it takes at least 26 weeks. The therapist coaches the mother and tells her what the baby wants, what the baby needs, how to connect with the baby, how to smile and praise the baby. The therapist actually *shows* her, because this not something that can be learned passively, nor can it be taught without intensive one-on-one modeling.

Evaluation

QUANTITATIVE ANALYSES OF CHANGE

Infant–Parent Psychotherapy has been implemented in the Dade County Court for the past 15 years. Evaluation of program effectiveness has been conducted through a pre–post design in which each family is administered various instruments before and after the program, including direct observations of parent–infant interaction behavior during laboratory tasks. This interaction was video recorded and coded by independent observers. Statistically significant positive change was observed for 9 of 14 measures from the Parent and Child Relationship Scale coded from these video records.

Following intervention, parents displayed significant improvements in behavioral and emotional responsiveness. Children displayed improvements in positive affect, less withdrawal, less irritability/anger, less noncompliance with the parent, greater enthusiasm, greater persistence at tasks, and greater emotional and behavioral responsiveness upon reunion with the parent.

Interviews with parents after treatment indicated strong satisfaction. In response to questions, 95% of parents indicated that they believed their relationship with their baby improved, 77% believed that their parenting had improved, 83% believed their child had changed positively, and 73% believed that their family life had improved.

Although abuse or neglect had been substantiated in 48 of 59 cases prior to treatment, only one dyad completing treatment experienced another report of abuse and this report was never substantiated. Of the 14 children who were not in the custody of their parent(s) at the beginning of treatment and who completed treatment, 12 had been returned to their parent(s)'s custody following treatment, showing a reunification rate of 86%. Although the national reunification rate for such families in the absence of treatment is not clear, it seems that the rate that we have found is significantly higher than the norm.

In a 5-year follow-up study of the original 59 dyads who participated in Infant–Parent Psychotherapy (Osofsky et al., 2007), evaluators were able to find 15 dyads. This is a very transient population, and we had not put into place mechanisms for long-term follow-up ahead of time. Of these 15 dyads, 10 had been reunified (two permanent guardianships and one adoption), and all 15 mothers had a legal right to visitation with their children. Finally, not a single case had come back into the system: The recidivism rate in that original group is zero.

Because only some families were selected to participate in this intervention, it is plausible that only the "best" candidates for positive outcomes were selected. Thus, a more rigorous test of the program's impact includes information about the rate of reentry into foster care among children who had been in foster care and were reunified with their families for the entire county over time, as compared with other counties in Florida. The Community-Based Care (CBC) Pilot Project Monitoring Report (2007) was completed to make these comparisons. Of the 2,225 children in Miami-Dade County who exited the foster care system for the first time in 2003–2004, 124 children, or 6%, reentered foster care within 12 months. In the 23,761 similar cases across the rest of the state, 2,678 children, or 11%, reentered foster care within 12 months. Although the relatively favorable outcomes in Dade County cannot be attributed solely to the Infant–Parent Psychotherapy program, these results certainly do not point to any ill effect of using the court to help families reach effective treatments.

A CASE STUDY

The reality of this program's effectiveness comes alive with a case study. Lucille came to court one day with her six siblings. They were all there. The thought was, typically, "Oh no, there goes another generation, because we are going to see these seven children now and we know we are going to see their children later." Lucille was born in 1984. All seven siblings had been removed from their mother's custody in 1994. We had put Lucille's mother through one of those parenting courses in which someone lectures to you 10 times and as long as you show up and keep your eyes open, you've successfully completed the program. We gave her the children back, and then we removed them again in 1999.

At age 15, Lucille was not progressing well developmentally. Her functional intelligence quotient, as a result of living in impoverishment, was much lower than her actual intelligence quotient. A psychologist who saw the children wrote, "The children of this family have been exposed to chronic emotional neglect and are experiencing symptoms of depression, emotional impoverishment and low self-esteem, low academic achievement and aggression. There are strong indications that they have been exposed to long-term family and community violence." So here we were again with this family.

Lucille and her sister both became pregnant during the pendency of this case. Her sister was rather defiant, but we tried to work with both of them. When Lucille and her sister came to court at the same time, it was impossible to work with Lucille; we separated their cases so that Lucille would come on another day, because we thought there was some potential in working with her. As we see so often, when a child of abuse gives birth, she does what she has learned. She neglected her child, sometimes leaving the child with her mother and running away. When we removed her child from her custody, she was defiant, saying, "Why have you taken my baby away? I am a good mom."

I thought that girls like Lucille were being defiant, or just obstructionist, but they *really* believe that they are good mothers. And it's something we need to understand before we can help them. In their minds, they are good mothers. It's not really hard to be a good mom in such families. Getting through that barrier of understanding *alone* is really very important.

Early on in therapy, Lucille demonstrated little affect with her little boy, no joy in being together. Sometimes she would be intrusive, and sometimes she would engage in parallel play alongside the baby. There was no exploration, no initiation, no real understanding of how to be reciprocal or how to meet the needs of this child.

By the end of therapy, Lucille had learned how to laugh with her son. She came back to us just a few months ago. At the age of 19 she had graduated from high school. She plans to become an assistant dental hygienist. She has had another baby, and her first child, Courtney, is on the honor roll. She is very proud. Last year, at age 23, Lucille returned to court to gain custody of her last two siblings who were in a foster home. She wanted to take them home and be responsible for them. I was a little reluctant because she was doing so well and I did not want to sabotage any of that improvement, but I let her take her brother and sister home.

CONCLUSION

Selma Fraiberg said, and this is something we talk to judges about, that working with children this young, because of the science and what we know about the science, is a "little like having God on your side" (Fraiberg et al., 1975). I think we—the courts, taking the lead, working in concert with scientists, experts in the field, and enlightened providers in the child welfare system—are having tremendous success in healing the infant–parent relationship because we are putting the focus on these young children and their parents. The court can be an instrument of change, and it can be a laboratory for testing the efficacy of innovative programs. It takes a collaboration among judges, scholars, and practitioners, and it takes a commitment to changing how business is done.

REFERENCES

Appleyard, K., & Osofsky, J. D. (2003). Parenting after trauma: Supporting parents and caregivers in the treatment of children impacted by violence. *Infant Mental Health Journal, 24*, 111–125.

Community-Based Pilot Project: Broward, Dade, and Monroe Counties. (2007, April). Chicago: Chapin Hall Center for Children, University of Chicago.

Fraiberg, S. H., Adelson, E., & Shapiro, V. B. (1975). Ghosts in the nursery: A psychoanalytic approach to the problem of infant/mother relationships. *Journal of the American Academy of Child Psychiatry*, 14(3), 386–422.

Lederman, C., & Osofsky, J. D. (2004). Infant mental health interventions in juvenile court: Prevention for the future. *Psychology, Public Policy, and the Law*, 10, 162–177.

Lederman, C. S., Osofsky, J. D., & Katz, L. (2001). When the bough breaks the cradle will fall: Promoting the health and well being of infants and toddlers in juvenile court. *Juvenile and Family Court Journal*, 52, 33–38.

Lieberman, A. F., Ippen, C. G., & Van Horn, P. (2006). Child–parent psychotherapy: 6-month follow-up of a randomized controlled trial. *Journal of the American Academy of Child and Adolescent Psychiatry*, 45, 913–918.

Lieberman, A. F., Van Horn, P., & Ippen, C. G. (2005). Toward evidence-based treatment: Child–parent psychotherapy with preschoolers exposed to marital violence. *Journal of the American Academy of Child and Adolescent Psychiatry*, 44, 1241–1248.

Osofsky, J. D. (Ed.). (2004). *Young children and trauma: Intervention and treatment*. New York: Guilford Press.

Osofsky, J. D., Kronenberg, M., Hammer, J. H., Lederman, C., Katz, L., Adams, S., et al. (2007). The development and evaluation of the intervention model for the Florida Mental Health Pilot Program. *Infant Mental Health Journal*, 28, 259–280.

Osofsky, J. D., & Lederman, C. (2004). Healing the child in juvenile court. In J. D. Osofsky (Ed.), *Young children and trauma: Intervention and treatment* (pp. 221–241). New York: Guilford Press.

Osofsky, J. D., Maze, C., Lederman, C., Grace, M., & Dicker, S. (2002). *Questions every judge and lawyer should ask about infants and toddlers in the child welfare system*. Technical Assistance Brief. Reno, NV: National Council of Juvenile and Family Court Judges.

Preventing Maltreatment or Promoting Positive Development— Where Should a Community Focus Its Resources?

A Policy Perspective

Michael S. Wald

As described in the previous chapters, a number of projects are under way in various states and localities that have the potential of reducing child maltreatment and providing better protection for children who have been maltreated. In this chapter, I reflect on the policy implications of the findings from these projects. Should more resources be devoted to expanding the reach of the various programs described in this book? Should communities try to establish a comprehensive set of programs focused on the prevention of child maltreatment? What system—child protection, health, education—should have primary responsibility for implementing prevention efforts?

POLICY ANALYSIS OF MALTREATMENT PREVENTION

I examine the preceding questions from the vantage point of a political decision maker, a mayor or a governor. This is a very different perspective from that of the researcher or program administrator. Researchers generally focus on whether a particular program or approach seems to work in terms of the goals for that program; most of the chapters in this book report on specific programs that seem to be successful in reducing maltreatment. Efficacy is, of course, an important issue for mayors and governors as well. However, a mayor or governor deciding whether to invest in a particular program, and especially deciding whether to try to implement a systemic approach to a problem, wants to know more than whether that program is likely to be effective. These decision makers will ask whether the program is affordable, whether it can be implemented at scale in their city or state with the same impacts as the model program, and what the politics of implementation are. In addition, these decision makers must focus on how any potential investment or approach compares with alternative potential investments.

Unquestionably, child maltreatment is a very serious problem. Child protection agencies investigate allegations of maltreatment of nearly 3,000,000 children each year, nearly 5% of all children. (U.S. Department of Health and Human Services, 2006). I estimate that between 10 and 15% of all children in the country will be reported to a child protective services (CPS) agency at some point before age 18 (Sabol, Colton, & Polousky, 2004). Unfortunately, for children from poor families, and particularly from poor African American families, that number goes up dramatically; as many as 25% of these children may be reported to CPS at some point in their lives (Sabol et al., 2004; Wulcyzn, Barth, Yuan, Harden, & Landsverk, 2005). CPS agencies conclude that nearly a million of the 3 million reported children have suffered from maltreatment, as defined under various states' laws. Maltreatment has a serious impact on children's health and development. Approximately 1,500 children are killed by abuse each year. Thousands more suffer serious physical harm as result of physical beatings. Approximately 100,000 children are victims of sexual abuse. The largest group of maltreated children, more than a half million children, suffer from inadequate parental care or parental neglect that hinders their academic, social, and emotional development (U.S. Department of Health and Human Services, 2006). It is certainly desirable to prevent such harms. Children should not suffer. Moreover, mitigating the impact of maltreatment after it has occurred is very difficult.

Yet despite the harms associated with maltreatment, if I were advising a mayor or governor, I would not recommend that he or she make major new investments in programs that are framed as child maltreatment prevention programs. Preventing maltreatment must be a *desired outcome*, but *not the primary focus*, of public investments in children. Governors and mayors must choose among many potential investments in children. Resources are not infinite, although advocates for various children's programs often act as if that were the case. In terms of the choices and tradeoffs that policymakers must confront, there are better frameworks to use in deciding investment policies and better places to invest resources than in programs designed primarily to prevent child maltreatment. I believe that the largest payoff will come from a focus on promoting the positive development of all children "at risk" of poor development, not from a focus on preventing maltreatment. Furthermore, the major institution for implementing this approach should be the early childhood education system, with a secondary role for the health system. Prevention activities should not be linked to the child protection system.

I recommend this approach for four reasons. First, there is likely to be more political support for approaches that are not framed as prevention of maltreatment. Second, the evidence does not support making major investments in *maltreatment* prevention. Third, focusing on preventing maltreatment will likely divert energy and resources from the critical need to improve child protective services to children who have already been harmed, as well as children in the juvenile justice and mental health systems, who greatly need improved services. Finally, the payoff for all children will be larger with a positive development, rather than abuse prevention, framework. Framing the issue as maltreatment focuses on the wrong outcome; we should seek positive development, not just the absence of harm.

A POLICY FRAMEWORK

Before assessing the desirability of different potential investments in children's well-being, a policymaker should determine the outcomes that he or she hopes will be achieved through any investments. Too often policymakers focus on inputs, not outcomes. Without a focus on outcomes, the efficacy of investments cannot be assessed.

Ideally, a society should try to maximize all children's health, educational attainment, and emotional well-being. But these are not realistic options for most investments, owing to either lack of resources or lack of knowledge of how to achieve the outcome. I would advise a policymaker to seek more modest goals—goals we are far from achieving at present. First, we should try to ensure a reasonable quality of life for all children *during their childhood*. This goal includes trying to ensure that all children have a minimally safe childhood. They should not be physically harmed or sexually abused by parents. Parents should have access to enough economic resources so that they can provide basic food and shelter on a continuous basis. Children should also be provided with caring and nurturing environments in school, preschool, and after-school settings (Waldfogel, 2006). We owe it to children to make investments toward these ends so that they can have a decent childhood.

Public investments should also seek to provide each child with the opportunities needed to lay the groundwork for a reasonably adequate adulthood. Again, many advocates call for investments that optimize children's potential; this is unrealistic, practically as well as economically. The political process should start with more feasible goals. I suggest that the two key elements of a minimally reasonable adulthood are being able to connect to the workforce in a regular fashion and being able to connect with at least one other person who provides positive emotional support on a consistent basis (Wald & Martinez, 2003). These are perhaps minimal outcomes, but at least 10% of adults do not achieve them. To reach these goals, children generally must be able to graduate from high school, not become deeply involved in the juvenile or criminal justice system, and not become seriously dependent on drugs or alcohol (Wald & Martinez, 2003).

In trying to produce these outcomes for children, policymakers must choose among many competing investments. There is a clear link between being maltreated as a child and failing to achieve the desired long-term outcomes (in addition to the outcome of a safe childhood). However, many other aspects of a child's environment also contribute to the likelihood that he or she will or will not achieve these outcomes. The development of children is often hindered by inadequate parental care that does not constitute maltreatment (Prinz, Chapter 3, this volume). In addition, the quality of a child's school, childcare, and neighborhood can make a significant difference.

In advising a mayor or governor about where to make investments, I suggest that the following considerations argue against a major focus on maltreatment.

Political Support

In allocating resources, a mayor or governor must consider not only the efficacy of particular forms of spending but also the political support for various alternative expenditures. Obviously, advocates of preventing child maltreatment are not the only group wanting public funds. They must compete with many other constituencies. In the competition for resources, it is highly unlikely that prevention of child abuse will receive high priority. The highest priority in all states is K–12 education. Most states spend between 30 and 50% of all general fund state dollars on public education, and the public wants more because of the many deficiencies in the education process (National Association of State Budget Officers, 2005). Schools affect all children, not just abused children, and thus they have a very strong lobby, including parents, teachers, and businesses. In most states, when more money becomes available, it will be going into schools.

In addition to primary and secondary education, there are four other areas for investment that command widespread support. First, children's advocates and elected officials are pushing for universal preschool. Universal preschool can promote children's well-being in many ways, if it is delivered in high-quality settings that involve parents in an adequate way. But high-quality preschool, like K–12 education, is expensive and will absorb a major part of new resources. Second, parents and child advocates want more high-quality childcare. More than half of all young children are in childcare and much of this care is of poor quality, especially for children from low-income families. Again, quality costs money; it requires low child–staff ratios and trained staff. Third, there is substantial support for really good after-school programs. Finally, there is the push for universal healthcare coverage, especially for children.

The fact is that there are not enough resources to fund all of these demands. This is true at the local, state, and federal levels. And, in many states, there is not much room in the budget to reallocate significantly more resources for children. In California, for example, children's programs, primarily schools, account for more than half the state budget, and medical care for the poor absorbs another 25% of the budget (California Department of Finance, 2008). Everything else competes for what is left.

The political support for schools, childcare, and health coverage has significant implications with respect to community efforts to prevent maltreatment. It is unlikely that most political leaders will support the level of resources needed to develop high-quality programs targeted at preventing maltreatment, which will be seen as affecting only a small portion of children. In fact, people and organizations concerned about maltreatment have been advocating for more prevention for nearly 40 years. Yet there has been only a limited response. "Child abuse prevention has not captured the imagination, or sustained attention, of the greater public" (Daro & Cohn Donnelly, 2002). As Gary Melton, one of the leading advocates for child protection, writes in this book (Chapter 5), there is little reason to believe this situation will change. Without widespread public support, it is likely that any systemic approach to prevention will be inadequately funded and supported, which will undermine its efficacy. Only by embedding efforts to prevent maltreatment in programs run by schools and health systems, with a focus on positive child development, not maltreatment, are we likely to generate public support for these efforts.

Efficacy

I am also hesitant to advise more investment in developing a maltreatment prevention system because, despite the attraction of the programs described in this book, I believe that we still do not know much about preventing maltreatment. This is especially true with respect to neglect, the most prevalent form of maltreatment (Daro, Chapter 1, this volume). Despite numerous efforts at prevention, there has been little change in overall rates of reported cases over the past 20 years. Although there has been a recent decline in reports of physical and sexual abuse, this is not true of neglect, the majority of reported cases (Finkelhor & Jones, 2006).

To be sure, few communities have tried comprehensive programs directed at prevention of maltreatment (Dodge et al., 2004). The most extensive efforts focus on making home visitors available, either universally or to targeted populations. Home visitor programs have much to recommend them, as discussed throughout this book. However, the research evidence regarding the effectiveness of home visiting in preventing maltreatment is mixed, and the research itself is limited (Daro, 2006). The major exception is the Nurse–Family Partnership developed by David Olds, who has meticulously researched its effectiveness for many years (Olds et al., Chapter 2, this volume). But even Olds suggests caution. His model is expensive, requires professionals to implement, works best for a small portion of the population—poor, teen, first-time mothers—and the payoffs are larger in general child development, higher high school graduation rates, and less delinquency, not specifically less maltreatment (Olds et al., Chapter 2, this volume). In addition, it is difficult to implement proven programs with any degree of fidelity (Ammerman, Putnam, Margolis, & Van Ginkel, Chapter 7, this volume). Moreover, there is a limited research base for programs aimed at families with older children (Daro, 2005; but see Prinz, Chapter 3, this volume).

In light of this situation, policymakers are far better able to make the case for programs aimed at improving general child development, rather than preventing maltreatment. And, as considered in the following discussion, it seems likely that more children will benefit from programs that do not focus on preventing maltreatment.

Alternative Needs

Given the limited evidence that prevention efforts will actually significantly reduce the number of children coming to the attention of protective services, policymakers must also consider the need to improve dramatically the way the child protection system responds to the needs of those children subject to more serious physical abuse, sexual abuse, and neglect who now come into the child protection system. A significant proportion of the children found to be maltreated evidence significant developmental problems (Wulczyn et al., 2005). Unfortunately, most children who come under the supervision of child protection agencies do not receive services, and the services now being provided are often inadequate (Wulczyn et al., 2005).

Theoretically, prevention and intervention activities are not mutually exclusive; they might even build on each other. However, in practice, efforts at prevention and intervention are often competing. It may be very difficult to improve child protection agencies while also trying to build a prevention system. Building systems requires people and attention, as well as dollars. Improving the child protection system in most jurisdictions will require the full attention of administrators in those systems.

In fact, there have been multiple efforts to reform the child protection system (CPS) for the last 40 years, but most commentators believe that we have made little headway. Despite major changes in federal and state legislation, and litigation in more than 40 states, very few child protection systems are able to provide high-quality services (Wulcyzn et al., 2005). Too many children are re-abused or neglected after coming to the attention of CPS agencies. Even if not maltreated again, their general well-being is not improved. The poor quality, instability, and length of foster placements remain a major problem. There is great difficulty in recruiting foster parents, who generally are poorly compensated and do not receive the necessary training and support.

It remains very difficult to recruit CPS workers, who often are poorly trained, lack support services, and are underpaid. This is not likely to change, especially because the demand for more teachers in K–12 and preschool and for more trained staff in childcare and after-school programs will affect the number of people attracted to CPS. These other jobs often pay more, have more prestige, and are less difficult. It has also been extremely difficult to improve juvenile court processes. Most judges still do not want to serve in juvenile courts, and court caseloads in most jurisdictions are very high. Not surprisingly, good judges often leave the juvenile bench after a short period. There are fine judges who have made a significant difference (e.g., Lederman, Chapter 10, this volume), but they constitute a small percentage of the juvenile court bench. Policymakers must take account of these realities.

The lack of high-quality services and personnel is especially problematic because many of the children now brought into CPS live in highly disorganized families, the families described by Judge Cindy Lederman in her chapter in this book (Chapter 10). They are extremely poor, they live in the most isolated parts of communities where the least resources are available to them, their children go to the worst schools, and they have limited access to health services. Helping many of these children and parents requires very intensive, high-quality services, delivered over a lengthy period by well-trained professionals. Few communities offer such services on an adequate basis. Far more resources will be needed to help such children.

Unfortunately, it is not just the child protection system that functions badly in most jurisdictions. Both the juvenile justice and children's mental health systems are plagued with problems in many, if not all, states and localities. These systems are supposed to be helping the worst-off children and youth—the very group that is likely to become "problem" parents. In fact, many youth incarcerated in the juvenile justice system are already parents. Services focused on their development, and parenting skills (future or current), are desperately needed. The same is true of children in the mental health system, many of whom are also in the child welfare or juvenile justice system (Mennen & Trickett, 2007).

Given the difficulty of helping children who have been maltreated, primary prevention certainly is desirable. But in terms of improving the well-being of children at high risk of developmental problems, investments focused on children who have already been maltreated or who are already experiencing mental health and behavioral problems may have greater payoff than investments in prevention. If society continues to ignore the needs of these children, it ensures another generation of very inadequate parents.

A Broader Focus

Beyond the political considerations and availability of resources, I believe that, except with respect to severe physical abuse and sexual abuse, the development of a child maltreatment framework is the wrong way to try to help most children to achieve the goals outlined earlier. Maltreatment is just one of many factors that seem to be causally related to poor outcomes for children; it is not likely to be the most prevalent. Especially with respect to academic development, parental education, income, and the quality of schools cumulatively are likely to have a much bigger impact. For example, nearly half of all African American and Latino youth fail to graduate from high school (Swanson, 2004). Dropout rates of as much as 50% cannot be primarily attributed to maltreatment, and programs aimed primarily at reducing maltreatment are not likely to substantially reduce this number, although they may have some effect.

Twenty percent all children under the age of 5 live in poverty, most with a single parent (Fass & Cauthen, 2007). It is estimated that half of all poor mothers suffer from some degree of depression and that their mental health affects their children (Knitzer, Theberge, & Johnson, 2008). These children are at risk of poor development, even if not neglected. In order to reach these parents and children best, the focus needs to be on parental needs, parent education, and positive child development. Framing the problem as one of parental dysfunction is unlikely to attract the support of the public or, even more critical, the parents. These families cannot be approached and engaged by helpers who come from a system that is viewed as accusatory and threatening (Melton, Chapter 5, this volume). The child protective system is not going to be made into the system that really promotes child well-being in this society; it cannot and never was intended to serve that role (Wulcyzn et al., 2005).

SOME FUTURE DIRECTIONS

Rather than trying to design and implement a system of community prevention of maltreatment, I would advise a mayor or governor to try to develop a comprehensive early childhood system of services focused on promoting positive child development. A high-quality home health visitor program would be one element. A difficult question is whether the program should be universal or targeted. Universal programs tend to get more public support and may be able to attract more qualified staff, and because a large percentage of children are born to poor and nonmarried parents, targeting may not be very efficient. In addition, a universal program may be more attractive to those parents we most want to engage; a targeted program may be viewed with distrust. However, a high-quality universal system is expensive and, I believe, the extra dollars could be spent better elsewhere. Therefore, I would try to get all jurisdictions to adopt a program targeted at young, higher-risk parents, based on Olds's model (Olds et al., Chapter 2, this volume) and developed with the tools described by Ammerman and colleagues (Chapter 7, this volume). The program should be based in the health system and not have a child protection justification, although it should be intensive enough to help prevent serious cases of physical abuse and the shaken baby problem described by Runyan and Zolotor (Chapter 6, this volume). Infants are at special risk of maltreatment (Wulcyzn et al., 2005). A high-quality home visitor program targeted at higher-risk mothers could reduce the number of cases of serious abuse and also help mothers suffering from postpartum depression or drug dependence.

With respect to all other children, I recommend that services be delivered through the childcare and education systems, including Early Head Start (EHS), Head Start, and other preschool programs. EHS already is designed to work with higher-risk parents and children (Ewen & Matthews, 2007; Schumacher, Hamm, & Goldstein, 2006). In addition to promoting general child well-being, there is evidence that early childhood and preschool programs focused on both parent and child can improve parenting and have a long-term impact on delinquency, graduation rates, and reduction of teenage pregnancy (Karoly et al., 1998). These positive results might be increased by the adoption of programs like the Triple P program described by Prinz (Chapter 3, this volume).

There certainly are legitimate concerns with, and drawbacks to, an education focus. A key question is whether an education-based approach will adequately reach high-risk families. Will these parents utilize such services? Only a small part (2.5%) of the eligible population is being served by EHS (Ewen & Matthews, 2007). Many disorganized parents do not send their children to center-based care, Head Start, or preschool. Clearly, outreach will be needed, but it seems likely that parents will be more responsive to outreach from the childcare and preschool systems than from programs associated with child protection.

Will education systems be willing and able to provide the type of services needed to alter the situation of these parents and children? Childcare and preschool personnel may be reluctant to engage in the intensive work with parents needed to help both the parents and children (Barth et al., 2008). Reports of high expulsion rates of preschoolers indicate that a great deal of work and training will be needed in many sites if they are to perform the desired role. However, changes have begun. Many EHS programs now work with children in the child protection system and are developing expertise in working with high-risk families. There are other parent–child programs that have been tested and appear to work for fairly severe kinds of problems, such as Triple P (Prinz, Chapter 3, this volume) and The Incredible Years (Webster-Stratton, 1998). It will be necessary to broadening teacher training and to add social worker support in these systems. Still, I suspect that building these institutions will be easier than building a system designated as a prevention of maltreatment system. Education-focused systems have the ability to recruit the highest-caliber staff and to generate broad community support. I would make my investment in the institution in our society in which we have the most faith for promoting well-being, even though that investment has many challenges.

Some people suggest approaching maltreatment prevention, and positive development, primarily through the public health system. A public health approach has strengths, especially with respect to children under 1 year of age. As discussed earlier, home health visitors should become a regular component of healthcare for infants. However, I have reservations about a public health framework regarding older children. Not surprisingly, the public, and many health professionals, think of the health system as treating people with diseases; thus, maltreating parents need to be "cured." This is not an approach that is likely to attract parents. In addition, health professionals may have difficulty deciding who the client and patient is—parent or child—and may feel compelled to choose between them. Even more important, although both maltreating parents and their children often have health needs, especially mental health needs, poor parenting is heavily influenced by economic circumstances and neighborhood stress. The impact of poverty and community conditions is too often ignored, even by the other writers in this book. The majority of "inadequate" parents need skills development or education, plus social support, not health treatment. Although many public health professionals recognize this circumstance and provide appropriate services, it may be hard to generate public support for altering the environmental situation of the parents through the health system. The limited success in achieving adoption of high-quality home visitor programs must be considered. Finally, it may be best to concentrate health system resources on expanding the capacity of the health system to work with children already exhibiting significant health problems, especially mental health problems. Unfortunately, mental health services may be available only to children in the child welfare system (Mennen & Trickett, 2007). All states and localities need far more mental health services.

If prevention of maltreatment becomes the province of the childcare, education, and health systems, and the focus is positive development, what should be the role of the child protection system? It is beyond the scope of this chapter to examine this issue fully, but I will comment on several issues.

One possibility is to provide services to families reported to CPS that do not now receive services, as the proponents of differential response advocate (Waldfogel, Chapter 8, this volume). Whereas services might be provided by community agencies, not the CPS agency itself, reports to the child protection system would be the entry point. In a differential response system, reports involving families in "less risky" situations would not be just closed without further action, as they now are in most states. Instead, these families would be referred for "voluntary" services. As Waldfogel discusses, many jurisdictions are moving in this direction.

Although it is too early to assess these efforts fully, I have reservations. In fact, there are many reasons why policymakers should explore the desirability of shrinking, rather than expanding, the reach of the child protection system. Given the limited resources, in both dollars and personnel, that are likely to be available to CPS and other intervention systems such as mental health, and the substantial deficiencies in current services, I believe that it is best to focus the child maltreatment system on the worst-off children and families and to try to make a real difference in the lives of these children. If investigations and interventions focused only on serious situations, caseloads could be reduced and services for the included families increased, although more funding is still likely to be needed for services if they are to be adequate to alter the situations of these families.

Whereas proponents of differential response would "divert" less serious reports to alternative systems, I believe that there is already too much reporting. CPS agencies currently receive 3 million reports involving 5.5 million children. One-third of these reports are closed without investigation. Maltreatment is substantiated for 900,000 children; only 600,000 families receive services (U.S. Department of Health and Human Services, 2006). Thus, substantial resources are being spent in investigations that could be used for services. Beyond the waste of resources, these investigations can negatively affect the parents and children. Investigations intrude on their privacy; for example, children are often embarrassed by being questioned at school (Coleman, Chapter 9, this volume). More important, they can negatively influence parenting and the psychology of families. We should consider repealing *mandatory* reporting laws or limiting the definition of reportable situations to those involving significant injuries or potential injuries and applying the laws only to medical professionals (Melton, 2005). Less serious situations would not be brought into the CPS system. Instead of trying to help these children through a differential response system, communities would rely on services provided through the childcare and education systems, supplemented by widely available family resource centers. I suspect that a widely available set of support services would be more beneficial to children in "marginally functioning" families than would a system built around differential response.

To enhance the impact of CPS interventions, CPS agencies should draw on the lessons that are presented in the other chapters in this book. Resources are best utilized when the personnel are trained to help specific populations. It is clear that a major focus should be on infants, inasmuch as they are at special risk. Specialized units of workers trained to help new mothers and to meet the developmental needs of infants should be established; these could be modeled on the treatment court or infant court such as the program Judge Lederman has developed in Miami (Lederman, Chapter 10, this volume), the home visitor model of Olds (Olds et al., Chapter 2, this volume), and the shaken baby program described by Runyan and Zolotor (Chapter 6, this volume). All of these parents, and many of these young children, need special therapeutic services.

In addition to focusing on mothers of newborns, I would concentrate on teens in foster care, especially those in group homes and youths in the juvenile justice system. These youths have substantial developmental needs, which are currently not being met. Many need therapeutic services as well. They currently lack services while in care and upon emancipation. Many are already parents; a large percentage of the rest will become young parents unable to provide adequate care for their children. Social service agencies at the city and county levels, including child welfare, mental health, and juvenile justice, need to join together to develop high-quality, developmentally appropriate programs for these youths. In designing and implementing such services, it is essential to incorporate the types of quality control procedures described by Ammerman and colleagues (Chapter 7, this volume).

My final advice to a mayor or governor is that if policymakers really are concerned with preventing maltreatment, they must confront the influence of poverty and continuing racial discrimination on the well-being of children. We will not substantially reduce maltreatment though any of the means discussed earlier unless we deal with the poverty and social isolation of a very significant portion of the population. To be sure, parents who maltreat children need help with their parenting skills. But they also need job training, reasonable housing, and protection from violence, as well as access to decent childcare, preschools, and schools. A community effort to prevent maltreatment must be embedded in much broader social change. Otherwise, we will continue to see the high rates of maltreatment that have been a major social problem for the past 40 years.

REFERENCES

Barth, R., Lloyd, E., Casanueva, C., Scarborough, A., Losby, J., & Mann, T. (2008). *Developmental status and early intervention needs of maltreated children.* Washington, DC: U.S. Department of Health and Human Services, Administration for Children, Youth, and Families.

California Department of Finance. (2008). *California Budget 2007–2008.* Sacramento, CA: Author.

Daro, D. (2006). *Home visitation: Assessing progress, managing expectations.* Chicago: Ounce of Prevention Fund and Chapin Hall Center for Children.

Daro, D., & Cohn Donnelly, A. (2002). Charting the waves of prevention: Two steps forward, one step back. *Child Abuse and Neglect, 26,* 731–742.

Dodge, K. A., Berlin, L. J., Epstein, M., Spitz-Roth, A., O'Donnell, K., Kaufman, M., et al. (2004). The Durham Family Initiative: A preventive system of care. *Child Welfare, 83,* 109–128.

Ewen, D., & Matthews, H. (2007). *Title I and early childhood programs: A look at investments in the NCLB era* (Series paper No. 2). Washington, DC: Center on Law and Social Policy Child Care and Early Education.

Fass, S., & Cauthen, N. (2007). *Who are America's poor children?* New York: National Center for Children in Poverty, Columbia University. Retrieved from *www.nccp.org/publications/pub_787.html.*

Finkelhor, D., & Jones, L. (2006). Why have child maltreatment and child victimization declined? *Journal of Social Issues, 62,* 685–716.

Karoly, L. A., Greenwood, P. W., Everingham, S. S., Hoube, J., Kilburn, M. R., Rydell, C. P., et al. (1998). *Investing in our children: What we know and don't know about the costs and benefits of early childhood interventions.* Santa Monica, CA: Rand.

Knitzer, J., Theberge S., & Johnson K. (2008). *Reducing maternal depression and its impact on young children.* New York: National Center for Children in Poverty, Columbia University.

Melton, G. B. (2005). Mandated reporting: A policy without reason. *Child Abuse and Neglect, 29,* 9–18.

Mennen, F., & Trickett, P. (2007). Mental health needs of urban children. *Children and Youth Services Review, 29,* 1220–1234.

National Association of State Budget Officers. (2005). *State expenditure report 2003.* Washington, DC: Author.

Sabol, W., Colton, C., & Polousky, E. (2004). Measuring child maltreatment risk in communities: A life table approach. *Child Abuse and Neglect, 28,* 967–983.

Schumacher, R., Hamm, K., & Goldstein, A. (2006). *Starting off right: Promoting child development from birth in state early care and education initiatives.* Washington, DC: Center on Law and Social Policy.

Swanson, C. B. (2004). Sketching a portrait of public high school graduation: Who graduates? Who doesn't? In G. Orfield (Ed.), *Dropouts in America*. Cambridge, MA: Harvard University Press.

U.S. Department of Health and Human Services, Administration for Children, Youth, and Families. (2006). *Child maltreatment 2004: Reports from the states to the National Child Abuse and Neglect Data System*. Washington, DC: U.S. Government Printing Office.

Wald, M., & Martinez, T. (2003). *Connected by 25: William and Flora Hewlett Foundation working papers*. Menlo Park, CA: William and Flora Hewlett Foundation.

Waldfogel, J. (2006). *What children need*. Cambridge, MA: Harvard University Press.

Webster-Stratton, C. (1998). Preventing conduct problems in Head Start children: Strengthening parent competencies. *Journal of Consulting and Clinical Psychology, 66*, 715–730.

Wulcyzn, F., Barth, R., Yuan, Y.-Y. T., Harden, B. J., & Landsverk, J. (2005). *Beyond common sense child welfare, child well-being, and the evidence for policy reform*. New Brunswick, NJ: Transaction.

Index